LateThoughts

PHILIP D. BEIDLER

The Legacy of Vietnam

on an Old War

The University of Georgia Press | Athens and London

© 2004 by the University of Georgia Press
Athens, Georgia 30602
All rights reserved
Designed by Kathi Dailey Morgan
Set in Berthold Baskerville by Bookcomp, Inc.
Printed and bound by Thomson-Shore
The paper in this book meets the guidelines
for permanence and durability of the Committee
on Production Guidelines for Book Longevity
of the Council on Library Resources.
Printed in the United States of America
08 07 06 05 04 C 5 4 3 2 1

Library of Congress
Cataloging-in-Publication Data
Beidler, Philip D.
Late thoughts on an old war : the legacy of
Vietnam / Philip D. Beidler.
p. cm.
ISBN 0-8203-2589-9 (hardcover : alk. paper)
1. Vietnamese Conflict, 1961–1975—United
States. 2. Vietnamese Conflict, 1961–1975—
Influence. 3. Vietnamese Conflict, 1961–1975—
Motion pictures and the conflict. 4. Vietnamese
Conflict, 1961–1975—Literature and the conflict.
5. Vietnamese Conflict, 1961–1975—Music and
the conflict. I. Title.
DS558 .B45 2004
959.704'31—dc22   2003016943
British Library Cataloging-in-Publication
Data available

For Mike Doyle

Contents

Late Thoughts on an Old War

After <u>Apocalypse Now</u>

Nearly three decades after the last U.S. helicopter lifted off from Saigon, countless Americans still struggle to make the Vietnamese war into history. I know. A former platoon leader in an armored cavalry unit, I'm one of them. At the same time, my life has brought me into contact with a large number of others attempting in their own ways to come to terms with the experience of the war. Some of them are in VA wards. Some of them take care of people in VA wards. Some hold high public office or win literary prizes. Some sell real estate, deliver babies, or write up insurance estimates on how much it will cost to get a crumpled fender fixed. Some, like myself, are combat veterans of the war. Some did military service in noncombat assignments. Others are lifelong civilians who have never been west of California, or maybe even Ohio. Some of them availed themselves of draft deferments or exemptions. Some did alternative service. Some were antiwar activists. Some lost friends or family members in the war. Some remained largely untouched by events. Most of the people I have thus far described are men and women now in their fifties or sixties. But there are plenty of others, much younger, like the high-school junior who interviewed me recently as part of an oral-history project, or the psychology students studying Posttraumatic Stress Disorder (PTSD) I sometimes get invited to talk to at the university where I work. I have a wonderful graduate student in English right now working on the literature of the war. She had an undergraduate accounting degree but decided life was too short not to do the things she liked best. Part of her motivation was her father's suicide after an adult lifetime of trying to overcome the psychological damage of his combat experiences in Vietnam. He shot himself in 1998 on the thirtieth anniversary of the Tet Offensive. One of the great lessons I believe I have gained from my generation's experience is that one surely did not have to go to Vietnam to get any special purchase on bad history. There was plenty of war to go around at home and abroad, and we are all veterans. And this does not begin to address the experience of the Vietnamese. While we may find the subject listed in the Library of Congress Catalog as Vietnamese Conflict, 1961–75, the Vietnamese do not call it the American War for nothing.

At the level of national understanding, ample evidence exists to suggest that attempts at collective comprehension are similarly unending. In the realm of geopolitical policy, success in the current campaign against terrorism, as in the Gulf War against Iraq a decade ago, has to this point been measured by how, in spite of the manifold warnings of imperialist history, *it has not turned out to be another Vietnam.* The ongoing Israeli-Palestinian bloodbath, like the Balkan horrors of recent years, elicits a reflexive horror concerning commitment of U.S. troops or even serious political alignment with one side or another in conflicts arising out of millennia-old antagonisms.

Apace, in the domain of popular culture and entertainment, contending representations of the war jostle for status as the currently prevailing version of national myth. The big Vietnam movie of 2002, *We Were Soldiers*–a much-publicized, high-budget Mel Gibson vehicle treating the 1965 Ia Drang Valley campaigns of the First Air Cavalry–was accorded for the most part respectful attention, albeit with accusations in some quarters of Hollywood GI movie cliché and in others of conservative revisionism. (The response of veterans, I suspect, was along the lines of the sentiment expressed by the full title of the book by Harold G. Moore and Joseph L. Galloway from which the script was taken: *We Were Soldiers Once . . . and Young.*) Meanwhile, *Apocalypse Now,* a film itself now about twenty-five years old, attempted to put new life into its claims as the ultimate cinematic metaphor of the American war in Vietnam by recycling itself in a director's cut version, as–what else–*Apocalypse Now Redux.* In chain bookstores and paperback buy-and-swaps, entire shelves remain devoted to popular titles about Vietnam special-operations units–snipers, LRRPs, Navy SEALs, and the like. Meanwhile, as another very bright graduate student of mine discovered recently, an entire new genre of postwar-generation travel narratives has come into existence. Her thesis title puts it nicely: "The Lonely Planet Does Vietnam."

About the business of the Vietnamese war and American cultural mythmaking, as suggested by some of my foregoing comments, I also know a good bit, having spent much of a university career reading and writing about the war in its relation to national memory. My own acquaintance with a vast literature–more than four thousand book-length texts in print and God knows how many articles, not to mention endless literary, cinematic, and popular culture representations with their attendant commentary–convinces me that no one has yet had the last word on Vietnam, nor does anyone seem to wish this to happen anytime soon.

I say this despite my serious fears, as well as those of others, about the unwillingness of Americans to confront responsibility for the war and its human consequences or to undertake the attendant work of cultural revision that so many of us have seen as demanded by the experience both at home and abroad. For my own part, I have staked such apprehensions not only on a willed obliviousness I saw all around me from the midseventies through the mideighties but also on a failure at the national level to come to terms with deeply rooted myths of providential destiny and historical exceptionalism that my studies as an academic specialist in early American literature and culture have identified to me as haunting the national consciousness from the earliest days of colonization to the present. On the one hand, from Cotton Mather through Herman Melville and Harriet Beecher Stowe and onward through Francis Ford Coppola, Americans have always wanted their apocalypses, and they have always wanted them now. On the other hand, as our most recent exercise in "democracy-building" in Iraq has shown, we have exactly in that measure become the most adept nation in the history of the globe at making things history. As in, oh yes, but that's history. This kind of millennial doublethink, I have frequently asserted, has been the basis of a cultural arrogance perhaps characteristically Western but exacerbated by a capacity for self-delusion uniquely American. It fosters the very habits of mind that made us delusional in the first place and that have consistently let us walk away without much further reflection. Redeemer nation, I have averred, reinvents itself over and over as amnesiac nation.

On the particular subject of the Vietnamese war, we may never know how the circuitry has gotten stuck. Have the voices, memories, and personal struggles of countless individual veterans kept the questions alive? Has the vast body of writing and popular-culture representation, for all its jangle and discord, passionate hyperbole and Hollywood nonsense, amounted to something? Did the end of the cold war open the door to a new climate of American historical self-assessment? Has the passing into history of the World War II generation with lavish outpourings of national gratitude and honor now redirected attention to a generation of Vietnam veterans moving into old age? Have the events of September 11, 2001, newly endowed Americans with a sense of their own historical mortality? Whatever the order of vectors, I find, with an ever deepening conviction, that individually and collectively Americans can't let go of the Vietnamese war, of what happened to us and the Vietnamese there.

The following essays on the war and its aftereffects in American life comprise an account, in composite form, of my own attempts as a veteran and a writer to combine personal memory with cultural reflection. Some use an autobiographical moment as an opening to cultural commentary. Others try to inform cultural observation with personal witness. Some address familiar topics: the war in literature, the war in film, the war in music. The reader will also find considerable attention devoted to some familiar figures: Richard Nixon, Robert McNamara, William Calley. By comparison, certain other essays examine curious or unusual subjects: the system of payments instituted by U.S. officials during the war to Vietnamese suffering losses of property and family as a result of military action, the life and career of a conscientious objector who chose to do alternative service in Vietnam and who has become one of the most important American poets writing of the experience of the Americans and the Vietnamese, the astonishing recent popularity of a vast paperback literature of the war centered on elite special-operations units.

Along the way, the book addresses the war and American remembering in light of what have now entered the vocabulary of cultural generalization as some fairly conventional categories of analysis: the race war, the class war, the media war, the draftee war, the minority war, the civilian atrocity war. It also takes up some of the commonplaces of academic and political discussion: that the American war in Vietnam was the first rock 'n' roll war, the first technowar, the first postmodern war; that it was a war lost from the start by the politicians and the Washington bureaucrats; that it was a war actually won on the battlefield but lost in the court of American public opinion; that, if not a "good" war, it was at least a necessary war. At the same time, the book eschews intentionally the perspective and, I hope, the manner of the academic specialist. One will find no footnotes here. One will find a memorial to a dead Vietnamese boy whose family received around thirty-five dollars as the U.S. Army's way of saying it was sorry. One will find a tribute to a dead U.S. general who got killed on the ground with his soldiers while Nixon treated his buddies to repeated viewings of *Patton*. Part autobiography and part cultural meditation, the book might be most aptly described as a memoir of living with Vietnam all these years. Accordingly, my title—*Late Thoughts on an Old War*—means just what it says. The homage to Bernard Fall is intentional. To this day, his book titles alone seem to tell the whole story: *The Two Vietnams, Vietnam Witness, Street without Joy, Hell in a Very Small Place, Last Reflections on a War.* As I approach late life, after a career of writing about Vietnam, I could only hope to honor the enduring wisdom he found as the prize of his ceaseless efforts to bear witness to the folly of the French, and later of the American, involvement in Indochina, not to mention the perseverance.

Especially the perseverance. From the standpoint of both personal and intellectual energy, I must admit that in a postmillennium America where *Apocalypse Now* has come and gone and come and gone again, both on the Hollywood screen and most recently in the rubble of New York and Baghdad, going for the easy irony has become increasingly tempting in writing about Vietnam and national remembering. At times, especially after the events of September 11, 2001, to choose a latest American epochal moment, looking back on one's own claims about one's own war as the end of the myths of American historical innocence and/or geopolitical invincibility, one imagines one's self something like a character in an old Peter Cook–Dudley Moore *Beyond the Fringe* routine—a lovely spoof of professional 1960s doomsaying, in which a clutch of goofy millennialists in sackcloth and ashes stand around waiting for the great moment. Over and over they chant, "Now is the end; perish the world. Now is the end; perish the world." Shortly, they begin their final countdown: "Ten, nine, eight," and so on. When they get to zero, nothing, of course, happens. Just silence. Finally a small, chastened voice observes, "Not quite the conflagration we anticipated." Then another, more cheery, dismisses the group, instructing them to reassemble tomorrow, same time, same place.

But that won't do either. The lives so violently cut short of fifty-eight thousand Americans and between two and four million Vietnamese still must cry out to us as a nation not to do the things we did there over and over again out of an obscene national solipsism that blinds us to the power of cultural difference. In the case of Vietnam, a proud nation with a three-thousand-year-old Asian culture really did not want to be a two-hundred-year-old Western democracy. The Vietnamese were nationalists, we discovered to our surprise, having assumed that such ideological categories could not rationally coexist, every bit as much as they were communists. They did not like American colonialists any more than they had liked French colonialists, not to mention the Chinese colonialists they had been fighting for millennia. Where they needed to, they also knew us far better than we would ever know them. "Americans do not like long, inconclusive wars," Premier Pham Van Dong observed in 1962 as the earliest American troops began to arrive, "–and this is going to be a long, inconclusive war. Thus we are sure to win in the end." And it was they who made us, the mightiest nation in the history of the world, believers, rather than the other way around, in what ought to be remembered by Americans as a monumental achievement of geopolitical humbling. The Vietnamese war is a national reality check we need to keep coming back to. It is also a geopolitical morality check that we need to keep putting in front of us. This is the way the world looks, we need to keep reminding ourselves, after *Apocalypse Now*.

On the one hand, as a personal survivor, I'm a lucky one, and I know it. I have a loving wife and daughter, faithful friends, and a dream job teaching in a university. On the other hand, in the years since the war I have also managed to rack up a good bit of the human damage– along with the attendant anger and regret–that so often strews veterans' lives. Alcoholic drinking, divorce, terrifying obsessive episodes, black depressions, chronic problems with authority, blinding impatience with everything from supermarket lines to administrative chickenshit, lifelong enmities with people who have tried to crowd me: such things constitute my personal inventory of what Philip Caputo has called *combat veteranitis*. To them may be added entries from his own more general symptomology: an intolerance for loud noise, inexplicable rages, a childlike fear of the dark. I have an abiding interest in PTSD in its relation to drug and alcohol awareness and in its extension into understanding the victims of rape, violence, and child and spousal abuse. I am a firm believer in psychological counseling and am particularly proud of how many Vietnam veterans are willing to get their heads examined. I wish the country could be as forthcoming.

In practical terms, I believe that getting our gringo asses kicked in Vietnam at the very least kept us out of Central America. I am also not surprised that the complete rebuilding of the U.S. military came about through the work of Vietnam veterans who stayed around and tried to make something out of the hard lessons of the war. More broadly speaking, even in a world of global terrorist threats that have prompted a dangerous new habit on our part of making preemptive war, I think as a country we have become at least somewhat more honest in looking at the hard facts of our racist and imperialist history, beginning with the enslavement of Africans and the wars of annihilation against native peoples and our subsequent adventurism in the Caribbean, Central and South America, Asia and the Pacific, and now the Middle East. Nor, on domestic grounds, do I find it remotely coincidental that, dating from when I returned from Vietnam, virtually every step forward we seem to have taken toward becoming a wiser or more humane country has been linked directly to the ascendancy of women, African Americans, Hispanics, and Asians into positions of voice and authority in the national discourse.

In my teaching and my writing I bring to my work an almost obsessive curiosity about the foundational myths of our culture, our historical assumptions about religion, national purpose, race, class, gender, and cultural difference, coupled with an intense skepticism of public pieties, past and present. Student evaluations of my teaching sometimes accuse me of saying mean things about Jesus. I don't. I say mean things about what people do in the name of Jesus, or Allah, or Yahweh. I believe that all totalizing systems of belief are bullshit. At the same time I expect people to work hard and deal fairly. I think life is pointless without commitment.

I am not saying that the experience of the Vietnamese war is at the bottom of all this. I am not going to lie and say it is not. Whatever the mix of the personal and the cultural vectors, having been present at the American apocalypse in question, I suppose I will always in a way find myself not unlike F. Scott Fitzgerald's Nick Carraway, on his return from

World War I, wanting "the world to be in uniform and at a sort of moral attention forever." Or maybe, to borrow the words and the sentiments of Paul Fussell, speaking for the American generation of 1941–45, I just think that somebody has to stand up for the viewpoint of the pissed-off infantryman. Out of my own war, it is the least I can do for the gift of survival and memory.

The Language of the Nam

gook /gook/ *n* an offensive term for an Asian person

or somebody of Asian descent *(slang)* [Mid-20C. ?]

(Microsoft Encarta College Dictionary)

For Americans serving in the military in Vietnam, "gook" was definitely

the operative term. Throughout the war, with the possible exception

of "shit" or "fuck," it may have been the most ubiquitous word in the

American soldier vocabulary. Ironically, as a piece of GI slang, it had

absolutely nothing to do with the Vietnamese people, their language

or their history, being (in its newest iteration, at least) a hand-me-down

from army and marine veterans of Korea, another lousy Asian war of ten to fifteen years earlier, where it allegedly derived from a disparaging native word for "people." In retrospect, that seems to have been just the point. One Asian war, officially undeclared, of dubious political provenance and indefinable strategic purpose, came to look like just another Asian war. One Asian people, indistinguishable as to those one was supposed to be killing versus those one was supposed to be fighting beside and/or protecting, came to look like any other Asian people.

To be sure, Vietnam War–era GIs labored extravagantly with their own creative elaborations: gooks, slants, slopes, zipperheads. The Cong: as in, "bong the Cong." Zips: as in, "feed a clip to a zip." An individual Viet Cong–the phrase itself derived from a belittling epithet applied by the South Vietnamese to their communist opponents, the VC, who insisted on calling themselves the National Liberation Front, the NLF–was Victor Charlie. Victor Charlie: the shadowed, elusive, deadly wraith of the ambush and the jungle, the mythological creature of the night, the great bogeyman of the war. Victor Charlie could be known by a host of other names as well. These depended on the unit, the region, the period of the war, and the degree of professional familiarity and/or appreciation: Charlie, Charles, Chas, Chuck, Old Clyde. Up north the marines called the bad guys "gooners." Down in III Corps we went mainly with "dinks." Not that any of us didn't appreciate the people on the other side with AK-47 automatic rifles and brass balls–highly motivated personnel, the army would have called them–whenever we went out to kill each other. "I love the little commie bastards, man. I really do," says a marine in Gustav Hasford's *The Short Timers*. "Grunts understand grunts. These are great days we are living bros. We are jolly green giants walking the earth with guns. The people we wasted here today are the finest individuals we will ever know." It was a question of respect. To my memory, nobody ever called the NVA, the regular North Vietnamese Army, by anything but the dreaded initials or their phonetic alphabet equivalent, En-Vee-Ay, November Victor Alpha. The same thing went for any main-force unit, VC, or NVA we found ourselves up against: we called it by name, usually a quite specific number or number-letter combination, and we did so invariably in tones of soldierly respect: the 24th; the 33rd; the 274D.

We saved the serious linguistic scorn for our South Vietnamese cohorts—allegedly, in the incessant cowboy parlance of the war, the good guys. "Our Vietnamese Allies," "our counterparts," we pronounced them, with a knowing smile and a jerk of the thumb over the shoulder: gookinamese; dinkinamese; squint eyes; rice eaters; little people; our gooks, as opposed to their gooks. Never has a military force had so many names of contempt for the people they were supposed to be trying to help. The South Vietnamese Army, the Army of Vietnam—allegedly working arm-in-arm with USARV (U.S. Army Vietnam) and MACV (Military Assistance Command Vietnam)—were the ARVN. The individual soldier was Marvin the Arvin, Marvelous Marv, Little Nguyen, Luke the Gook. The RF-PF, the Regional Force–Popular Force militia, were the ruff-puffs. The CIDG were the Civilian Irregular Defense Group. Other irregular fighters were Montagnards, Yards for short, as opposed to Hmongs, Nungs, Meos, and the like, all of them border and mountain tribes working with the special-operations people, the sneaky Petes. Early in the war, there were also all the crazy factions and militias, the Catholics, the Buddhists, the Taoists. The Hoa Hao were a shadow government. The Binh Xuyen were organized crime, an infrastructure of gangsters, murderers, and thugs. The Cao Dai were a religious sect, with a pantheon of saints including Buddha, Jesus Christ, and Victor Hugo. The LLDB were the Vietnamese Special Forces. The Vietnamese national police were the white mice. A statue erected to members of the Vietnamese military fallen in battle against the communists, two soldiers charging forward as one, in somebody's bad joke of a Saigon answer to the Iwo Jima Memorial, was called the National Buggery Monument. What could you expect of an army where you could see privates walking down the road holding hands? As one character says in Martin Russ's *Happy Hunting Ground,* one of the early novels of the war, "Steve says the reason the South Vietnamese have such a lousy army is because everybody's all the time goosing each other." And then there was all that talking and gibbering that strange musical language in those high little voices, the skinny little fatigue pants and shirts, the tiny feet, the kid-sized heads slopping around in steel pots.

On either side, dead Vietnamese, of which there were plenty, came in for the standard accounting formulas and statistics, a daily bureaucratic bag of numbers and letters. If remotely plausible that they could pass for enemy, mostly they wound up as BC, body count: as in, "3 VC KIA CBC"–three Viet Cong killed in action, confirmed body count. Because, in fact, the many ways in the American inventory to kill people so often rendered the manner of death largely unrecognizable, the general rule was, bag 'em and tag 'em. If they're dead, they're VC. To be sure, it could be hard to claim a corpse from a traffic accident as VC, spilling out all over the roads as the Vietnamese did on foot with their buffalo carts or in their wheezing buses and cyclos and Lambrettas: a bad case of road rash, you might hear a tank driver say; somebody taking a Honda nap. Or a dead five-year-old kid or two with their mothers, the result of somebody's opening fire at movement in a treeline or calling an air or artillery strike too close to a village, a pile of civilians with no weapons or adult males in sight. Then it could be time for the odd solatium payment–that was the actual word–around thirty-five dollars a corpse, plus ten or twelve cartons of cigarettes, maybe some foodstuffs or building materials, along with a ceremony featuring high-ranking officers delegated to tender an official expression of regret. When all else failed, there was always the TOG rule. TOG: "They're Only Gooks."

A place to buy imitation GI stuff and crappy souvenirs was a gook shop. A skin problem that refused to heal was a gook sore. A place to take a nap was a gook hammock. A quick wash-off under an upturned bucket was a gook shower. The great entertainment moment of any unit standdown–an infrequent two- or three-day base-camp respite from field operations for rest and refitting–was the appearance of a gook stripper and a gook band. Somebody who had been around too long was in danger of turning into a semigook. In Larry Heinemann's *Close Quarters,* gook is the word of the day for a typical ugly day in the Nam. During a sweep through a village, somebody drops a grenade down a well. Somebody throws another one into a bomb shelter and hoses down the inside with a burst of automatic rifle. Somebody else sets a thatched house on fire. A Vietnamese woman squats and watches, slapping her hands helplessly on the ground. "Fucken' GI," she mutters. In response, Heinemann's narrator-protagonist, Philip Dosier, slowly, coldly, calmly, proceeds to

est ownership of the other big magic word, which was DEROS (Date Eligible for Return from Overseas). Sometimes it could even be a guy with months left to serve, a pretender trying to act hard-core, what the marines would have called salty. Not that having months left ever kept people from sounding off. By day two, anyone could take small happiness in being technically shorter than somebody just arrived—by his cherished personal calculus, at least, already a bona fide short-timer. (Not for nothing was a quick encounter with a Vietnamese prostitute also called a short time—as in, "Me give you short time." GIs and women: in a war, they are almost always the two main classes of people getting fucked.)

People marked down the days on flak jackets and the camouflage covers of their helmets, on latrine walls and the hulls of armored personnel carriers. In the rear, everybody had a short-timer's calendar—usually a *Playboy* foldout with the Bunny of the Month divided up into numbered sections like a meat-company diagram of a beef cow or a pig. No imagination was required, of course, to guess which of the choice cuts were saved for last. To be sure, the technical definition of short was under a hundred days. Then the short-timer became a true prince of the realm, a two-digit midget, with the privilege of a new manner of speaking and yet another special vocabulary. Now it was "twenty-six and a wake-up," the latter, of course, being the day of departure. Short-timer graffiti took on the attributes of an art form: "So short I need a ladder to get out of bed in the morning." "So short I have to roll down my socks to take a shit." "So short I'm gone." The numbers also garnered their share of superstition. I know I never wrote one down. At some point, in fact, most people I knew—including myself—stopped counting. It seemed too much like asking fate to come up and take a giant dump on you at the last minute. Bad dreams could always come true. Speaking with the authority of the near miss, I remember only two things, for instance, about my last morning in Vietnam, after an overnight in the barracks at the allegedly safe and stateside-seeming Ninetieth Replacement Detachment. One is waking up to the smell of diesel exhaust and burning shit. The other is watching a VC 122-millimeter rocket take out a water tower about one hundred fifty yards downrange.

Afoot in the land we never knew, neither did we much speak the name of the place we desperately wanted to get back to. That, too, seemed some sort of bad magic. Nobody went home. They DEROSed. They went back to the World. They finally got on the Freedom Bird and headed for the Land of the Big PX (post exchange)–that is, unless they "extended," took a "delay," usually with the promise of some safe, non-combat reassignment; maybe tried to get a "drop" or an "early-out," a reduction or cancellation of enlistment time remaining back in the world; or if all else failed, decided to reenlist again, usually for a safe assignment and a pay bonus. To re-up: go for the bennies, stay with the green machine, take a burst of six. A man had to be really desperate–or hooked on war, as certain people actually came to be–to do the latter. Most people just kept on counting, crossed their fingers, said their prayers, or notched their short-timer sticks, tried not to listen to the heartbeat of time, tick-tick-tick.

The immediate world of the war for most soldiers in line units began with arrival at a major air base–Bien Hoa, Tan Son Nhut, Cam Ranh Bay. And yes, the opening scene revisited in countless novels, memoirs, and the like really did take place. A chartered civilian airliner makes a high-speed landing and taxis quickly to a gate. The door opens and cheery American stewardesses, all short skirts and panty-girdle curves and lacquered sixties hair, bid good-bye to a planeload of jet-lagged, sheepish-looking arrivers in rumpled khakis and dress summer greens. The engines remain running. As the deplaning passengers move to an assembly shed, they pass by an equal number of jeering, wisecracking, grab-assing veterans going the other way to get aboard. For people so happy, many of them have the strangest, saddest vacant look in their eyes. Those with the haunted stares are usually not the ones yelling things like "Fresh meat!" and "Short!" and "You'll be saaahreee!"

Arrival was usually followed by at least a glimpse of a division or brigade main base camp–usually a U.S.-style installation: wooden barracks; mess halls; EM (enlisted men), NCO (noncommissioned officer), and officer clubs; a library; a PX; sometimes even a swimming pool. (Oddly, the other first thing a lot of people noticed was all the construction equipment around–PA&E and RMK-BRJ–making hay while the war raged.) In-processing, as it was called, began at Long Binh, Da Nang, Cam Ranh Bay, or one of the big unit bases: the marines at Dong Ha; the 101st Airborne at Camp Eagle; the First Air Cav at Quang Tri; the Fifth Special Forces at Nha Trang; the First Infantry at Di An; the Fourth at Pleiku; the Ninth down in the Delta at Can Tho; the Twenty-fifth out on the III Corps border at Cu Chi. Cu Chi: I still marvel at the overhead photographs after all the years—the headquarters quadrangle; the unit insignia carved into the vegetation; the parade ground, honeycombed underneath with thirty years of tunnels, some of them running all the way to Cambodia.

My unit, a separate light infantry brigade, had a headquarters compound all the way back at Long Binh Post we just called by a workmanlike set of initials: BMB, Bee-Em-Bee. Brigade main base—or, in the phonetic alphabet we used on the radio and, more or less unconsciously, across the range of our everyday speaking, Bravo Mike Bravo. Any of these we infinitely preferred to its official designation, Camp Frenzell-Jones—that hyphenated phrase comprising the last names of the first two members of the brigade to be killed in action.

Base-camp geography alone could be a history of the war. I've compared photos, for instance, with a friend from the First Cavalry, a survivor of LZ Albany in the Ia Drang. His are of An Khe, 1965. His best buddy sits on his helmet, reading a letter from home. In the background is the pup tent, rigged up from two infantry shelter halves, where they sleep. Mine are of Long Binh, 1969. My best buddy and I pose, on a stand-down at BMB, with the mess sergeant in front of the supply room, marked by a sign with the 199th Light Infantry insignia and a big wooden red-and-white cavalry guidon. (My friend's best buddy, for the record, died at LZ Albany; mine survived the war and, like me, became a college teacher.) Behind, one can see barracks and painted sandbag bunkers. This was the place my war radiated out from, Redcatcher Rear. Early in my tour Redcatcher Forward was at a place called the Fishnet Factory, down on the southwest approaches out of the Delta to Saigon. I found my new unit, a troop of armored cavalry in which I was to command one of the three platoons, across the highway, at a compound guarding the gates of Cholon, just beyond the Racetrack, where a predecessor of mine was killed during Tet. In midtour, we went east, out toward the South China Sea, taking over the old Eleventh Cavalry main base camp at Black Horse. In the shadow of a mountain called Nui Dat, we worked out of hard, angry places like Xuan Loc, Gia Ray, Dinh Quan, Vo Dat, Tanh Linh. There, staking themselves outward from the brigade forward headquarters and battalion command centers, came new satellite firebases with names like Mace, Libby, Mary Ann and, beyond these, hasty perimeters carved out by combat-engineer bulldozers, a cleared space with a protective berm, sandbagged bunkers with overhead cover, barbed wire encirclements of tanglefoot and concertina, and, inside, maybe a battery of artillery, a security force, a small tactical-operations center.

Every unit had its own topographical memory, stations of the cross. For the big III Corps units out on the Cambodian border, the Eleventh Cavalry, the First and Twenty-fifth Infantry, the names were An Loc; Loc Ninh; Lai Khe; Quan Loi; Nui Ba Den, the Black Virgin Mountain; eventually Snoul and points west. The Ninth Division in the Delta knew the Ho Bo Woods and the U Minh Forest. The Central Highlands marked the big battles of the First Air Cav: Pleiku, An Khe, the Ia Drang, the A Shau. In I Corps, up by the DMZ, it was the same for the marines at Con Thien, Khe Sanh, the Citadel at Hue. Meanwhile, out by the coast, the Americal wrote a permanent chapter of dark history on the Batangan Peninsula in the Song My village complex, at a hamlet eventually known to the world as My Lai. Sometimes we just went ahead and renamed the landscape to our own designs. We'd written its name in a lot of people's blood, after all: Indian Country, Ambush Alley, the Arizona, Tombstone Territory, Fort Apache, the Alamo, Dodge City, Death Valley, Dogpatch, Pinkville, the Michelin, the Rockpile, the Iron Triangle, the Parrot's Beak, War Zone D.

For those serving in small-unit operations, the war of the battalions, the companies, and the platoons, this was further subsumed in a workaday geography of topographical map sheets, overlays, plastic laminations covered with grease pencil, abbreviated mission orders, grid coordinates, call signs, radio frequencies. These were the true boundaries of a world, a vision delineated and encompassed in the concept of the

AO, the area of operations. To this day, I have several of mine completely memorized. I see terrain features that jump right out, contour lines translating horizontal space into up and down: ridges, plateaus, valleys, defiles, plunging ravines, major hills with numbers denoting feet of elevation; road junctions, major trails, abandoned railroad tracks. A big road, a hardball, is red. A dirt road or a big foot trail is black. Streams are blue. The jungle is green. There is a lot of green. Sprinkled everywhere are the names of many villages. On the ground, the places usually turn out to be nonexistent: an abandoned well, a broken shrine, heaps of scattered stone and brick. On each of these maps, in grease pencil, in my own hand, are intersecting arcs of artillery coverage from various units in the area. The command radio frequencies and call signs I need are also there, battalion and brigade, artillery, forward air control, medevac, as well as various useful locations designated in grid coordinates—positions of nearby units, checkpoints, preplanned targets, and so on.

The farther out one went, the more language itself seemed to change into pure number and letter: six-figure grid coordinates for location, alphabetical and numerical designations for units and mission activity. Tactical communication was usually in code. SOP, standard operating procedure, officially required the use of an SOI—a little mimeographed book of signal operating instructions, replaced monthly and containing radio frequencies and a fairly simple enciphering system called a shackle code. You were required to use this—unless you were obviously in the shit, at which time, nobody bothered. Contact, we called it—" 'Quakin' and Shakin',' " wrote Michael Herr, "great balls of fire." Then it was allowed to send all information in the clear—that is, without any attempt to encode or disguise—to say exactly who was where, what was going on, who was doing what to whom, how many on either side, and at what coordinates, precisely, one wished to have an artillery or air strike ASAP—as soon as possible.

Indeed, for anyone who participated in field operations in Vietnam, surely some of the strongest memories aside from actual combat must involve the incessant noise of radio traffic—yet another whole language within a language, complete with its own vocabulary, syntax, and alphabet. Founded on a formal code—RTP, or Radio-Telephone Procedure—

it demanded precise observance of protocols, of rules and regulations. There were even rules on profanity, soldiers being a notoriously foul-mouthed lot. Curiously, the insistence was usually repaid. Even the most irreverent, toilet-tongued GI could see that there was just too much at stake. Here was a mission language, make or break—designed to eliminate confusion—in which errors of communication procedure could spell life or death. A crucial instance: Confused about a message, you don't say, "Repeat"; you say, "Say again." "Repeat" is a command used exclusively for calling artillery missions, where you want them to shoot an exact replay of what they just shot for you—as in, "Repeat, battery three, hotel echo, on the deck." Or, as opposed to old war movies, you can't say, "Over and out." You can say, "Over," which means, "I still have more to say." Or you can say, "Out," which means, "Message ended: move your ass."

The baseline elements of discourse actually became the formally pronounced letters of the military phonetic alphabet. Again, as opposed to the old war movies, Vietnam predictably had a new one, updated from World War II and Korea. For Audie Murphy it may have been Able, Baker, Charlie, Dog, Easy, and so on. In Vietnam, it was Alpha, Bravo, Charlie, Delta, Echo, and the like. The same went for numbers. Fourteen was pronounced one-four. Forty was four-zero. Fourteen and forty sound alike, after all, and when someone called in artillery or an air strike, ambiguity was tragedy waiting to happen. A last lingering bad movie cliché persisted in official call signs, letters and numbers, changed on a monthly basis along with frequencies and invariably dreamed up, one observed, to invoke the alleged Asian inability to pronounce *r* and *l:* "Flaming Dagger Three-Seven," "Rapid Pillows Four-Four," "Learned Slogan One-Three." Again, once this got down to the level of ground action, common sense simplicity took over. A six was a unit commander, as opposed to a three, an operations officer. A one-six, two-six, or three-six denoted a First Platoon leader, a Second Platoon leader, a Third Platoon leader, as opposed to a one-five, two-five, three-five—their platoon sergeants. An actual was the officer speaking, as opposed to a radio operator. A tango was a tank commander, as opposed to a delta—a driver.

20

In the field, and then radiating backward through the system, everything tended toward a tactical shorthand. Operations jargon became the official language of the country that was the war, at once strangely hermetic and spilling out into everyday expression. Experience reduced itself to short words, one or two syllables, or sometimes just phonetic letter combinations. Charlie Alpha: combat assault. Lima Zulu: landing zone. Cold: no enemy. Hot: a world of hurt. Whiskey India Alpha: wounded in action. Kilo India Alpha: killed in action. One lived and died in the empire of the acronym, sometimes in phonetic pronunciation, as often in the letters themselves. MOS: military occupational specialty. ETA: estimated time of arrival. RTO: radio-telephone operator. FO: forward observer. DMZ: demilitarized zone. CO: commanding officer. XO: executive officer. NCO: noncommissioned officer. EM: enlisted man. MP: military police. EOD: explosive ordnance disposal. OP: observation post. NDP: night defensive position

Here, as with everything else in Vietnam, there was always the power of a bad example from the MACV Mission down in Saigon or the USARV headquarters over in Long Binh, the Pentagon West. JUSPAO was the Joint U.S. Public Affairs Office. CORD was Council on Revolutionary Development. USAID was U.S. Agency for International Development. Sometimes the acronyms really stood for other acronyms. USAID, for instance, usually meant CIA. Sometimes there were even acronyms for acronyms. SEER stood for System for Evaluating the Effectiveness of the RVNAF, RVNAF in turn being Republic of Vietnam Armed Forces. Meanwhile, on the bottom line, GIs made their own acronymic adjustments. "FTA" read a thousand helmets and flak vests and latrine walls from the DMZ to the Delta: Fuck the Army. Ditto the marines, mocking their own globe and anchor insignia. "Fuck the Apple," they wrote everywhere they could find a space. "Eat the Corps."

In either case, "fuck it" seemed the necessary grunt response to what theorists, planners, or other advanced thinkers of the time called the tactical environment, as their cohorts now refer to war-space or battle-space. For people in close combat, Vietnam became its own lexicon, a thousand words for the "country," as Michael Herr has put it, that was "the war." It was the air over our heads, the terrain in front of us, and the ground under our feet. It was a world of weaponry—ordnance: stunning blasts and sheer walls of explosive energy, flames, flying metal, high-velocity rounds, air strikes, artillery, mortars, rockets, miniguns, cluster bombs, napalm, machine guns, automatic rifles, grenades, land mines, booby traps.

Language filled itself up to the breaking point with names for the machines and equipment of war. In the air alone, one witnessed an astonishing array of technology, beginning with a nearly endless inventory of helicopters. An LOH was a light observation helicopter, a "loach." Next above came the Bell UH-1, "Huey," in its ubiquitous and varied configurations, something of the master symbol of the war. A "slick" was a troop carrier. An "eagle flight," also known as an "Alpha Mike Charlie" (airmobile company), was a cluster of slicks flying in formation. A "log bird" was a cargo ship; a "dustoff," a medical evacuation; a "hog," a gunship mounted with cannon and rocket pods, ARA, aerial rocket artillery. Next up the line was the Cobra gunship, the "snake," and then the bigger cargo helicopters: the fat, two-rotor Chinook, AKA the "hook," the "shithook," the flying supply truck, with its carrying impedimenta—donuts, straps, sling loads in cargo nets, huge fuel and water bladders variously known as blivits or elephant turds; and above that, the CH-58 Flying Crane, the "skycrane," capable of carrying whole buildings or, as in one case legendary in my own unit, lifting out an armored personnel carrier sunk to its top deck in the Delta mud. Meanwhile, there were the poor bastard marines, for the better part of the war so helicopter poor that they flew everything from troops to cargo and medevacs in Korean War–era Sikorsky H-38s not all that different from the bizarre eggbeater Mickey Rooney flies in the *Bridges at Toko-Ri*. More imposing were the big air force and navy search-and-rescue ships, the "sky master," the "sea stallion," the "Jolly Green Giant."

Above the helicopter battlefield flew fixed-wing aircraft in equally myriad configurations. Many were old-timers, in new Southeast Asian dress: early in the war, propeller-driven support aircraft, modified navy and air force trainers, and Skyraiders so venerable that their pilots and crews proudly called them "spads"; World War II– and Korean War–era C-47s (cargo versions of the old civilian DC-3) or military C-130s, workhorse transports, rigged up as flareships and flame-spitting gun platforms, and known variously as "smokey," "spooky," "Puff the Magic Dragon." Then there were all the jets, the "fast movers." In big units, coordination came from special controllers on the ground, air force liaison officers. For individual formations in active combat–platoons, companies, battalions, working on the tactical radio–air strikes were usually directed by a pilot (a FAC, or forward air controller) flying a small propeller airplane overhead, most often a twin-tailed OV 10 Bronco. Aircraft on call could range from the F-4 Phantom and converted fighters such as the F-100, F-101, or F-105 to medium-sized bombers. (One time, working with an Australian FAC, I got a B-57 Canberra. It was carrying one bomb, a five hundred pounder. We backed off a full kilometer before the strike. When it went off, a piece of shrapnel the size of a concrete block hit a tree head high about twenty feet behind me.) High-level mission planning was required for a B-52 strike. When that happened, it was exactly what people called it, an arclight: you could actually feel the ground shake miles away and see the night sky lighting up like an incredibly violent storm.

On the ground, a comparable rain of destruction was as close as any commander's tactical radio, with artillery on call twenty-four hours a day in every caliber imaginable: 105-millimeter, 155-millimeter, 175-millimeter, and 8-inch cannon, towed and self-propelled; 81-millimeter and 4.2-inch mortars, ground- and track-mounted. Equally spectacular was the array of ammunition: high explosive–Hotel Echo; white phosphorus–Whiskey Papa, Wilson Pickett (Willy Peter, make you a buh-liever); delayed fuse, for bunker busting; smoke, for marking a target, adjusting fire, or sometimes just finding out where the hell you were. Antipersonnel rounds included beehive, canister, flechette, along with corresponding tank versions, as a last resort fired over open sights with the tubes horizontal. Somewhere in the field, somebody always seemed to be firing something: a marking round, an airburst, a fire-support mission; defcons (defensive concentration); TOTs (time on target); H&Is (harassment and interdiction). The stuff was inexhaustible.

When in doubt, the wisdom went, call arty. The lowliest ambush commander or patrol leader knew how to bring it down in all kinds of combinations:

"Fire mission. Grid, three-five-six, two-one-seven. Direction, one-three-two. Adjust fire."

"Shot, over."

"Shot, out."

"Right one-hundred, drop five-zero. Fire for effect."

It was as simple as that to "bring smoke," "bring pee," "bring the max," "bring max pee" on somebody's ass. Call arty, then the gunships, then the fast movers. Then start the cycle over again. Put them in the hurt locker, big time.

On the ground, the world seemed in constant machine motion. Jeeps and trucks ran everywhere, alone on the hardballs or in low-flying convoys, scattering pedestrians, bicyclists, farmers and their oxcarts; roaring down backcountry trails, horns blasting, throwing rocks and gravel, in the wet season spewing mud, in the dry leaving long contrails of dust. Everything was rated for capacity. A Jeep was officially a quarter ton. A light truck was a three-quarter ton. A heavy truck was a deuce-and-a-half, although in actuality more often a five ton. There were cargo trucks, fuel trucks, water trucks, dump trucks, tow trucks, American and ARVN. Everything towed a trailer—a cargo trailer, a water trailer, a commo (communications) trailer, an ammo trailer. Meanwhile, on tracks, there was the ubiquitous M-113 APC, a boxy armored personnel carrier, generally refitted for Vietnam service in various kinds of mechanized units—cavalry, mech infantry—as an ACAV, armored cavalry assault vehicle, with a front-mounted .50-caliber machine gun, side mounted M-60s, and gunshields all around. Here too, the mutations were various: line tracks, mortar tracks, scout tracks, infantry tracks, flamethrower tracks—with the latter invariably called zippos, not least for their own tendency to go up in flames. Also in use toward the end, and a close competitor in the instant incineration sweepstakes, was the highly touted ARAAV (airborne reconnaissance armored assault vehicle) 551 Sheridan, a light tank distinguished for its incessant mechanical malfunctions and its terrifying vulnerability to rocket-propelled grenades. Heavy-armored units were equipped with the M-48 main battle tank, a fifty-ton behemoth already replaced in the United States and Europe by the newer and more efficient M-60. Engineers ran bridge tracks and did defoliation work with armored bulldozers called Rome plows—big D-9 blade Caterpillars fitted out with cages to stop falling trees but not so good with booby traps like suspended Chicom (Chinese communist) claymore mines. Meanwhile, out on the periphery swarmed a vast reptilian universe in endless armored mutations: 106-millimeter recoilless rifle tracks; 155-millimeter self-propelled artillery tracks; tracks mounted up with quad .50s, 40-millimeter cannon, and Vulcan miniguns. Up north, the marines ran their big, armored amphibious landing vehicle, the Amtrac, and a bizarre tracked platform mounted with four 106-millimeter recoilless rifles. They called it Ontos—"the Thing."

Then there were the weapons in the hands of individual soldiers, the tools of the trade. The standard automatic American infantry rifle, with its black plastic stock and handgrip, was the frequently malfunctioning M-16. The CAR-15, a rakish-looking commando version with a collapsible stock, was even more notorious for stoppages. The Communist-bloc opposite number was the sturdy, blowback-operated, virtually unjammable AK-47. Its ubiquitous companion weapon, simple enough for a sixth grader to operate, was the rocket-propelled grenade (RPG) launcher, variously known as the B-40, the RPG-2, and the RPG-7, with the acronym itself used interchangeably for the weapon and the projectile. The American equivalent was the LAW (light antitank weapon), small and disposable, but much more complicated to use, albeit with detailed instructions written thoughtfully on the side. The VC and NVA infantry machine gun was the SPD; the American was the M-60, alternatively known as the "60" or the "pig." American tracked vehicles were mounted with the much heavier and more devastating .50 caliber. Much less frequently seen, except as an antiaircraft weapon, was the Communist .51. Ground-mounted mortars, again emphasizing the communist knack for utilizing stolen or abandoned ammunition, standard, cold war, NATO (North Atlantic Treaty Organization) caliber, were the American .81 and the VC/NVA .82.

A host of weapons filled out the antipersonnel inventories. Communist stocks included the obsolete SKS rifle and the 9-millimeter pistol, not to mention a full range of stolen weaponry. On the American side one could find everything under the sun—.38- and .45-caliber pistols, sawed-off shotguns, submachine guns, Browning automatic rifles, and the ubiquitous, astonishingly useful M-79 grenade launcher, the "blooker" or "blooper," so named in either case for the sound of the projectile going out of the tube. Hand grenades came in fragmentation, concussion, gas, and smoke varieties, not to mention a white phosphorus version that could inflict hideous burns. Mines and booby traps studded the landscape. Punji stakes were wood or bamboo, sharpened, fire hardened, and dipped in shit, animal or human, for maximum septic potential. Dud artillery rounds rigged as mines literally vaporized people or turned bodies into legless, armless, headless trunks. Bouncing betties went off at groin level. Toe poppers took off feet. Enormous, shotgunlike claymores, American and their Chicom equivalents, emplaced singly or rigged with C-4 plastic explosives and a detonation cord into sprightly daisy chains, took out everything in front of them with a deadly wall of shrapnel.

The language of personal mayhem held precedence. To shoot was to "bust caps." To shoot blindly in the absence of targets was to "recon by fire." To fire off everything simultaneously *and* blindly was a "mad minute." Full of our fears of dying in a hundred different ways in any given moment, we mocked and baited death, tried to call it hard names that showed how hard we were. People didn't die. They got wasted, waxed, dinged, zapped, greased, lit up, blown away. They bought the farm, ate the big one, went west. "Har, har, har," wrote Michael Herr. "Get some." "I waxed the son of a bitch." "I lit the motherfucker up." "I blew the bastard away." And it could happen to you too, a long litany on finding yourself in deep shit. Even if you had your shit together, you could still step in the shit and get your shit packed or get your shit blown away. The army got more and more theological. To distinguish dead Americans from NVA and VC WIA (wounded in action) and KIA (killed in action)—and to separate out those killed in accidents and other noncombat events—U.S. WIA became WHA (wounded by hostile action), and KIA became KHA (killed by hostile action). BC (body count) became CBC (confirmed body count). Meanwhile, nobody got any more or less dead. Anything involving napalm was called operation crispy critter. Even the defoliation people were proud of their killing power. The ranch hands, they called themselves, proclaiming, "Only we can prevent forests."

Everybody knew the mission words. In the air it was the new religion of helicopter warfare, combat assault—insertion, extraction, rapid reaction—what the tacticians liked to call airmobile, vertical envelopment. On the ground, for the average GI, movement mainly translated into humping the boonies—busting jungle, wading paddy mud, fording streams and canals, sliding up and down treacherous hillsides—with the unit of measurement the kilometer, the klick. During daylight there was the war of movement: the sweep, the cloverleaf, the cordon, the block, the hammer and anvil, and occasionally the rare civilian assistance activity, the medcap or the dentcap. Darkness became the time of the static NDP (night defensive position), the OP (the observation post) and the AP (ambush patrol). As ever, the enemy waited with the landscape to see where we would blunder next.

As to clothing and equipment, the things we carried, to paraphrase Tim O'Brien, were truly myriad: weapons, grenades, claymore mines, entrenching tools, machetes, bayonets, combat knives (in the marines, called K-bars), canteens, combat rations, first aid packets, and endless belts and bandoliers of ammunition. Personal gear included a steel pot, jungle fatigues, jungle boots, and, in a rucksack, a pair of socks and maybe a poncho or poncho liner. On tracks and tanks, or in engineer and artillery units, there were pioneer tools, barbed-wire rolls, and even aluminum fencing. Any kind of overhead cover—straw, sticks, wood, screen, canvas, sandbags, concrete—that was not a bunker was a hooch. Food was mainly C-rations—canned turkey loaf; boned chicken; pressed ham; spiced beef; ham and eggs; spaghetti and meatballs; ham and lima beans, and hot dogs and baked beans—with the latter known respectively as ham and motherfuckers, and beans and dicks; fruit cocktail; peaches; date bread; pound cake; packets of sugar, salt, coffee, and hot chocolate; a plastic spoon; toilet paper; and cigarettes. A can opener was a P-38. Much better than Cs were freeze-dried LRRPs—what the army now calls MREs, Meals, Ready to Eat—developed for the long-range-reconnaissance units. But best of all were "hots," officially called class-A rations, served in mess halls or brought from the rear in insulated mermite cans. We drank anything: water with purification tablets and without; iodine-tasting Kool-Aid; reconstituted milk; beer and sodas, in names that themselves have become part of history—Carling, Falstaff, Schlitz, Pabst Blue Ribbon. The field in Vietnam was the land of the off-brands. I do not recall a Budweiser or a Miller. Likewise, instead of a Coke or a Pepsi, it always seemed to be a Fanta or a Shasta. The local brew was Thirty-three Beer—Ba Mu'o'i Ba—universally drunk and known, for its distinctive skunk-cabbagy aftertaste, as "tiger piss." The active ingredient was allegedly formaldehyde.

Other impedimenta of daily living were thoughtfully provided. Money, allegedly to forestall illegal speculation in dollars, was called scrip or MPC (military payment certificate). Vietnamese money was in Ps, piasters. For correspondence home, no one had to buy stamps. In the corner of an envelope headed back to the world—just as congressmen could do, we were reminded—we scribbled the word "free." Through the MARS network (Military Affiliate Radio System), we could actually phone our families back in the world in stupid conversations where everybody forgot to say "over." "I'm OK, Mom, over." "I love you, Honey, over." "How's Bobby, over."

Meanwhile, in our fear and our rage—the self-torturing agony of a war with no mission, impossible a good deal of the time to tell friend from foe, a million different ways to get killed, anywhere, anytime by a skilled, intrepid, almost insanely brave, suicidally committed, and incredibly deadly enemy—we spent a lot of time working up hard words for each other.

Terms of admiration bristled with prowess, resulting in martial epithets of every imaginable variety. Hot dog commanders devised custom call signs like "gunfighter" or "whispering death." Unit nicknames spoke of grisly bravado—Executioners, Widowmakers, and the like—or invoked older regimental and divisional traditions: the Wolfhounds, the Old Reliables, the First Team, the Big Red One, the Screaming Eagles, the

Tropic Lightning, the First Horse, the Black Horse, the Quarter Horse, the Three-quarter Horse. (A new unit like my own 199th Light Infantry Brigade, one of several ginned up for Vietnam more or less ex nihilo, had to invent an appropriately brave moniker. With our fiery spear insignia and alleged prowess in rooting out communist insurgents, we were called the Redcatchers. The troops, as inventively, dubbed the design the "flaming pisspot.") Mottoes blazoned forth everywhere, official and unofficial. "Second to None." "Noli Tangere." "Audaces Fortuna Juvat." In Josiah Bunting's groundbreaking novel *The Lionheads,* the fictionalized titular division rallies to the heraldic "Nemo Me Impune Lacessit." In George Patton's Eleventh Armored Cavalry, the traditional "Allons" found itself restyled into "Find the Bastards, Then Pile On." Even quartermaster and transportation units got into the act. "You Call, We Haul," they proclaimed. "Humping to Please."

Then there were the specialized outfits. A teams, B teams, red teams, white teams, pink teams, blues; LRRPs (long-range reconnaissance patrol), Rangers, SEALs (sea, air, and land), marine force recon. Assassination teams went out under the code name Phoenix. There was even the ultimate war party of one, the sniper: Charlie Bravo Kilo; they called him in my unit: Cold Blooded Killer.

Our terms of disparagement frequently emphasized racial and ethnic divisions. Race words carved themselves mainly in black and white: nigger, spade, jungle bunny, soul brother; versus honky, chuck, whitey, peckerwood, redneck, pale motherfucker. Others broke out across a range of predictable ethnicities: dagos, micks, wops, kikes, Jewboys, Polacks, spics, beaners. Still others marked compliance to authority. To blacks, a black collaborator with the system was a "uniform tango"– Uncle Tom. A model soldier of any complexion was put down as a lifer, an RA–regular army–as opposed to an EM, a draftee or straight enlisted. Divisions could even arise over intoxicational preferences. Those who drank were juicers. Those who smoked were heads.

As often, our hard words for each other were full of what would now be called gender anxiety. "Erry swingin'd dick," crowed the drill sergeants, and every American boy got the message. "C'mon, girls," "Let's go, ladies," they taunted, part of the making of a soldier. The last thing anyone wanted to be was a pussy, a cooze, a cunt, a snatch, a slash, a gash. A cherry. Even combat soldiers had to wait to be blooded so nobody could call them cherries any more, or fresh meat, newby, FNG—a fucking new guy.

Names conferred estate. An army infantry soldier was a grunt, a troop, an eleven bravo (shorthand for the official MOS designation, 11B10), or an eleven bush. The marine equivalent was a gomer, a snuffy, an enlisted puke. Officers became the six, the LT, the skipper, the old man; a new second lieutenant was a brown bar; a new marine second lieutenant was a boot brown bar. Old-line sergeants—top, gunny, mess daddy—mingled with instant NCOs—Pillsbury, Shake and Bake, Ready Whip—young enlisted guys fresh from special academies mass-producing them for the war. In-country christenings abounded. People named Bob or Jerry or Ramon became Deadeye, Killer, the Assassin, the Entertainer, Homicide, Doc, Day Tripper, the Sandman, Jax, Happy, Monk, Boom-Boom, Polack, Ski, Preacher, Cookie, Catman, Reverend, Queenie, Bunny, Mick, Red, Junior, Tiny, Psycho, Shake, Bagger, Baby Cakes, Ogre. Included might be the occasional officer: the Boy Ranger; Mad Mark; the Prince; or, in the case of some one-in-a-million warrior, Hard Core. In the alternative, scorn was generic and pithy: Dufus, Dipstick, Numbnuts, Hand Job, Shithead, Turdbird.

The larger world configured itself according to standard Tables of Organization and Equipment (TO&E). Every unit battalion-sized or bigger had a set of staff sections: S-1 for personnel; S-2 for intelligence; S-3 for operations; S-4 for logistics; and a Vietnam add-on, S-5, for civil affairs. At division and above, the model was replicated with the S for staff replaced by G for general staff. Ranks were broken out according to officer and enlisted: O-1, O-2, O-3, and so on; E-1, E-2, E-3, and so on. E-4, the commonest enlisted rank in Vietnam, was specialist fourth class, or spec four. The specialty—denoted by the MOS—could be anything from killing people to running a projector at the base theater. It was all in the 201 file, the personnel record: qualifications, schooling, decorations, infractions, punishments.

Myriad other numbered forms addressed finance, supply, medical, and legal issues. A 1049, the request for transfer, was known as a dream sheet. A section 8 was a mental discharge. A profile was a certified medical condition, frequently authorizing limited duty, including a reprieve from the field. Other forms of exception might come through a congressional inquiry, a Red Cross emergency leave, or a military compassionate reassignment. A self-contained legal system operated out of its own self-contained text called the UCMJ–the Uniform Code of Military Justice. The commonest proceedings were at the unit level in the form of the Article 15 proceeding–in the marines called the captain's mast. Guilty parties received what was called nonjudicial punishment, involving restriction, extra duty, possibly a fine or reduction in rank. More serious matters became the province of the CID–Criminal Investigation Division–a special branch of the military police, the MPs. At that point there would be lawyers as well, from the JAG, the Judge Advocate General branch. Convictions for serious offenses meant prison time in the LBJ–the Long Binh Jail–or the Da Nang Brig.

Our fellow members of the various military services existed in a pecking order of derision. Marines were jarheads or seagoing bellhops. Sailors were swabbies. Aviators were zoomies or helicopter drivers. Artillery soldiers were redlegs or cannon cockers. Support troops were variously REMFs–rear echelon motherfuckers–pogues, clerks and jerks, titless WACS, Remington raiders. Lowest on everybody's food chain were the Mike Papas, the military police, who were deemed not worth shooting.

Domestic Vietnamese included mamasans, papasans, babysans; barbers, KPs (Kitchen Police), and shitburners; house girls, pimps, and prostitutes. Non-Asian women, mostly nurses or USO (United Services Organization) and Red Cross workers, were round eyes. The most allegedly ubiquitous of the latter were "donut dollies," "Delta Deltas," "Dixie cups." I may have actually seen some in a firebase once out toward the South China Sea. I was getting aboard a Chinook going out to resupply one of the platoons and caught the blue seersucker uniforms at a distance. The only Caucasian women I even vaguely remember in person were nurses when I went to check on people from our unit in the hospital.

Women in general were mainly "pussy," "poontang." "Avoid innimit contack with indigenous females," inveighed sergeants and medics everywhere. This was something not about to happen. "Hello, I love you," was the standard introduction. People got short time or all night; they went to whorehouses and massage parlors—steam and cream, they were called, the Old Cocksucker Shop, going to a blow bath to get a steam job. VD came in the standard permutations. Gonorrhea was the clap, the drip, the crud, the gunge. Syphilis, also rampant, was rumored to come in obscure, incurable Asian variants. The Legend of the Black Syph included a secret island where people were warehoused for the rest of their lives instead of being sent home. Sex without a condom—called going in bareback—was an automatic dip in the septic pool. Even scrupulous participants observed a VPCOD, or Vietnamese pussy cut-off date.

Another major in-country malady, malaria, likewise came in two versions: vivax was disabling; falciparum was a killer. For these, the Mission handed out two kinds of pills, one pink and one white. Both produced instant watery diarrhea—as if everyone in the place didn't already have the chronic shits, which were themselves universally known to the troops as the Ho Chi Minh revenge.

A whole history could be written of the distinctive pidgin of the era, in this case not only of the American war but of the French war before that. *Boo-coo* meant "many"; *ti-ti* meant "little." *Same-same* meant exactly what it said. A *bac si* was a medic—for the marines, a corpsman; a *co* was a girl; a *trung uy* was a lieutenant; a *dai uy* was a captain. A *Chieu Hoi* was a surrendered enemy soldier working for the Americans, a Kit Carson scout, also known as a *Hoi Chanh* (for the amnesty program, Open Arms). A *do ma* was a motherfucker. *Lai day* meant "come here"; *dung lai* meant "stop"; *sin loi* meant "sorry"—most often as in, "Sorry 'bout that." Or "Sorry 'bout *that* shit." *No bic* (from the Vietnamese *khong biet*) meant "I don't know." *Cho oi* meant "Oh My God." Meanwhile, up North, there was also all the marine patois, hybrid Japanese, imported from Okinawa: *skoshi-skoshi, ricky-tick, hayako. Dinky dow* was allegedly Vietnamese for crazy, and also, according to GI lore, a synonym for American. Nuoc Man, a smelly, fermented fish sauce, the national condiment, became a universal adjective: Air Nuoc Man, Radio Nuoc Man, Operation Nuoc Man, and so on. Number one was the best; number ten was the worst; number ten thou was the absolute worst. (Honoring the local linguistic trend, the Tenth ARVN Division, in reality one of the worst divisions in the whole South Vietnamese Army—and that was saying a lot—was actually renamed, while I was there, the Eighteenth. They were wiped out, fighting with an astonishing bravery of desperation at Xuan Loc during the last days in 1975.)

As in most wars, the language of the skin trade required no translation. Boom-boom. Fuck-fuck. Suck-suck. You buy me tea? You want short time? I love you too much.

In its multifarious crossings of language, the war seemed somehow to levitate above its own horror in some vast, unreal polyphony. From atop the chain of command, Mission-speak trotted out phrases like "Winning Hearts and Minds," "Fortified Hamlets," "Revolutionary Development," "Pacification," "Vietnamization," and names of operations like Rolling Thunder, Linebacker (Nixon was a big pro football fan), Cedar Falls, Attleboro, Hastings, Masher, Junction City, White Wing, and Forward Together. The plans and the names came and went with equal celerity. Frances Fitzgerald recalls the "*Ap Doi Moi,* the 'Really New Life Hamlets,' . . . standing over the ruins of the New Life Hamlets, which in turn stood on the ruins of the Strategic Hamlets."

On the ground, down at the level of daily tactical operations, "search and destroy," after a lot of bad back-in-the-world publicity, became "search and clear," which became "reconnaissance in force" (RIF, pronounced *riff*), which in turn became "ground reconnaissance" (Golf Romeo), which of course meant "search and destroy." Commanders doled out formulas about "orchestrating forces," "insertion," "extraction," "an element of unknown size," "denying the enemy valuable resources and cover." A situation report was a "sitrep." Any briefing became the Five o'Clock Follies; Jive at Five. Performance was "excellent," "first rate," "real fine," "outstanding."

From the commanding general down to the lowliest grunt, the language bristled with hard words for hard guys, fervently anatomical. Somebody tough was hard core, a guy with balls, a hard-ass. Somebody aggressive was a hard charger. Anger was a case of the ass, a case of the red ass, a case of the reds. A chewing out was getting your butt reamed, somebody tearing somebody else a new asshole. When the pucker factor went up, you learned to cover your ass, keep a tight asshole. When all else failed, you prepared to bend over and kiss your ass goodbye.

Even saying a simple yes somehow turned into a labor of profane love. "Roger that," someone would say, and then just keep following it up and following it up: That's a rog. That's affirm. That's affirmative. That's an affirmative. That's most affirmative. You got *that* one right. Damn straight. Fuckin' A. Damn fuckin' straight. Fuckin' a diddy-bag.

Meanwhile, down on the very bottom line, we turned the war into hard non sequitur. Doing our best Don Adams/Maxwell Smart, we piped "Sorry 'bout that" and "Sorry 'bout *that* shit." "*Sin loi,* mother-fucker," we said. "There it is," "Don' mean nothin'," and "What can they do, send me to Vietnam?"

Even today I remember Vietnam in language as intensely, almost imprisoningly, hermetic. I expect further that with every passing year each veteran's world probably gets even more solitary in its enclosure according to branch of service, specific unit, mission, equipment, and area and period of operations. Somebody once described Vietnam as a one-year war we fought ten times. If you adjusted the latter figure to around 3.5 million–the number of Americans who actually served there–I think you'd get closer to the truth still going around in people's heads. To this day, for instance, I haven't the foggiest notion, outside of a few terms I've read in books or seen in movies, of how the air force and navy aviation people talked: MIGS, SAMS, wild weasels, going downtown, and so forth. On the other hand, I know just enough about the marines, poor bastards, to believe that they really should have had their own language–"utilities" instead of fatigues, "corpsmen" instead of medics, and the like. They had their own war, invariably lousier than anybody else's. And it was not just the standard military poor-mouthing. Wherever they went, they could count on the lousiest food, the lousiest equipment, the lousiest weaponry, the lousiest missions, the whole "sour reek of obsolescence," as Michael Herr observed, "that followed the Marines all over Vietnam." Look at old photographs of those hellish bases up on the DMZ. You see Guadalcanal, Peleliu, Okinawa, jungle rot, sweat, uniforms disintegrating off their bodies, and further back beyond that the mud soldiers of the Somme and Petersburg.

Whatever the language of your war, you never forget it; instead, you continue to live in it in ways that never stop surprising you. One of the most jarring experiences any Vietnam War veteran can still have even today is hearing a baseball announcer tell how a homerun hitter really lit up somebody's fastball or a teenage kid swear how he's completely blown away by somebody's new record album. On a popular TV series about the Mafia these days, disposable people get wacked. Is that like waxed? Or more like wasted? How strange a pang of recognition arises to hear somebody your age use the expression *boo-coo* or *ti-ti*? How close in certain moments do you hear yourself almost calling something number one or number ten?

Viet-speak. *Slang for a mixture of standard English, slang, and Vietnamese or other Asian languages, often used in Vietnam.* So the definition reads in one of several encyclopedias of the Vietnam War. The time has probably come now to update the reference, to give it a lengthening historical definition. *Viet-speak:* The in-country language adopted and developed by American soldiers in the Vietnamese war to communicate with each other during the war and afterward about their experience. It is what a discourse theorist would call an archaeology of knowledge—an episteme, a whole field of consciousness, a self-contained grammatology. To this day, numerous books about the Vietnamese war include a glossary. There are at least two freestanding dictionaries. A major criterion of excellence for established works in the Vietnam canon—novels, poems, plays, memoirs, histories, works of journalism and reportage—is that they still read as if somebody had a tape recorder in their ear. Ditto movies: *Apocalypse Now* is a spotty film with a great Michael Herr–Martin Sheen voice track; similarly, *Full Metal Jacket* (Herr again) and *Platoon* succeed best when they get the words right *and* the music. But pretty soon it will all start to go, because many of us are starting to go. In our books we will sound like Norman Mailer or James Jones. In our movies, we will remind people of Frank Lovejoy or Aldo Ray. Eventually our war will be a dead language. The sooner the better, one wishes to say.

However, at the same time, there is a discourse of national memory; and for one word alone, it is surely worth preserving for its burden of tragic knowledge. Gooks, we called them: a lousy name for Asians from another lousy Asian war. In the largest sense, it is an object lesson in naming the enemy as old as warfare itself: the bigger the language disconnect the better. In the same moment, as a particular etymology it speaks a whole history of American empire. The Korea story, for instance, probably holds its own portion of truth: in the word Koreans used for themselves, *Han-Guk,* as opposed to Americans, *Mi-Guk.* Along a different, but equally documentable path, however, are others taking it further back, to the army in the Philippines and the marines of the banana wars of the early twentieth century in the Caribbean and Central America. (One account dates the word to 1920, used in Haiti as a term for native servants; another locates it slightly earlier in the Philippines.) The most likely etymology, however, carries all the way back to the Spanish-American War, where it derived from a derisive term for white American anti-imperialists—called goo-goos, for "good government"—advocating self-determination for Cubans, Puerto Ricans, Filipinos, and other formal colonial subjects of Spain.

Gooks, we called them. What did they call us? Interestingly, from a cultural and a linguistic standpoint, the great problem of Vietnamese history has always been *their* trouble with outsiders. Nuoc Viet they have termed themselves from prehistory—with Nuoc meaning roughly "the water nourishing the land"—as opposed to Nuoc Cambot, Cham, Khmer, and so on, not to mention the Chinese, all of them traditional invaders whom the Vietnamese have been fighting off for more than two millennia. Of other bloods, we were just the latest in a long line. And for all the destruction and death we wrought, the language couldn't seem to find the energy to rise much above everyday accommodation. In the South, the official term was *Ong my*—as in, "My! My!" ("American! American!"). Common slang was "long nose." As noted earlier, GI legend had it that *dinky dow*—the pidgin phrase for crazy—was a direct translation of the Vietnamese word for American. It was not true, but it should have been. They thought we smelled bad and had too much hair on our bodies. They found us loud, boorish, and clumsy. In the North they had their own variety of expressions. The "devil Americans," bombing victims were said to call us, the "murderous Americans," the "death sowers." The communist phrasings, of course, were what we would call propaganda. The more common coinages, in contrast, remain a way of looking at us that we might have found profoundly instructive, even illuminating. In a war that prided itself on information, these were things we might have known if we had bothered to take even a short course in the language of the Nam.

Solatium

More than thirty years later, and not a week goes by when I don't think
of the dead Vietnamese boy at Gia Ray. Actually, I go through periods when I see him every day. I zip open the body bag, and out he
comes, face first, the rest of him in a fetal crouch, arms and legs drawn
up in front like some dreadful insect mutation. Later I find out that is
what dead bodies often do. Everything–head, limbs, torso–is covered
in a kind of viscous, translucent slime, the stuff used in monster movies.
A combination of mucus, chest fluid, urine, and dissolved fecal matter,
it smells oddly sweet. Later I find out that is how dead bodies often
smell.

It's dusk. Earlier in the day, I've sent this boy out on a helicopter with a depressed skull fracture. The mechanized unit in which I'm a platoon leader—tanks, armored personnel carriers, and assorted other vehicles—has been moving through his village, and a big tank retriever has knocked down the corner of an old, ceremonial stone gate. A heavy piece—about the size and weight of a cinder block—has fallen on the boy's head, caving in one side of his skull. When I pick him up and carry him to my track, I notice that the indentation is in the exact shape of the rock.

My next recollection has me inside a nearby firebase—Mary Ann, I think it's called—kneeling on the helipad, with the boy in my lap and a PRC-25 radio beside me. I'm yelling into the handset, begging for an army medevac helicopter, a dustoff. Voices on the other end keep telling me that no dustoff is available, and that even if one is, I can't call a dustoff for a Vietnamese civilian. In between sessions of screaming at the bastards on the radio, I keep looking down at the kid, patting him and stroking him, telling him it's going to be all right, we'll get him out of there, and somebody will take care of him.

He seems to be just barely breathing. Under his short, black, shiny hair, I can see the big rectangular dent in the side of his skull. As I remember, it's finally the brigade executive officer, a colonel, who with much impatience finally agrees to land his command ship and take the boy to the Vietnamese Army compound at Xuan Loc, about ten miles away, where the Vietnamese have their own medical evacuation unit. When the helicopter lands, I give him to one of the door gunners. I go back to my platoon.

In the years since, I have tried every way I can to put together the rest of that day, but it just doesn't exist. We may have patrolled the jungle with tanks and armored personnel carriers like we did most days or set up blocking positions for the infantry sweeping the other way. We may have done convoy-escort or roadblock duty. It was bad country up there. On the roads, we kept passing burned-out hulks from the last American unit to operate in the place a year or so before—a hot-shit armored cavalry regiment, commanded at the time by George Patton Jr., that obviously had not won all that many hearts and minds. Once, in the middle of a jungle clearing, we found some kind of aircraft fuselage with French markings. Boy, I remember thinking, is this going to be a long war.

Whatever happened that day in late July or early August 1969, my platoon was back inside the firebase by late afternoon, setting up for night perimeter security. The boy was waiting for us when we pulled in. Also waiting were orders to get him cleaned up and ready for a ceremony in the morning, when he would be returned to his family for burial. Because I had the only field medic, he got the job. I went with him to see if I could help. As a platoon officer, I knew that there would be times when I would never ask anyone to do something I wouldn't do. I decided this was one of those times. That was when I opened up the body bag. It was also when my medic went temporarily insane. He was a decent man and a brave soldier, the kind of medic everybody called Doc, and he had been through a lot. He took what he saw as an insult to the dead. He screamed, he raged, he wept. He cursed every curse he could think of, mainly at the fucking ARVNs. It seemed to be a professional matter. Who would let something like that happen to a kid and then not clean him up? After a while, the thing seemed to pass. He settled down and went to work, wiping the boy's body and straightening his limbs. I offered to stay and help or at least keep him company. He told me in a kindly voice that he wanted to do it by himself and that I should go on back to the platoon.

The ceremony didn't take place until midmorning. It probably took that long to gather up all the brigade bigwigs from the rear. The Vietnamese boy's parents were going to be brought in to the firebase to claim him. They were also going to get something called a solatium payment. That was the official name for it. It was a cash payment made by the U.S. government to Vietnamese civilians who lost property or family members as a result of accidents of war. The figure, as I recall, was alleged to be around thirty-five dollars. The procedure was administered by a special staff officer in the brigade called the S-5. This was something the army had added during the Vietnamese war. Traditionally, S-1 was personnel; S-2, intelligence; S-3, operations; and S-4, supply. In Vietnam, S-5 was the officer for civil affairs, who provided civilian medical and dental care, helped rebuild damaged property, involved villagers in agricultural and sanitation projects, and the like. This was another thing the S-5 did: find Vietnamese civilians who had lost loved ones due to military operations and arrange solatium payments. He was also in charge of arranging the ceremonies, like the one at Mary Ann.

I watched from a distance. The meeting was held in the back of a big armored command vehicle, full of radios and situation maps, with a ramp that dropped to the ground and a tent attached like an awning, making a kind of pavilion. Lots of high-ranking functionaries had flown in for the ceremony, including a couple of field-grade officers from the brigade staff and the local ARVN commander. The S-5 did the honors. The parents looked numb and bewildered. They made strange smiles and bows. Every time they did, the Americans smiled and bowed too, and then the parents smiled and bowed some more. Besides the cash payment, the parents received a couple of big ration-supplement boxes like those given to units in the field once a week or so—SPs, or sundries packs, they were called—full of candy, snacks, and toilet items, and each with about ten cartons of American cigarettes in all different brands.

That was it. An infantry company moved in to secure the firebase, and the next day I was back in the jungle with my platoon. Eventually I left the platoon and became the executive officer of my troop, a company-sized unit. When my year was up, I went home. I went back to graduate school and used the GI Bill to get a Ph.D. in English. I've spent my career teaching American literature in a university. As part of my work, I've written a good deal about the literature of the Vietnamese war. On the one hand, I suppose it's been my way of coming to terms with the experience. On the other, not much of it has dealt directly with what I did or what happened to me personally, and I can only infer that until lately, at least, I have wanted it that way.

I'm fifty-eight now and a parent for the first time. My wife and I have a daughter who is nine. I have an obsessive fear that something bad is going to happen to her. There are times when I put her in the car to go somewhere with her mother or someone else I really trust and I worry that I'm never going to see her again. One weekend about three years ago, when my wife and I were at the beach and my daughter was staying with her aunt, I convinced myself that they were both going to be freakishly murdered. For a day and a half I sat in a chair, staring and mute, bludgeoned with medication. My wife took me home. A VA psychologist who has become a friend tells me this is all typical of what he calls "recurrent unpleasant thoughts," a form of PTSD called delayed posttraumatic stress disorder. It's all through the literature, he tells me. Deep down somewhere, he says, it's the dead Vietnamese boy at Gia Ray I'm thinking about. He's right, I've decided. I've also checked the DSM IV, and he's right there too. It's all in black and white: intrusive memories, persistent anxiety, excessive vigilance.

Oddly, as many Vietnamese as we killed in what were called accidents of war, you don't see much written about solatium in the literature. A scene such as the one I witnessed appears in an early chapter of Josiah Bunting's novel *The Lionheads,* in which the major general commanding the fictional Twelfth Infantry Division and his chief of staff meet with a Vietnamese couple whose son has been killed and their house destroyed. The ceremony takes place in the general's imposing office at the division headquarters. "Mr. Tranh," says the general, addressing the father, "this is a great tragedy you've sustained, and we know what a blow it is for you. It's something we feel terrible about here. We want you to know that we have made arrangements with Captain Kramer to see that you get every assistance rebuilding your house. And it's a terrible, terrible shame about your son. I know how much you must have loved him." The general mentions that he also has sons. No, he replies to the Vietnamese father, they are not in the army. The chief of staff, a colonel, surprises everyone, including himself, by quoting some Lincoln he has learned at the academy. "Nothing could beguile you from a loss," he intones, "as overwhelming as this one is." The bereaved parents receive the payment in an envelope embossed with the Lionhead crest. Typewritten and carefully centered in capital letters, the envelope reads: FROM THE MEN OF THE TWELFTH INFANTRY DIVISION IN DEEP CONDOLENCE. When the Vietnamese couple are escorted to the jeep that has brought them to headquarters, "a trailer has been attached to it, filled with tools, burlap sacks of rice, and some cartons of C-rations."

Misspelled as "solacium," the policy is mentioned anecdotally in James William Gibson's *The Perfect War: Technowar in Vietnam,* where a former army enlisted man assigned to the U.S. civilian aid mission angrily remembers it as emblematic of the American bureaucratic attitude toward the Vietnamese: "an adult civilian over 15 years who was killed was worth $35 to their family; a child under 15 was worth $14.40. The United States government paid people off for their dead children, or their dead husbands and wives, or whatever, at the rate of $35 or $15, depending on their age."

Another brief reference appears in a glossary, *Words of the Vietnam War,* as "Grievance Payment," under which are listed not only "Solatium" but also "Compensation Payment" and "Go-Minh Money." Solatium procedures, it says, involved "cash payments ranging from a few dollars to several hundred dollars made to Vietnamese as compensation for property damages to buildings, crops, farm animals, and personal possessions, and also for grief suffered as the result of the loss of a loved one." However, as with virtually everything involving money among Americans and Vietnamese, it goes on to explain, a built-in potential for shamming and scamming quickly became a two-way street. Initially claims were to be made either to the U.S. military directly or to the U.S. Mission through the Vietnamese district and/or province chief. In the latter case, a problem with fraudulent inflation of claims and awards quickly arose, including the skimming of high percentages of payments into official pockets. As a result, eventually the Vietnamese government was *required* to have citizens submit claims directly to Americans. Thence, in the idea of applying for and receiving compensation directly from the Americans, arose the local nickname: go-minh money. In Vietnamese, it can be roughly translated as "extracting oneself from a predicament."

Ironically, the most detailed historical description of solatium policy now available probably comes from an official source, a Department of the Army pamphlet titled "Law at War." Written by a Major General George S. Pew, it is a history of activities during the period of Vietnam operations of the army's legal branch, the Judge Advocate General

Corps. Under the heading of Claims Administration within a general framework addressing civilian problems caused by military operations, the description is worth quoting in full:

> In South Vietnam it was the custom for a representative of the United States to pay a visit of condolence to a Vietnamese injured by military activities or to the survivors of a deceased victim, and for a small amount of money or goods such as rice, cooking oils, or food stuffs to be given. The visit and payment took place when U.S. personnel were involved in the incident that caused injury, regardless of who was at fault, and even if the incident was technically caused by combat. The donation was not an admission of fault, but was intended to show compassion. By caring for the victims, the United States could assist the civic action program in Vietnam. The recipient of the solatium payment would also be advised of the procedures required to present a claim against the U.S. government, if appropriate, and the location of the nearest U.S. foreign claims commission office.
>
> The condolence visit was successful in that the personal expression of compassion by a representative of the United States made a favorable impression on Vietnamese victims who had previously regarded the American claims system as efficient, honest, fair, and generous—but cold.

That, apparently, was the explanation of the scene I had witnessed at Firebase Mary Ann. Whether the desired results had been achieved I couldn't tell. As Michael Herr would say later in *Dispatches,* trying to read the war was like trying to read the faces of the Vietnamese, and trying to read the faces of the Vietnamese was like trying to read the wind. Still, the word stuck with me. Solatium. Obviously it was some kind of civil affairs policy term—another bright idea, no doubt, from the people who gave you "Winning Hearts and Minds." And if it was a policy term, like anybody who had been in Vietnam for five minutes, I could rate the chances at around 100 percent that it was also some kind of bullshit language game. At the very least, solatium was obviously some kind of payoff. Like anybody who had struggled through ninth-grade Latin, however, even I could see that the term had something to do with solace.

Whatever uses the army was trying to make of the term, I wondered, how had a word of such strange beauty sneaked into the war? Everything else seemed such an acronym stew. As if to mock the absolute reality of fear, weapons, and bodies, language seemed to have reduced itself mainly to strange combinations of sounds and initials. Sorting out the names of all the people trying to kill each other alone was nearly as hopeless as identifying them on the ground: Americans officially belonged to MACV or USARV; South Vietnamese were ARVN or RF-PF. Enemy soldiers could be VC one day and NVA the next. At closer range, while you rode your ACAV on a RIF, you could get killed by an AK, an SKS, an SPD, or an RPG, not to mention a dizzying array of things coming back at you—usually stolen from the ARVNs and RF-PFs or abandoned by them on the battlefield—carrying analogous nomenclatures from your own vast inventory. If you wounded or killed one of them, you got a WIA or a KIA. If one of them wounded or killed you, you were designated WHA or KHA, as if the change of a letter made some kind of difference.

Most of the time in Vietnam, even if something looked like a real word, chances were good that it was trying to say anything but what it meant. "Pacification" was forced resettlement. "Revolutionary Development" was political indoctrination. "Phoenix" was political assassination. "Forward Together" meant "Americans fight and ARVNs watch."

For years I tucked "solatium" away, as if trying not to disturb it. On one hand, it seemed a kind of beacon in the general muddle; on the other, I was almost afraid to find out what kind of linguistic freak show it would turn out to be. Eventually, I looked it up and found that my intuitions on both counts had been dreadfully correct. The good news was that it did have a direct connection with "solace"; indeed, by some accounts, the word "solace" itself actually derived directly from "solatium" as a past participial form of "solari," to comfort or console. The bad news was that I found the word only in obscure legal lexicons, conceptually a bizarre inheritance of English law from Scottish law, which in turn, because early Scottish lawyers did most of their study on the Continent, derived from Roman law by way of the medieval church. "*Solatium,*" read the entry in *West's Legal Dictionary,* "(se-lay-shee-em),

n. [Latin 'solace'] Scots law: Compensation; esp., damages allowed for hurt feelings or grief, as distinguished from damages for physical injury."

I shouldn't have been surprised. What I had seen, then, that morning at Firebase Mary Ann was the attempt during U.S. military operations in Vietnam to put a price on mental anguish. To say this another way, you weren't doing anything as crass as trying to pay people off for their actual loss of a loved one or some other kind of injury to family or property; you were trying to compensate them for their emotional loss, as if those could somehow be separated.

In all these respects, it was a very Western concept, a function of what Frances Fitzgerald called states of mind: a way of dividing the world into reason and emotion, mind and spirit, body and soul, on the assumption that everyone everywhere was naturally inclined to think that way. Because the gospel of American progress, of moral assurance and rational certainty, assumed politically that any nation enlightened enough to want to be America's ally—even the remnant of a three-thousand-year-old Asian culture—really wanted deep down inside to be a two-hundred-year-old Western democracy, it only followed that such a nation wished a similar vision of legal equity to be effected in its understanding of death. In sum, the policy must have once been exactly the kind of thing a Mc-Namara, a Bundy, or a Rostow could have cooked up in a memorandum and then slept better knowing about. Now, like everything else in the war, it seemed pointless and irredeemable.

Like most company-grade officers, I got to see my share of dead people in Vietnam. So increasingly I wonder why over the years it's the dead boy at Gia Ray who keeps coming back to me and not the ambush patrol leader we picked out of a minefield a few days later with the back of his head blown off; the ghostly looking kid from Texas in a ditch, bled white from a single bullet; the heap of dead civilians who came back to earth one day after their Lambretta ran over a booby-trapped artillery round; or the God knows how many Vietnamese I saw on convoy runs with their brains all over the pavement. Surely it has to do with coming late in life to being a parent, to understanding that peculiar lesson in mortality no childless person, I believe, can really comprehend.

In my particular case, I also think it has to do with an analogous version of that lesson as embodied in words. Even longer than I've been a parent, I've been a teacher and a writer who has spent his life working with them, trying to comprehend their queer conjoinings of presence and evanescence, their power quite literally both to make and unmake the world in the space of a breath or a line: how they sound, how they look, what they can do, what they can't do, where they come from, where they go, the exaltations they inspire and the dishonesties they conceal, the corruptions they put on and the debasements they resist.

This particular word, as it turns out, still has a place in the government inventory—now on the Internet, not surprisingly, in an official Department of Defense dictionary of military and associated terms. "Monetary compensation given to alleviate grief, suffering, and anxiety resulting from injuries," the entry reads, "and property or personal loss." However, you still won't find it in the histories, or even in the personal accounts, like this one, except as some queer, haunted memory. Nor, of course, will you find it in the DSM IV. This is as it should be.

I think that when the army came up with the word "solatium," it set some very strange magic loose in the world. For me it will always be a reminder, even amid the latest revelations of the sheer amplitude and indiscriminateness of our killing and destructiveness in Vietnam, of something every bit as horrifying, and that is of how totally, appallingly, even insanely resolute we remained in believing in our good intentions. Solatium. What's in a word, I ask, when now, as then, there's still so little solace for anyone, American or Vietnamese, who had anything to do with that war? As an American, still trying to come to terms with what we did there, I hang on to it for two very specific reasons. It won't bring that boy back; and it won't make him go away, either.

Just Like in the Movies

I begin this examination of the strange and often dreadful reciprocity between American life and American entertainment—a commemorative essay, one might call it, in several meanings of that term—by adducing two parallel narratives, both essentially factual and both spanning roughly the same period more than thirty years ago. Each begins in early April 1970 and ends slightly more than a month later, after the U.S. Army invasion of Cambodia and the killing of four students by Ohio National Guardsmen at Kent State University. The first involves a U.S. president and his obsession with a war movie. The second involves a U.S. Army lieutenant and his experiences in a war being conducted at the time by that president. The president was Richard Nixon. The war movie was *Patton*. The army lieutenant was me. The war, of course, was in Vietnam.

It was on April 1, 1970, according to one account, that Richard Nixon saw *Patton* for the first time. Another says it may have been on April 4 at a family viewing. And according to biographer Stephen Ambrose, whose choice of phrasing is noteworthy, Nixon may "have started watching" the film in late March. Whatever the exact date, the appearance of the movie and the president's instant identification with it coincided with a crisis Nixon quickly and directly associated with General George S. Patton–the inspired, unpredictable, headline-grabbing, victory-loving hero depicted in the film.

With the United States attempting to wind down the Vietnamese war, communist forces suddenly seemed to be taking advantage of the apparent American weakness by widening the war with military actions against the new Cambodian regime of Lon Nol. According to Ambrose's account, it became increasingly clear to the president that–as he dictated in a 5 A.M. message to Henry Kissinger on April 12–"we need a bold move in Cambodia to show that we stand with Lon Nol." Still, for a while, it was unclear what kind of bold move would eventuate. The administration could send arms. It could send a Vietnamese force with U.S. support. Or it could actually commit U.S. forces–an appealing but risky option. The latter would certainly not help negotiations, and there was bound to be tremendous political opposition at home. Yet such an attack could penetrate the major communist sanctuaries long used to prosecute the war across the border in Vietnam with relative impunity. It might even locate and destroy the fabled COSVN (Central Office South Vietnam) headquarters, said to be the nerve center of all Viet Cong operations. Nixon agonized.

Meanwhile, he could at least carry along for support the freshly inspirational image of George S. Patton–or, more properly, of Patton as depicted by George C. Scott. And when the real crunch came, Nixon did not hesitate to call on it. On April 25, we can isolate at least one repeat viewing, and possibly two, that proved crucial. The date in question was a Saturday following a late-week debate at Camp David over whether to enlarge an already planned South Vietnamese invasion of the Parrot's Beak border region of Cambodia by introducing an all-out U.S. attack on the Fishhook region. Nixon returned to Washington. There, accompanied by Kissinger, John Mitchell, and his friend Bebe Rebozo, the president took a long cruise down the Potomac on the official yacht *Sequoia*. Military discussions continued, now involving a good deal of alcohol and punctuated by a boozy pass-in-review off Mount Vernon. The river outing was not the crown of the evening, however. That role was reserved, back at the White House, for a special showing of *Patton*.

Actually, there is good reason to believe that the movie treat may not have been the first of the day, at least for the president. According to Hugh Sidey's *Life* magazine account, Nixon may also have watched it earlier with Kissinger "in the Saturday stillness of the White House." And Kissinger, in describing his manner of begging off from part of the late show, seems to support the idea. "It was the second time he had so honored me," he notes archly in his memoirs, and "inspiring as the film was, I managed to escape for an hour in the middle of it to prepare for the next day's NSC meeting."

Whether April 25 was a single- or double-feature day for Nixon, we will probably never know. The important thing is that a viewing of the movie punctuated the day on which the die, as Caesar would have said, had been cast. Likewise, we cannot know if Nixon's screening of the film continued after the invasion of Cambodia. Certainly the film's influence on Nixon continued, in an eerie recapitulation of the film script.

That recapitulation began with Nixon's composing of a saber-rattling address to the American people, scheduled for national television on the night of April 30. Though his text made advisors such as William Rogers and Melvin Laird "cringe," Nixon refused to moderate the tone. What's more, he chose to deliver it from the White House war room as a stand-up, quasi-military soliloquy, complete with maps, overlays, and a dancing pointer—what staffers would have called eyewash or the whole dog-and-pony show. A real commander would have used a briefing officer, who in turn would have used a sharp enlisted man to do the pointer work. Nixon did it all solo, at once master strategist, briefing officer, and bold captain at arms.

He outlined options. He defended his choice to commit major U.S. forces as "going to the heart of the trouble." He invoked the memories of previous presidents pressed to take the military reins and make similar lonely choices in the same room: Wilson, Roosevelt, Eisenhower, Kennedy. After all, the issue was really victory, he concluded, even if it cost him his political life. "Whether I may be a one-term president," he noted, "is insignificant compared to whether by our failure to act in this crisis the United States proves itself to be unworthy to lead the forces of freedom in this critical period in world history. I would rather be a one-term president and do what I believe is right than to be a two-term president at the cost of seeing America become a second-rate power and to see this nation accept the first defeat in its proud 190-year history."

Decisive, beleaguered, prepared to be dismissed for a belief in the correct military option—Patton was all there. One could almost hear the stirring music, the tapping of the drums, the rising melody of the fifes. And it continued into the next morning, as chronicled by Ambrose, where Nixon, still in high martial fettle, attended a Pentagon briefing on the operation's progress. Ever the no-nonsense guy, the commander on the scene, he asked the tough, probing questions and refused to settle for warnings about political consequences, saying that was his business. With a flick of the hand, he ordered the assembled joint chiefs to "take out all of those sanctuaries," including ones previously uninvaded. "Make whatever plans are necessary," he said, "and then just do it. Knock them all out so that they can't be used against us again. Ever."

Then, just outside, came an impromptu extension of the performance. One young woman thanked him on behalf of a husband in Vietnam. Another described her admiration for his resolve. "It made me proud to be an American," she said. In response, Nixon launched into a tirade against student protestors, whom he characterized belligerently as barracks loafers and sick-bay commandos whose radical posturing stood in contrast to the real "stand-up" heroism of "those kids out there" in Vietnam. The college types were "bums," he said.

With little effort, one could see Scott in *Patton* getting ready to pull his .45 on Tim Considine and getting ready meanwhile to be wrestled into submission by calmer heads around him. "Why, the son of a bitch ought to be shot," and "Hell, I ought to shoot the son of a bitch myself." Then, as the anger subsided, would come the general's sly smile, the one Patton's daughter called mirthless. The histrionics were over, having made their point in words that could shoot no one. It was, in military terms, a demonstration.

By evening, the incident had been widely reported. Nixon was castigated for his political insensitivity and gratuitous truculence. For the moment, he put a lid on it, but not without another aggressive military decision. Through back channels, he secretly ordered MENU, a new air offensive against North Vietnam. Meanwhile, with the "bums" speech and the bombing resumption now making for more upheaval than the ongoing invasion, campuses predictably erupted everywhere.

By May 4, the United States had experienced not only the killings of four students at Kent State University in Ohio but also, too often forgotten, the deaths of two others at Jackson State in Mississippi. Nixon offered a brief, bellicose call for quiet on the nation's campuses in the name of "peaceful dissent." On the student deaths he wasted no words of regret, instead falsely justifying the official violence as a necessary response to what he described as violent protest. Basically, he told the university communities, those who played war with the government should expect to be warred upon in return.

Meanwhile, the moviegoer gloriosus, seemingly unchastened, continued to parade and orate his militarism. By midmonth, indeed, as Hugh Sidey would record in his *Life* magazine account, Nixon was emboldened to extend the histrionics so far as to bring the movie text out of the closet as a source of explicit reference. Most notable was his meeting with business and economic leaders who were called in, with the invasion still in progress, for their share of inspirational briefing. Midway, he played his trump card: "Hey, has anyone seen *Patton*?" As if genuinely pleased with the originality of the insight, Nixon compared his own actions to Patton's rescue of Bastogne during the Battle of the Bulge after it had been deemed impossible by other leaders. Then, softening the self-flattery, he joshingly recalled Patton decorating a chaplain for an apparently successful prayer for good weather and said that every chaplain in Vietnam was now accordingly praying for rain so that the communists could not easily move into their bulldozed sanctuaries.

A week later, a copy of the film went with the president to California–not, according to Sidey, for Nixon's further delectation, but rather (apparently as counseled by presidential assistant Robert Haldeman) for viewing by young aides so as to help them accurately gauge the president's frame of mind at this important historical moment. And as late as the end of May or early June, Secretary of State William Rogers is said to have remarked to *Patton* producer Darryl Zanuck that "the movie comes up" in every Nixon conversation. (Apparently, it also surfaced in important conversations about Nixon. According to Kissinger, *Patton* later made the viewing list of Chou-En Lai, who ordered a copy as a way of helping assess Nixon's likely behavior as a negotiator in China.)

If April Fool's Day 1970 truly was the day that Richard Nixon first saw and became hopelessly enamored of the Hollywood film biography of the father of modern armored warfare, I must confess to wishing I had never found out about it. Halfway around the planet, that same day– the first day of my last month in Vietnam–was the worst of the war for D Troop, Seventeenth Cavalry, the company-sized armored unit I had joined eleven months earlier as a platoon leader and currently served as executive officer.

The trouble had started early that morning, when an artillery convoy, escorted by tanks and armored personnel carriers from the Second Platoon, was attacked by a large and unusually well-armed ambush force along a stretch of road in the northern part of the brigade's area of operations. After receiving a weak radio transmission from a wounded artillery lieutenant in one of the trucks–the only thing that probably prevented the convoy from being overrun–the First Platoon was brought in from the north to assist, and it too came under attack. By the time things stabilized, six D Troop soldiers were dead. Three had burned to death in a Sheridan tank. One had been cut in half by a rocket-propelled grenade. Another had bled to death from a bullet wound in the leg. The last–one of the platoon sergeants, commanding another Sheridan–had been killed by a direct rocket hit that had penetrated his gun shield and blown off his arm.

My first knowledge of the attack came as part of an urgent request from the brigade helipad for all the extra machine-gun barrels we could round up. The same message conveyed the information, albeit unconfirmed, that the troop's commanding officer had accompanied the First Platoon into the ambush zone, had been wounded, and had possibly been killed.

As the troop's second-in-command, I asked to be flown in with the machine-gun barrels. When I arrived there, I found the troop commander unwounded and firmly in charge. For the rest of the day, I ran around the perimeter—a fairly useless and very scared short-timer—trying to do what I could. All the casualties had been evacuated except for the dead platoon sergeant. I found him on his turret floor. His arm was beside him, still in its jacket sleeve, buttoned at the wrist against the morning chill. Half his face was gone as well. With two volunteers pulling from the back deck of the abandoned tank while I pushed from below, we hoisted him out.

The sergeant, however, was not the final American soldier to die that day, a distinction that went to the brigade's well-respected and popular commander, a one-star general. Leading from the ground, as was his custom, he was shot through the heart while participating in an afternoon sweep of the ambush positions. He died just after his pilot picked him up. The troop continued to fire up whole sling loads of ammunition, which had been carried into the perimeter by huge CH-47 helicopters. There had also been continuous air strikes and artillery and a flank insertion of an infantry company. The enemy disengaged, and the troop rolled out with what was left of the convoy to a night defensive position.

For me, the rest of April mainly involved hanging around at the brigade base and waiting to go home. Late in the month, my orders finally came. I reported to the Ninetieth Replacement Battalion at Long Binh and got my port call. Nineteen hours later, I landed at Travis Air Force Base in California. Five hours after that, I was out of the army, on my way to the San Francisco airport in a cab. At the airport, I bought a newspaper; on the front page was a photograph of three soldiers from my brigade in Cambodia. The next newspaper picture I remember seeing after that was the famous shot of the girl at Kent State, the one of the girl with her arms in the air—a teenage runaway, it turned out—keening over a dead student facedown on the pavement.

Later on—as virtually everyone else in America already had, I supposed—I went to see *Patton*. It struck me then, as it does now, as the oddest kind of guts-and-glory comic book, a film that couldn't decide whether to be heroic or funny and therefore opted for both. According to film historian Lawrence Suid, apparently that caused the lead actor, George C. Scott, considerable pain. Somehow he had come to admire the insane energy that seemed to radiate from the historical character; at the same time, he knew that those willing to identify with the image of the military genius would wishfully connect those feelings with their dissatisfactions about Vietnam, which he personally felt to be an "obscenity." To resolve the problem, he later confessed to an interviewer for the Sunday *London Times,* he had "to load the part with pyrotechnics, with smoke screens, with every dirty actor's trick to bring out what [he] want[ed] to bring out," even at the price, he admitted, of being "thoroughly disgusted with the project."

The way Scott played the role of Patton, I have to admit, reminded me of some strange, hard-charging people I had known or heard about in Vietnam. He certainly made me think of the general's own son George Patton Jr., a recently promoted brigadier still much talked about in his old command, the Eleventh Armored Cavalry (the Black Horse). The younger Patton had earned fame for rewriting the regimental motto (from the somewhat quaint "Allons" to the more graphic and serviceable "Find the Bastards, Then Pile On") and for distributing a Christmas card featuring a picture of Viet Cong bodies with the legend "Peace on Earth." But the movie most closely recalled for me a brigade executive officer I had dealt with often, a senior colonel bucking for brigadier. He was a tiresome, somewhat comical, little man who seemed to spend most of his time flying around to units in the field trying to impress them with what a fire-eater he was—not exactly what the troops were looking for.

In sharp contrast, none of the dead or wounded people in the movie looked to me even remotely like the sergeant on the turret floor. Actually, they all looked like the private who had bled to death from the leg wound, seemingly unmarked but very, very pale, and covered with the finest red dust. I remembered crawling into the ditch where he was lying after the helicopter had gone. I felt like asking him if he was really dead. I think I did ask someone that.

This is where Nixon comes back in, along with *Patton,* Vietnam, Cambodia, Kent State, and, for me at least, the last thirty-odd years. To be sure, I am not going to propose that Richard Nixon opted to invade Cambodia with U.S. troops and thereby precipitated—with his pseudomilitary prating and strutting and his "bum" soliloquy—the killings of students by National Guard troops at Kent State as a direct result of his excessive viewing of *Patton.* Yet for the sake of all those who shortly after found themselves under fire in Cambodia or Ohio, I wish we'd all known more at the time about the commander in chief's film preferences and their likely effect on his decision-making abilities.

My main objective here is to lift the Nixon-*Patton* business out of the realm of political anecdote, where it has been reported for years as if it were merely curious or psychologically and historically piquant. Surely Cambodia and Kent State and the rest of the tragedies of Southeast Asia during that era were none of those things. Neither should any of us find it curious or piquant, then or now, that an American commander in chief was somehow allowed—when he should have known better, and when people around him certainly should have known better—to make large life-and-death decisions by confusing the Vietnamese war with things he saw in a war movie. (And this is not even to begin to get into historians' controversies over "hard" information available at the time indicating that the Cambodian business was likely to achieve exactly 0 percent of its objectives from the start.)

The Vietnam period is one of many in American history that have been garishly mythologized, and not nearly all of them in times that were earlier and more innocent. We are, after all, the country that just a decade ago unveiled to the planet a skilled, articulate field commander named Norman Schwarzkopf and then within weeks had him appearing everywhere (including at Disney World as an adjunct of Snow White and Mickey Mouse) doing a Norman Schwarzkopf imitation. We are also the country that, roughly around the same time, took seriously the advice of the Speaker of the House of Representatives that we would do well to envision a chain of national orphanages modeled on *Boy's Town*–the movie, not the place.

So let me state directly what happened and why we should not excuse or forget it: Richard Nixon spent at least the month of April 1970 in a decision-making frame of mind that was deeply–perhaps even obsessively–constructed by his repeated viewing of a Hollywood movie that starred the extremely gifted, protean, and controversial actor George C. Scott in the role of the equally gifted, protean, and controversial military leader George S. Patton. The result was not just the Cambodian invasion, although that took center stage. The result, abroad and at home, was a leadership performance that became as big a comic-book reenactment as the film itself–except that this performance actually killed many people.

I don't care that Nixon later denied any connection outright when asked directly in a famous 1977 interview with David Frost. I don't care that George Patton's name goes utterly unwhispered during all 1,090 pages of the official Richard Nixon Library Edition of the president's memoirs. Patton was in fact a constant presence in Nixon's life and a frequent reference.

Indeed, the frustration at having to squelch the slightest mention of Patton from the entire text of the memoirs, lest the particular episode of movie foolishness be unpleasantly spotlighted, must have been enormous. In truth, Patton had been everywhere. In the years just before his death he had been a much talked about choice for the Republican election vacancy that Nixon eventually filled against Jerry Voorhis. He was the source of the flattering analogy Eisenhower had resorted to in praising Nixon's courage (after the "Checkers" speech) for acknowledging his mistakes, thereby further making Patton the hip- and lip-shooting military subordinate Eisenhower could not afford to keep, and Nixon somehow the hip- and lip-shooting political running mate he could not afford to fire. And surely most important for a man as insecure as Nixon himself was the psychological analogue, a ready-made heroic type wishfully constructed in unerringly parallel contours: tough, inspirational, controversial–ready to be hated, even, for doing what he believed in a nearly mystical sense to be right–and all the while wrestling with a profane soul he knew to be capable of the most unbelievable hypocrisy, from the disguise of a legendarily foul mouth to the affecting of a deep religiosity.

Ironically, the glaring absence of Patton becomes most explicitly pronounced in the detailed historical sections of Nixon's own political autobiography *RN* that deal extensively with the events of April and May 1970. The same is true in some later passages of *In the Arena* (described by Nixon himself as the candid memoir he wanted to write in the first place) that also deal pointedly with Nixon's motivation and conduct during the Cambodia–Kent State crisis. (There, he settles for the historical analogue of Lot's wife: "Don't look back.")

After all, put yourself in his place. Would you be willing to admit for posterity that, during the most crucial decision-making period of the most divisive American war since 1865—not to mention a tragic bloodbath that had now engulfed Indochina for at least three decades—you basically made the decision to invade a country next to the one your nation had already been at war with for more than five years by identifying excessively with a war movie? That you celebrated that decision by getting drunk and treating your inner circle of advisors to a special viewing of that movie to seal your camaraderie? And that the renewal of identification affected you so thoroughly that for the ensuing month or so you behaved and talked as if you were actually in the movie? Remember, *you* are the president of the United States—not George S. Patton in a movie. Not even George C. Scott in a movie.

History, of course, will record that neither an overdose of Patton nor Cambodia and Kent State combined actually killed Richard Nixon. Nor did Watergate, resignation in disgrace from the presidency, phlebitis, the loss of his beloved wife, or any of the other ailments and heartaches that came to him in later years as part of a person's usual earthly portion. When he died in 1994, he was full of years and generally rehabilitated of all the bad old Nixon things, Watergate included. He was selectively remembered and memorialized, most recently on a U.S. postage stamp.

When my brigade commander died in Vietnam he was fifty. The platoon sergeant, who had seemed to us at the time an old soldier, was in his thirties. The other D Troop soldiers and the students at Kent State were all in their late teens or early twenties. Even though most of these American dead of April and May 1970 haven't been as adequately remembered or memorialized as Richard Nixon, I am not dancing on his grave to even up the score. I just want us to remember that, if it is reprehensible for people to die in war, it is even more reprehensible for them to die because of someone's failure to distinguish between a war and a war movie. That is an elementary observation, as obvious and painful now as it should have been more than thirty years ago.

How I Flunked Race in Vietnam

Years later, when I look back on the personal performance of my duties as an armored cavalry platoon leader in the Vietnamese war, I do so with a mix of modest satisfaction and profound unease. In combat I sometimes met the test of average competency. Recalling certain occasions, however, I cringe with something close to shame over the dumb luck that kept people from having to pay with their bodies and their lives for my callow errors in response and decision making. Outside of combat, the one place where I failed miserably in Vietnam was with race. In an army literally tearing itself apart from the inside over race in black and white I failed abjectly, almost absolutely.

Although minimal efforts were actually made to inform Indochina-bound American soldiers about Vietnamese life and culture, the army didn't have anything resembling racial sensitivity training in 1969. Ironically, the lack was most pronounced with regard to the internal divisions between black and white with which, by the mid- to late sixties, everyone from privates to generals could see it struggling. In turn, my cultural background could not have made me more unprepared. A descendant of Quakers and Mennonites, I spent my youth as upper-middle-class Presbyterian in southern Pennsylvania with hardly an African American in sight. My English forebears, from the upper part of Adams County, a section in fact called Quaker Valley, could rightfully claim their historical bona fides as active abolitionists. From an early age, I knew to identify a springhouse on one of the valley farms as a stop on the underground railroad. In my upper-county school district, completely rural and small town, during a full twelve years of public education, I remember a single black student in continuous residence, himself an inhabitant of the valley, the descendant of freed slaves. One or two black Floridians, sons or daughters of migrant laborers, came through with their families in the fall during apple harvest and vanished before Christmas. Gettysburg, the site of the great battle in 1863, was the county seat. It had inhabitants who dated their origin to a community of free blacks formed before the Civil War. Their descendants lived on a place called Washington Street, dominated by an AME Zion church. They too, as far as most white people's lives in the town and the county were concerned, seemed absolutely invisible. Again, perhaps there was the odd individual one met through the county high-school band competition or playing on some athletic team.

Other small memories summon up the casual racism of the times mixed with at least one episode of complete cultural incomprehension. My father frequently had to travel to one of his food company's processing plants in West Virginia. His route took him through a black community informally called Darksville. A threat in response to misbehavior—one that my siblings and I all found consistently hilarious—was that I would be exchanged on one of those trips for a black counterpart named Snowball Jackson Brathwaite. I also recall my mother's disapproval, in the early 1960s, of our minister's attempt to integrate a Gettysburg barbershop. It wasn't the integration she disagreed with so much, as I recall, as the fact that her minister, the minister of the Gettysburg Presbyterian Church, of all people, was going around acting like a racial agitator.

Another recollection is more serious, arising from an early experience I had at Boy Scout camp when I was nine or ten. We were crowding around a cage to watch a great blacksnake being fed live mice. All of us shoved forward, everyone wanting a place in the front row. Suddenly I found myself propelled back into the crowd with a series of hard, painful raps on my sternum. Administering the blows was a black kid, a member of the Crispus Attucks Troop from York, a midsize city. As quickly, he vanished, yanked out of the crowd by a black scoutmaster by whom he was severely berated. I remember the exchange vividly. "What you doing to that white boy?" the black scoutmaster kept whispering in silent fury. "I was beatin' him on the chest," the kid kept saying, as if that were somehow sufficient explanation. I suppose in these days we would call it a racial incident. At the time, my response was complete befuddlement. The black kid and the black scoutmaster could have been men from Mars. I hadn't the foggiest notion of what I had done to warrant the particular aggression, nor could I fathom at all what the chastisement had to do with my being a white boy.

College took me southward in the midsixties to Davidson in North Carolina, which despite its high admissions requirements and elite status, was considered by its communitarians an exemplar of enlightened meritocracy, the kind of place that prided itself on seating the scions of wealth and privilege at the same table with the scholarshipped sons of Presbyterian ministers. It also remained notable, however, during the time I was there, for its nearly total absence of black students. The only black member of my class—a person, I believe, with whom I never exchanged a word—was a Francophone Congolese, there on some kind of missionary grant. Ensuing groups of matriculants through the midsixties brought in only a handful of other African Americans. Although the college proudly claimed a high-profile Kennedy man among its illustrious graduates—a Rhodes scholar of humble Presbyterian origin named Dean Rusk who, as we never ceased to be reminded, had worked his way through the college by waiting tables—it did not partake greatly of the new climate of racial liberalism that seemed to infuse the national politics. During the four years I was there, the great events of the civil rights struggle in the South, ranging from those in far-off Alabama and Mississippi to more proximate upheavals in Greensboro and Winston-Salem, seemed to take in a world far outside the gates. Accordingly, in contrast to what I recall about the general atmospherics of many of my classmates' and professors' genuinely felt Kennedy-era liberal intellectualism and egalitarian earnestness, my most concrete racial memories—albeit surely accentuated by having grown up in a world in which no one except whites really existed on the social horizon—center on black cooks, black barbers, black shoeshine men, black janitors, all employed in housekeeping duties. Every morning for four years, after I went to class, a hall man cleaned my room and made my bed, as no doubt the practice had been since the college's beginnings more than a century earlier.

Next, a Woodrow Wilson graduate fellowship for a master's in English took me to Thomas Jefferson's University of Virginia for essentially more of the same. During that year of graduate school, I do not remember a single black person. Only after that did I have a modest first experience of direct and fairly intense interracial involvement: a year teaching public school as part of an experiment in large-scale integration in Greensboro, North Carolina, a new senior high built purposely on the town's exact demographic interface of blue-collar white and poor and working-class black. I was young and enthusiastic. I brought personal copies of current paperbacks to class to supplement the dismal textbook offerings. I played basketball in the gym after school. In both the classroom and the gym, the students, black and white, came and cautiously warmed, bemusedly and tolerantly, to my enthusiasm. One black sixteen-year-old—at the time all gangly arms and legs, shy and affable, with a saintly smile—went on to Atlantic Coast Conference basketball stardom at the University of North Carolina and a pro career that eventually carried him to the NBA Hall of Fame. Another, among the smartest and most verbal of my students as well, was a hotshot quarterback on his way to a scholarship at Chapel Hill, in a time when major-college black quarterbacks were rare in the South or any-where else.

Once, I noticed one of my black students—at the time, an athlete even more gifted than the two noted in the previous paragraph, not to mention a hard and sharp questioner in the classroom—missing for sev-eral days and decided to visit his mother. It turned out he'd been in jail after a tussle with a railroad detective, who had arrested him on a phony trespassing charge. He was taking a shortcut after school to play basket-ball; he'd had the ball with him when he was arrested. Another teacher knew some political people and helped to get him released. Later, on leave from the army, I visited him. He had gotten a scholarship to a local private college.

The event of my brief high-school teaching career I remember best, however, was the worst: the day Martin Luther King was shot. That awful day turned into an awful week, tremendously tense, with students milling about in crowded confusion and a lot of tears. The young people handled it better than the teachers as I recall. Greensboro, at least, did not burn.

My experience with race in the army proper began after college with ROTC camp. Or, it began, as everywhere else at the time, with what there was of such experience to be had, which was not much. Not a single black officer candidate was in my platoon. In the next company over, we all admired one of the tactical officers, a black engineer captain, his airborne crest jaunty on his overseas cap, his jump boots immacu-late. Everyone in the whole cadet brigade could see he was the single sharpest TAC in the group. His officer candidates loved him, would do anything for him. Everywhere they went, they went screaming his motto. "WETSU, WETSU, WETSU," they chanted. *"We eat this shit up."*

In my own training platoon, a black noncommissioned officer was in charge, a senior master sergeant who became my first military men-tor from the NCO ranks, and not my last. I remember with pride his praise for my conduct as the designated student platoon leader during the attack portion of the final field-training exercise. He said I could have hardly done it better. The only problem, he added, is that I, having run around in the open as if I were in some kind of John Wayne movie, would have wound up dead in the first thirty seconds. Still, I was glad, moved really, by the fact that a senior sergeant I thought of as a wise teacher and a model of the professional soldier seemed proud to take my first salute upon my commissioning as an officer and then, smiling, to receive the NCO's traditional obligatory dollar.

In my first active-duty assignment, to the Armor Officer's Basic Course at Fort Knox, I remember one black lieutenant in my group of fifty or so. Again, much like the TAC officer at Fort Bragg, he was a hot guy who would have been a standout in any group, a very smart, very witty Afro–Puerto Rican, a charismatic leader in a quarterback's body, so completely at home with himself as to represent his own category of person. To the best of my recollection, there were no others. Shortly following was my assignment to a famous old armored cavalry regiment. Likewise here, as hard as I try to recall things, I do not believe I found a single black officer in my squadron. However, in my troop, a young black staff sergeant and I did build a mortar platoon from scratch, studying up on the field manuals at night and practicing each day's training exercise early the next morning so that we could stay one step ahead of the privates. Together we rewrote the record book on live-fire proficiency. Another, more senior, black NCO—as is the story of so many young lieutenants and captains—on several occasions took me quietly aside and taught me how to become an officer. In a chickenshit dispute over the early relief of a furnace-firing detail of which I was the duty officer, the black squadron sergeant major, a man of great repose and authority, undertook to remind me of a rule that I had forgotten—that the sergeant major takes orders only from the colonel—and, more importantly, that I might be an officer, but I was still a lieutenant.

From Vietnam in 1969 and my platoon of armored cavalry, I still have a set of pictures I took one day at a muddy firebase where we had circled up for a couple of hours, long enough to drop the back ramps, eat chow, clean weapons, dry out in a patch of sun, write a letter. In the whole platoon, numbering around forty soldiers, I find one black guy, Jay Flowers, sitting on the back ramp of his track with two white fellow crew members. He is bare chested, fit and muscular, with wraparound shades. On the back of the picture, I have noted that he is from North

Carolina, making him my idea, I suppose—because that was my military home of record—of a fellow Tarheel. In contrast, I find a pronounced representation of Hispanics, including one of the scout NCOs and several gunners and drivers. Mostly the platoon is white, however, from white places: Ohio, Idaho, California, Texas, Kentucky.

Aside from Flowers, I have in fact a memory of only one other black soldier during my whole time with the platoon. And *it* turns out to be of one of the strangest experiences I ever had in Vietnam. It's so long ago I don't even remember the man's name, but I know that he was a staff sergeant, a career NCO, just assigned to our troop, a company-sized unit. Apparently to help him get acclimated, the troop commander sent him to spend his first night in the field with me. I don't know whether it was because I had considerable experience and good NCOs or because we were just the nearest platoon available. I remember showing him the whole ambush drill, the claymore mines, the fields of fire, the guard shifts, and so on. I also remember vividly making a mental note that I knew he was going to die. And sure enough, a month or so later, while he was up north with the Third Platoon, an RPG through the gun shield blew him in half.

To be sure, as to race or unit configuration, my platoon in Vietnam was not representative. It was an armored cavalry outfit, even at a fairly late stage of the war staffed with a full complement of specialist personnel and NCOs and, to that degree, relatively insulated from the intense racial turmoil occurring in the brigade of four line infantry battalions of which it was a part. Only later, as the executive officer of the troop, working closely with command and headquarters units of the latter, would I find myself personally immersed in that larger conflict and eventually watch the war in black and white come to ravage my own unit as well. When it came, the experience was one that, in many ways, has become over the years nearly as strong a source of violent, angry memory as combat itself.

A lot was written over the course of the war and afterward about the preponderance or—the current word—overrepresentation of blacks in combat units in Vietnam. Much information of the sort has assumed the status of in-country legend. Even today people repeat stories about running into numerous infantry units in the bush that were 50 percent or more black. It is hard not to argue that black enlisted soldiers were far more likely than their white counterparts to wind up in combat units in the field, unless the white soldiers in question came from comparably disadvantaged social, economic, or educational backgrounds; class seems to have been the great leveler. And it is even harder not to argue that, once African Americans got slotted for assignments in the field, they had far more trouble again than their white compatriots in being awarded after some length of combat service relatively safer jobs in the rear.

At the same time, the numbers issue itself turns out to be more complicated than has frequently been alleged or understood. Much of the complication has to do with the extended duration of the war and the attendant racial makeup of the armed forces over the period in question. It is now substantially accepted that blacks did in fact experience an unusually heavy share of hazardous duty early in the war. This was in part due to the presence of a considerable proportion of professional black noncommissioned officers in the military forces generally–around 20 percent–who had found soldiering a career path with advantages and opportunities for promotion frequently blocked in the civilian economy. When the war got hot, the longtime professionals were the first to do repeat tours. Further, the enlisted ranks at the time contained high proportions of black volunteers for specialized units, such as airborne infantry, offering rapid advancement in rank and hazardous duty pay. Accordingly, through the early period of heavy U.S. involvement, with experienced NCO leaders and regular combat formations the first to go, black soldiers accounted for between a fifth and a quarter of those killed in action. From around 1966 on, however, with an expanded draft, both the racial percentages of black and white Americans in the field in Vietnam and of casualties reported came into rough congruence with the national demographics of the military-age population.

Toward the end of the war, however, a new ingredient of racism was indisputably added to the draftee mix with what was called the McNamara Project 100,000, an experimental program to induct soldiers who would have not been accepted previously because of low intelligence- and aptitude-test scores. Blacks with poor educations, literacy and numeracy problems, and poorly developed testing skills, were among the first swept up in the net. Actually, 240,000 recruits eventually entered under the program. Forty percent were estimated to be black. Concurrently, although not represented in official records, an unusually high percentage of black soldiers, as opposed to white, wound up in the army or marines as a result of being offered military induction in lieu of jail sentences for civilian crimes. Statistics remain uncontroverted that, at the very least, once in the army or marines in Vietnam, blacks were far more likely than whites to get in serious trouble with the military justice system. By mid-1968, jail populations at the U.S. Army Long Binh Stockade and the III MAF Brig in Da Nang, mainly a marine facility, stood at around 50 percent. Uprisings at both took the form of full-scale race riots. Overall, 45 percent of bad-conduct discharges during the war also went to blacks.

As to service in the field, no question exists that, in combat units themselves, blacks tended to be placed at the sharp end—in the line companies, platoons, and squads—and sometimes, even further, at what might be called the sharp end of the sharp end: made to walk point, to ambush, and to occupy listening posts. Beginning with their combat-branch assignment and extending to their specific distribution as members of platoon- and company-sized formations, even among line units—as my platoon revealed—blacks in the field were consigned predominantly to the infantry, rather than armor or artillery. But as big a problem throughout the war was what happened to black soldiers, as opposed to white soldiers, in combat slots in the field once they were assigned. Not only were they invariably put at the sharp end but also they were made to stay there frequently long after white counterparts had been relieved. Corollary problems occurred once they started trying, both legally and extralegally, to get out of those positions. With each of these problems, the testimony of black soldiers, in its sheer volume and consistency, carries the full weight of historical evidence.

The fact was that in virtually all combat units black guys tended to stay in the field as white guys moved back to the rear when the occasional headquarters job opened up. And make no mistake about it: if you had to be in Vietnam, the rear was the place to be. It was alleged to be a war of no front lines, of constant danger from an invisible enemy who could strike at any time in any place without warning. The fact of the matter is that some places were better than others, and among them were definitely the headquarters installations handling the administration and logistics of major American units. There, especially for a field soldier, the safety and comfort factors took on the attributes of something like a parallel universe—hot chow, clean clothes, cold beer and soda, a dry place to sleep, showers, a fully manned bunker line at night, movies, an enlisted men's club, maybe a PX. With the exception of the occasional rocket or mortar attack, headquarters was really close to being back in the world. It also featured back-in-the-world protocols, and as such, it was a place where the lifers were definitely in charge. Accordingly, for the plum reassignments, the lifers tended to pick model soldiers. Given the fact that being a model soldier meant knowing how to play the lifer game, that usually meant white selectees.

On the one hand, a great part of this was surely due to the favoritism of white officers and NCOs, themselves in most cases occupying the preponderance of privileged positions at the company and battalion levels and above. On the other hand, not a little of this was visited on black soldiers as a result of the attitudes of uncomprehending black career NCOs. Frequently called uniform tangos and Oreos by their younger racial compatriots—Uncle Toms, black on the outside, white on the inside—they themselves had made it in a white man's army through a willingness to make certain attitude adjustments and social and political concessions to white racism as a military fact of life. In turn, they looked for black soldiers who inclined toward the compliant, adaptable, and disciplinarily reliable—those, in short, who were willing to cultivate and exercise political skills similar to their own. As increasingly fewer such soldiers emerged from the African American community, black NCOs moreover were the first to turn their backs on younger black racial militants.

Whoever did the choosing, the result usually played out according to a dismally racist script concerning assumptions about who might be a competent orderly room clerk, supply clerk, finance clerk, mail clerk, and so on down the list. Those assumptions included basic literacy skills, coupled in many cases with basic mathematical and analytic competencies. Almost every combat unit had a number of white guys who had some college, albeit people who had foolishly dropped out, flunked out, or found some other way of fumbling a student deferment. They were frequently more like the officers than they were like the other enlisted men, schooled in the ability to navigate a white institutional world, adept at catching the eye of a prospective patron or mentor. And particularly, as the war went completely sour in the late sixties and early seventies, with duty in the rear increasingly proliferating as a form of compassionate reassignment, these networking skills definitely paid off. A new component of white bias and privilege was added to the witches' broth of a disintegrating army already dreadfully replicating, under pressures of institutional military discipline and combat, the racial conflicts of the larger society. White guys, trying to hold together military units and minimize casualties in a world of shit, focused their limited abilities to salvage the situation on their own white cohorts. The reaction of black GIs, as Tim O'Brien describes in an account roughly contemporary with my own experience, was essentially to complete the racial choreography of a vicious circle. Faced with the racist favoritism of white officers, as O'Brien notes, "many blacks react as any sane man would. They sulk. They talk back, get angry, loaf, play sick, smoke dope. They group together and laugh and say shit to the system." He goes on: "And this feeds the problem. Pointing at malingering and insubordination by the blacks, the officers are free to pass out jobs to white men. Then the whole cycle goes for another round, getting worse."

Once I was promoted to executive officer and had to work with all three platoons in the troop, my own perspective on this quickly became larger. In the field, where I still spent most of the time, albeit in a support role, frequently living out of my jeep; shuttling fuel, ammunition, and supplies to forward firebases; hooking up cargo nets at helicopter pickup points; riding in with the loads and riding out with back-loaded equipment and GIs with business in the rear, I found a new friendship with the black First Platoon sergeant, a wise, funny, tremendously competent career NCO whose combat trademark became the bedroom slippers he put on at night in the tank. He was a deer hunter back home. One afternoon on a sweep up north, he had one of his gunners pop some kind of jungle elk he saw moving in a treeline. Before night ambush, we had a field-expedient barbecue, eating venison off our rifle cleaning rods.

On another afternoon, in the middle of a big ambush, I got to watch some of the coolest work under fire that I ever saw. The work was that of a buck sergeant named Joe Bell, a black telephone repairman from Atlanta whose ACAV I was riding in. While I worked the radios for artillery support, he charged right into the fight, slinging the big .50-caliber machine gun around in the command cupola like it was an ax. His platoon came into attack formation with him like something in a field-training exercise back at the armor school.

When I started out, the brigade main base support contingent I worked with had a couple of black old-timers—a sergeant in the arms room and a clerk in the motor pool. But what I remember most vividly is how the rear detachment at brigade main base quickly started filling up with crowds of black temporary assignees, back for personnel actions, medical problems, legal counseling, and the like. One guy we acquired from the LRRPs spent a month in the troop, attached to the rear party, filing multiple requests to be reassigned to other units in the brigade. He never served a day in the field. We finally pawned him off, I believe, on the infantry battalion next door. There was also a flood of attempts to get medical profiles—assignment to limited duty that ruled out field conditions of hardship and physical exertion. The most desperate candidate I remember for one of these managed to contract overlapping venereal infections resulting in symptoms requiring day-to-day treatment. Another guy got himself dusted off for a piece of shrapnel in the back of his hand that a five-year-old would have picked out and then asked for a Band-Aid. Once he got back, we couldn't pry him out of the place.

Once in the rear, such temporary assignees usually had their stays prolonged by legal matters arising from minor military offenses. As might be expected, officers and NCOs in rear areas were only too ready to jump on uniform violations (haircuts, headgear, footwear) and minor military courtesy infractions (failure to salute, disrespect to a superior, violation of a standing order). Most penalties meted out were company-level Article 15s, known as nonjudicial punishments. Determined by unit commanders, in this case the captain commanding the troop, these could include such things as fines, deductions in pay, demotions in rank, or extra duty. In turn, convicted Article 15 offenders could increasingly be seen each morning shuttling between the orderly room and the brigade Judge Advocate General's office, seeking the counsel of and making appeals through army lawyers, thereby insuring extended stays in the rear. Shortly the legal standard was well established: anything short of the Long Binh Jail was good time, one day closer to home.

In my unit, mid-1969 was when things started to go really bad. Ironically, all this was happening in a brigade that had been singled out as a showpiece for racial progress. In fact, the previous commander had been Brigadier General Frederic Davison, the first black general officer commanding a major unit in the field in Vietnam, and a leader much admired by his troops, both black and white. He left in April. By August, things had turned violent. One night when I happened to be at brigade main base, an infantry battalion came in on stand-down. I could hear a band playing in its area. The scene was like a block party, with a lot of beer drinking, shouting, general grab-assing. Then I heard a couple of explosions. They sounded like mortar rounds, with that ugly crump that means incoming, not outgoing. A couple of hand grenades had been tossed into a fifty-gallon drum where a bunch of white guys were congregated. Two were killed. No one ever found the perpetrators. Everyone assumed it was "racial."

Another night, with my own unit in from the field on a three-day stand-down, I bailed out of my hooch barefoot in my fatigue pants, waving a .45, and chasing down a runaway Sheridan tank on its way to the EM club. Two white guys were going to pivot-steer through the back wall and hose down the place with the .50-caliber machine gun. Fortunately, the one in the driver's seat was too drunk to steer and the one trying to mount the .50 was too drunk to get it loaded. The incident, of course, was "racial."

I got to the point where I spent most of my time in the field. It was safer. Generally speaking, the scale of the action was not much changed from my first days with the platoon. The point was that in the field you expected to get mortared, mined, sniped, booby-trapped, and ambushed; and when that happened, it was just us chickens. In the field, as most combat veterans of the war, white and black, will testify to this day, the color of the basic GI never changed from being anything but olive drab. In the rear, by contrast, the air breathed hate; one felt the anger, the menace, the hostility, the violence waiting to erupt. For the first time, people, nearly all of them black, were being sent back to brigade main base to talk with the lawyers for what in those days was called "combat refusal"–that is, when a field soldier disobeys a direct order to go on a mission or remain in a forward area, a serious charge. Article 15s were turning into court-martials. Nonjudicial punishments were turning into sentences in the Long Binh Jail. Now when I walked back to the transient barracks behind the mess hall, I carried my .45.

Portraits of a late-sixties Vietnam army in complete racial meltdown abound in the literature of the period to the degree that they contend with descriptions of combat itself in detail and intensity. They are clearly part of the indelible memories of anyone who was there. Especially in the big rear installations, but extending forward to the larger firebases, everyday GI life became swept into an elaborate choreography of difference, a drama of mutual incomprehension. Working, eating, and sleeping arrangements became almost completely segregated. There were white tables versus soul tables in the mess hall, the EM club, and the PX snack bar. Entire buildings and unit areas split into black and white turf. A part of every barracks got walled off into a place called the soul shack. White territorialists responded with intensified forms of counterracial display, confederate flags being a particular favorite. Portions of base camps and adjacent areas became unsafe for whites to travel through after nightfall.

Accounts of numerous outbreaks of racial violence at major U.S. installations–Qui Nhon, Da Nang, Tien Shau, China Beach–may be found in military records of the era, in some cases appearing as serious brawls and in others as personal assaults and even murders. We will never know how many clashes went officially unreported; nor will we ever really know how many were, in fact, racial, as opposed to the results of drunkenness, drug abuse, or rivalries over Vietnamese women, all of them exacerbated by GI fear, frustration, boredom, and misery.

The same goes for fraggings, primarily assaults on officers and NCOs by enlisted men with grenades and other explosive devices. Mainly occurring in rear areas, these could involve grenades tossed into sleeping or living areas, or more complicated booby traps rigged to explode with the opening or closing of a door. These showed a dramatic increase during the years of heightened racial tension. At the same time, no one will ever know, given the anonymity of the method, how many were racially motivated or carried out by black perpetrators on white victims of whatever rank. Toward the end, an officer could be fragged for anything from overzealous operational endangerment of his troops in the field to insistence on spit-and-polish lifer protocols in the rear, as could an NCO or any other member of a garrison party—an arms-room sergeant, a motor-pool mechanic, a mail clerk. Rear-area murder became just one more specter of violence hanging like a miasma over the whole racial scene.

On the street, in the mess hall, the orderly room, the motor pool, race among black soldiers became a performance. Haircuts flirted with the stateside Afro, frequently with headgear perched precariously on top or to one side. Alleging Muslim religious mandates, militants asserted the right to grow facial hair. There were "bad"-looking little wire sunglasses, carved ebony sticks, and black-power jewelry, frequently fashioned from GI shoelaces, now reappearing as bracelets, necklaces, amulets, and hat decorations. Reminiscent of the old rituals practiced during centuries of slave resistance, blacks became slow to salute and respond. In a kind of people's theater, they enjoyed elaborate forms of greeting, beginning with the raised fist salute but more frequently sequencing into the ritual variously known as the dap, the soul shake, the Afro-salute, or passing the power. A combination of handshake, dance step, palm slap, head butt, and hip bump, it could take minutes to perform, sometimes working all of that and then coming around again. Officers and NCOs looked on and fumed. More important, they took things tolerated among soldiers generally—long hair, peace signs, helmet slogans, decorated bush hats, increasingly informal behavior toward NCOs and officers, even drug use—while cracking down heavily on blacks. Meanwhile, white enlisted counterparts, who heavily scrutinized it all for some symbolic significance, found themselves increasingly puzzled and resentful, even hostile.

The default cultural mindsets about group identification into which whites and blacks retreated as the war started to go bad further exacerbated the situation. For whites, the attitude basically remained something like old-time army group esprit, the kind of adolescent, athletic-style bonding learned in small-town and city high schools or in shit jobs after graduation, with its emphasis on teamwork, fair play, and sharing the load. "As long as we're in this," whites seemed to say, "let's all pull together." The black guys, frequently the product of inner-city ghettos or public-housing projects, in contrast, had spent their adolescent schooling learning survival instincts—solitary, combative, violent skills of self-preservation. One made it only by being the baddest guy in a bad lot. Binding them together, not surprisingly, was not so much a team mentality as a classic gang mentality, with each member measured by a code of toughness, wary allegiance, and naked threat.

Meanwhile, the political anger in the streets of America found a home in the country that was the war as well. Suddenly, many black soldiers—hearing their GI brethren call people "gooks," "dinks," "slants," "slopes," and "zipperheads"—understood what Muhammad Ali had meant when he noted that no Viet Cong had ever called him "nigger." Suddenly, many found themselves enlisted in a new belief that it wasn't just Black Panther rhetoric when H. Rap Brown described the war as a conspiracy of white people to get black people to kill yellow people to protect a country originally stolen from red people. Once the endgame politics of the war started to be played out—Vietnamization, the first withdrawals of U.S. units, followed by the steady disengagement of American troops from large-scale combat operations—it was trouble enough persuading white draftees to fight in a war where the last person out was probably going to get shot, let alone a black kid who thought the LBJ was just another jail.

After the war, I returned for another graduate school stint in Charlottesville, this time four years. As before, I met or knew no black graduate students. I knew informally one young black faculty member, at the time Virginia's prize UCLA Victorian-literature specialist, albeit a professor who had made his own risky decision to come out of the closet as an African Americanist. What I remember about him is that he could be numbered among the handful of faculty members who had the audacity to believe—and to visibly act on the belief—that graduate students were human beings. Ironically, the only black graduate and professional students I met anywhere, I met through Hanan Mikhail, later Hanan Ashrawi, the Palestinian spokesperson, who was studying for a Ph.D. in medieval literature and was a known favorite of the FBI. My guess is that my new black acquaintances were on the watch list as well.

Oddly, standing out in my mind from those years as well is another strange "racial incident," in this case an assault I witnessed at a convenience store. Waiting to buy a six-pack of beer, I looked on incredulously from the back of the line as a teenager entered with a baseball bat and smashed an older man standing at the cash register in the head. I chased the boy on foot and ran him down to an address. Later I was picked up by the police to make a positive identification. They brought him out of his mother's house. I made the identification. "Why did you do that?" I asked the boy as I rode with him in the backseat. He looked straight ahead and did not answer. The police said I might have to appear in court. I never heard anything more of it.

Finally my academic career took me to Alabama, where I have lived for nearly thirty years, teaching at the University, the place where Governor George Wallace stood in the schoolhouse door. To name the cities of the state is to recite the stations of the cross of the civil rights movement: Tuscaloosa, Birmingham, Selma, Montgomery. It is a world where race is still everything. Among my students, generally the academic elite as far as public university education is concerned, the upper-tier demographics of race in the state are at least reflected. They are between 10 and 15 percent black. Some belong to the black upper-middle classes of the big modern cities: Birmingham, Montgomery, Mobile. Some are first-generation college students. In the main, they are the living incarnation of W. E. B. Du Bois's talented tenth. After three decades, however, I find that they still live in one world while my white students, especially those in the student government and Greek systems, live in another. At the faculty level, in my department we currently have two extremely forceful and popular black faculty members, both men. As with black colleagues who preceded them, as well as other candidates we have tried to recruit, we are faced with utterly cutthroat competition from peer institutions. Recently, we made an effort to vie for at least two African American figures of some seniority. One was ludicrously out of our price range. The other fell between the cracks when affirmative-action hiring money dried up. Meanwhile, we are hardly helped in our work by a fraternity and sorority system that makes the newspapers in New York and Los Angeles each fall when it stays segregated for another year.

A very particular experience of race at my university, however, brought me to compose these reflections. That experience involved a recent encounter, at once professional and personal, with the African American playwright August Wilson. As one of the organizers of an academic symposium on writing race across the Atlantic world in the early modern era, I agreed with my codirector that a major public event should be scheduled involving a literary figure of note currently address- ing race in America. On a wild hope, we invited August Wilson. To our delight, and that of the audience that packed the auditorium the night of his lecture, he came and spoke clearly and passionately. Meanwhile, I got to know him and found that we have some of the strangest things in common. For one thing, we are nearly exact contemporaries. For an- other, as members of some shadow geriatric fathers association, we both have young daughters. We both grew up in Pennsylvania, he in the Hill District of Pittsburgh, I in the apple orchards of Adams County. Surely the most bizarre connection, however, for a black guy and a white guy anyhow, was the humorous realization that we are both half German. Historically, I split right down the middle between English Quakers and Black Forest Mennonites. Wilson's father was actually a German national.

It was there, however, just on the edge of literary irony, that we both realized how we also have virtually nothing in common. He knew nothing about white eastern Pennsylvania, the land of Quakers and Mennonites, of quaint little hamlets with names like Mount Tabor or Bird-in-Hand. I knew nothing about Pittsburgh and the Hill District, the vibrant, flourishing cultural center that—as reported recently in the *New*

York Times—once housed the *Pittsburgh Courier,* the nation's most influential black weekly newspaper; that fielded a baseball team with legendary players including Satchel Paige and Josh Gibson; or that so moved the poet Claude McKay with its vitality to make him call it "the crossroads of the world." We weren't fooling anybody. For all our pleasant conversation and easy amicability, we knew that we had grown up in different worlds. We also knew that we continued to live in worlds that could not comprehend each other.

Wilson's public lecture mingled a profound sense of his fame, his wealth, and his first-class style in every sense of the phrase with a bitter anger at the never-ending harassments, frustrations, and humiliations of being a black person in America. As he has done in other places, he asserted his proud identity as a "race man" in both art and life. He argued the unconditional necessity that a black aesthetic and a black arts tradition should aggressively and unapologetically cherish its own independence in celebrating the terrible beauty and sorrow of the black experience in America, not only through the arts but also through a political and institutional apparatus: fellowships, writing programs, endowments, public theaters. He also unapologetically grounded his aesthetic politics in the politics of the everyday personal experience of being an African American in this country. He related an anecdote about a patronizing white acquaintance at a cocktail reception given for him. Surveying the crowd of invitees, save Wilson, all white, he seized the occasion to inform the guest of honor that when he looked at him, "he didn't see race." That might be so, Wilson replied, but he didn't notice the guy finding himself impelled to make that claim to anybody else in the room. He then went on, with some anger, to describe the frequency with which he finds himself subjected in airports to "random" security checks. "I guess," he concluded, "I am just a random kind of guy."

As he talked, I thought about Wilson out there in the world. He is, with his presence, his manner, his genius, one of the most imposing persons I have ever met. He is, in every respect, one of the few individuals whom I would be tempted to style, in the archaic phrase, a fine figure of a man. Immaculately dressed, with the bearing of a general or a prince or a president, he radiates pride and self-possession. At the same time, in any given moment, he is hard, truculent, and prepared, just waiting to be fucked with.

I also thought about the person I had invited to introduce Wilson, a person who had in fact generously accepted my invitation after the university president had been forced to bow out to go make, as fate would have it, a speech to other university presidents on issues of racial and cultural diversity. He was a student of mine at the university, one of my first and lifetime best, as well as the first and to this day the only student government association president at the University of Alabama of African American descent—his supporters, for their pains, got a cross burned on the Kappa Kappa Gamma house lawn. A Marshall scholar, Harvard Law School graduate, successful attorney, and corporate executive, he had also become a long-serving and courageous trustee of the University of Alabama. After nearly twenty years, he was about to resign over the selection of a new chancellor. As is his way, he thoroughly approved of the new chancellor; what he thoroughly disapproved of was the insider selection process.

In addition, I thought about some colleagues at the university I saw in the audience that night. One is a young cultural-studies specialist, a black Marxist postcolonialist, a serious theoretician, intellectually demanding with a formidable vocabulary, albeit a great undergraduate favorite as well. In everything from his Lauren khakis and polo shirts to his BMW, he is also the most prepped-out assistant professor I have seen south of Sewanee, Tennessee. Another is a jazz specialist, a very hip guy with the style of the black intellectual: sharp clothes, rimless glasses, a graying natural. A third, from the Department of American Studies, has a big headful of long dreadlocks. On some days he wears a dashiki or djellaba. On others, it's a flannel shirt and corduroys. A fourth is a dancer, a member of the fine-arts faculty. He's wiry and muscular and has a completely shaven head. He's also 2002's CASE national award winner for teaching in a doctoral university.

They all have something in common with August Wilson, I realized that night. And the fact that they are all visibly successful black men does not matter one jot. It's the same thing they have in common with a day laborer, a welfare mother, an inner-city teenager, or somebody reading meters for the gas company. And it's exactly the thing that they all don't have in common with me. Somewhere, somehow, some way in America today—and tomorrow and on any given day in the rest of their lives—someone is going to fuck with them because they are black. They'll wait extra long in a grocery checkout line. They'll get asked for more than one ID. They'll need to mind their traffic manners and make sure the brake or the turn-signal lights are not out. When their spouses or other family members are with them, they'll have try to be proud without acting angry. For them, there will always be a part of life that people like me don't understand. That's what I didn't understand about race when I was in the army. And it's still, I believe, what anyone who is not black can't even begin to comprehend about race in American life right now.

This has been a story about men. That fact is dictated by the pattern of personal experience it describes. The Vietnam army as I knew it was exclusively a world of men; and in my interracial experiences during a career in the academy, for whatever reasons, I seem likewise mainly to have moved in the world of African American men. If I knew enough to do it, I would write a parallel narrative about white and black American women and their lives, but I don't. In any event, let me claim from my particular strand of narrative at least a few elements of insight about why we are still flunking race in America. My experience from my time in the Vietnam army until now shows how little we continue to know about each other after all these years. Accordingly, it also shows how depressingly little, as a consequence, we have changed. From where I stand, the lifers still seem to be pretty much in charge; and if you're black, on any given day it's pretty certain that you're naturally going to get fucked with. As a white guy, I am at least starting to see why, for so many black guys, all those years back there in Vietnam, the LBJ was just another jail.

Late Thoughts on Platoon

One Saturday morning not long ago, I sat down alone and watched the movie *Platoon* for the first time. More than thirty years had passed since I came home from Vietnam. More than fifteen years had passed since the movie first appeared. I had heard strangely conflicting things about it ever since. On one hand, it was supposed to be the most realistic movie made about the war, notable for its GI authenticity on everything from the sheer day-to-day misery of humping the bush (the endless patrolling, the heat, the moisture, the vegetation, the insects, the fear, the fatigue) to the bloody shock of jungle combat (the ambushes, the mines, the booby traps; the bunker complexes, the tunnels, the night perimeter attacks; the mortars, the air strikes, the artillery). It was said to depict accurately the life of the firebase—the slang, the food, the beer, the dope, the music—and it was also regarded as one of the few films that, without resorting excessively to the claims either of World War II–movie cliché or of post-Vietnam conservative revisionism, somehow managed to honor the experience of the common infantry soldier in the war. On the other hand, I had also heard that it contrived at length to the make the combat initiation of the young GI protagonist Chris Taylor—"ChrisT," as more than one sharp-eyed critic pointed out—into a Manichaean parable of the struggle between the forces of good and evil, light and darkness, compassion and hatred, symbolized on one hand by the dope-smoking, humane, and spiritually enlightened squad leader Elias and on the other by the heavy-drinking, murderous, even demonic platoon sergeant Barnes. And when not actively giving itself over to such allegory, it allegedly bogged down even further—particularly through the intrusive voice-over narration of the main character, on the pretext of letters home to a beloved, wise grandmother—in its own struggle after a certain kind of didactic "meaningfulness."

For all of these reasons I had resisted seeing the movie until that Saturday morning. On the first point, if it was as authentic as had been claimed, I didn't need it. Although I had been a platoon leader in the armored cavalry, busting jungle with tanks and assault vehicles, as opposed to a small-unit infantry commander, I had spent most of my time miserable and scared down in the triple canopy of III Corps where the movie was set, and the combat had been pretty much that of the infantry war. Daytime sweeps were called RIFs (reconnaissance in force) by the time I got there, but the mission was still search and destroy. Every night we ambushed or did firebase perimeter defense. Mechanized missions included running convoys and setting up cordons and checkpoints. A favorite task was the hammer and anvil, with the armor serving as a blocking force for infantry sweeps coming in the other direction. Sometimes there was even the actual cavalry-to-the-rescue drill, charging into an enemy bunker complex to extricate a pinned-down infantry unit. In bizarre contrast, we could also spend the odd peaceful day on what was called a medcap, carrying a doctor, a dentist, and a medical team to a village for such things as shots, tooth extractions, and malaria treatments.

Most often the real war shook itself out as the battle of the latest road bend: a mine, more often than not command detonated, blown beneath an ACAV or a Sheridan; or automatic weapons fire, maybe some RPGs, enough to keep us stopped and shooting, laying down a mad volume of fire, until the perpetrators were long gone. Then it was time for a dustoff, maybe the call for an artillery strike, or another hulk to tow back to base camp so that, presumably, the enemy couldn't keep count of how many vehicles were destroyed. I almost had to call the Pentagon one time to obtain an order allowing me to blow an ACAV in place. We were somewhere in a defoliated area outside of Black Horse, a big firebase. After a mine went off under the ACAV, exploding ammunition had burned it down to the road wheels, which in turn had fused to the hull. The crew got out, but the brigade didn't want to leave it as a VC monument. The fact that more vehicles could get blown up and more GIs killed and wounded while trying to figure out how to get rid of what was essentially a twelve-ton ingot of melted steel, rubber, and aluminum, did not seem to register.

As opposed to the straight infantry war, mechanized operations had both an upside and a downside. On the one hand, riding into war was certainly less physical strain than humping incredible weights of ammunition and equipment, along with minimal food, water, and personal gear. Tanks and ACAVs contained cargo space for a change of fatigues or socks, usually enough food and water, maybe even, if you'd been around the artillery or the engineers that day, a chunk of ice in an Igloo cooler. The tracks also provided modest protection in a war of weapons and booby traps designed mainly for close-range individual killing and maiming. On the other hand, every day in the field was an incredible orgy of bumping, gouging, and bruising, the hardest kind of machine work, putting thrown tracks back on road wheels and hooking up tow cables to get mired vehicles out of the jungle mud. The vehicles were incredibly hot. They were also unbelievably loud. Riding in them was just asking to get bushwhacked, almost always on the enemy's terms. Vehicle walls and gun shields might deflect small arms. However, inside was the worst place to be when a mine detonated or an armor-piercing rocket burned its way through the hull. Then it was time to be splattered all over the roof or the turret, macerated by flying metal and explosives, or consumed by flash fire as the ammunition cooked off–tons of it, including, in the case of the Sheridan tank, the combustible cartridge cases of the big rounds for the main gun. Meanwhile, out on top, you were meat for small arms and rocket shrapnel. The varieties of booby traps could get you coming or going. Under the ground were enormous antitank mines and rigged dud artillery rounds. Chicom claymores hung from the trees, along with nature's own jungle surprises–poisonous centipedes and cascading waterfalls of red ants. To borrow a phrase from Michael Herr, humping Vietnam anywhere came down to varieties of religious experience. Whether in the infantry, the armor, or the artillery, whether riding down a road in a jeep or a truck, slogging through paddy mud, or clawing up the side of a jungle ravine, when contact with the enemy occurred, it was astonishingly loud, violent, and terrifying–a world of shit. For all these reasons *Platoon,* over the fifteen years that I had refused to watch it, had come to menace me as a movie that accurately reproduced something I had no wish to relive.

On the second point, that *Platoon* was an overblown parable, I had been violently angry at the allegedly "big" Vietnam movies that had preceded it, which in turn had played a large role in making me stop paying attention to movies generally, let alone going to see them or renting them on video. For it hadn't been the attempts at combat realism that I had found so disturbing as much as the ostentatious conversion of the war into cinematic conceit. (I should say that back in 1969 I walked out of Sam Peckinpaugh's *The Wild Bunch,* absolutely outraged and disgusted, after a year of combat, at the graphic violence of the new Hollywood wounding-as-entertainment technologies unveiled there.) *The Deer Hunter* in particular really made me nuts: Robert De Niro, the returning Green Beret, with a fucking goatee; the Natty Bumppo moment with the great stag in the upstate Pennsylvania woods; the Russian roulette motif– exactly the kind of "concept" some hot-shit twenty-four-year-old graduate of the UCLA film school would invent as "a metaphor of the insanity of Vietnam"; all the people down at the social hall singing "God Bless

America." *Apocalypse Now* had its moments: the opening, for instance, with the napalm strike in the treeline, the helicopters darting about, Jim Morrison singing "The End"; the combat assault footage; the airmobile insertion into the village. But meanwhile it couldn't help laying down all that dreadful, insulting stuff about the surfing. There were commanders every bit as nuts as the Robert Duvall character all over Vietnam, and they loved the smell of napalm in the morning, but–presumably again, except at the UCLA or NYU film school–they didn't stage complete air-mobile operations in search of the perfect wave. And the Kurtz business, of course, was completely off the scale. For an ex-GI, *Coming Home* was downright piquant: the radicalization of Jane Fonda from marine-officer wife to protesting hippie-chick adulteress was like some kind of bizarre metascript where Barbarella meets Hanoi Jane. The music seemed right at least, as did the VA stuff–the John Voight character with his anger and his remorse. Even Bruce Dern captured some of the stone craziness of the marine lifer, if you let go the pretty hair and the *Star Is Born* final wade in the surf. There was also, of course, *First Blood,* which, in isolated moments under all the murder and mayhem, really did say some important things about veterans coming home and getting jacked around and finally cooking off into violence. But then came all the hoopla about *First Blood II* and *Rambo III*–not to mention *Missing in Action 1* and *2*–none of which I have seen to this day or ever plan to see. All of these had gotten me to thinking for a long time that I just didn't want my experience or my intelligence insulted by any more Hollywood Vietnam shit.

So I didn't come to *Platoon* exactly cold. I certainly knew my prejudices, both experiential and cinematic; and this, worked in with the curious emotional mathematics of a double anachronism–in effect, happening to put myself at thirty years distance from my own experience and fifteen years from the cultural moment of the movie's much heralded appearance–seemed actually, if anything, to bring me to it with a sense of curious transparency. What I experienced was the strange and powerful reciprocity of the personal and the cultural in shaping our knowledge of ourselves in any given moment of our lives. In waiting thirty years to see a fifteen-year-old movie about the war, I had confronted simultaneously both the memory of the war and the life of memory and reflection

in countless novels and personal narratives, in more populous circumstances. The location is usually a big air base: Bien Hoa, Da Nang, Cam Ranh Bay. The plane is a commercial jet. A whole planeload of arriving soldiers disgorges, blinking and scared looking, into a blast of heat and light, as a whole outgoing planeload of joyous, profane veterans waits in a big shed to take their seats for the flight home. The disembarking troops are subjected to a ritual hazing—howls of derision, name-calling, predictions of how they'll be going out in body bags. They respond with sheepish grins and curiosity. As part of a wise foreshortening, Stone has set Chris Taylor's arrival scene closer to the end of the line. The airstrip is big enough to move major cargo and to fly planeloads of soldiers in and out, both the living and the dead. The new guys have flown in there by C-130, the in-country workhorse transport, from the place of their initial landing from back in the world. Accordingly, Stone has avoided the usual literary run-up, beginning in civilian life, possibly with debate over the rightness or wrongness of the war; the inevitable draft notice or choice to enlist; basic training or OCS (Officer Candidate School); the flight, complete with movies and in-flight meals served by stewardesses; and finally, arrival, and the realization that one is at last in-country. Stone concentrates all this in a glimpse, through the swirling dust, of bodies in body bags being off-loaded from helicopters. Then, as quickly, he brings forceful closure to the ritual scene as Chris Taylor locks eyes with the last of the departing veterans. The latter has the look in the eye called, in World War II, the thousand-yard stare, now ratcheted down—as described by novelist Larry Heinemann, himself a Twenty-fifth Division veteran—to the stare of the ambush, bushwhacking distance, ten meters or maybe even three. The man in question looks demented, so profoundly damaged as to make one suspect he's had a head injury. His eyes are completely unpitying, almost hostile.

Cut to the rifle company Chris has joined on a jungle operation. Chris is with the lead platoon. The caption on the screen reads "B Company, 25th Division, Somewhere on the Cambodian Border." Here, the veteran in me realizes that Stone is trying not to confuse the civilians. Anyone who knows the infantry, the big divisions or the separate brigades, expects an infantry company to have as its main designation a battalion identity—B Company 5/12 or 3/7, for instance—with the numbering derived from an older regimental system, the brigade and division assignment notably secondary. Stone's actual unit, in fact, had been B for Bravo Company, Third Battalion, Twenty-second Infantry, Third Brigade, Twenty-fifth Division. Quickly, however, the objection passes, as a familiar, dreary subject arrives on screen. The subject is humping.

The soldiers hump the jungle, the mud, the miserable heat, the stifling humidity, the triple canopy darkness, the impenetrable vegetation, the impossible footing, the endless uphill and downhill, one slimy ravine after another. The soldiers hump their weaponry: M-16 automatic rifles; M-60 machine guns; M-79 grenade launchers; belts, boxes, and bandoliers of ammunition; hand, smoke, gas, and white-phosphorus grenades; plastic explosives; mortar tubes, sights, and base plates; disposable antitank weapons, called LAWs, for bunker-busting. Their wet fatigues hang on them; their steel pots bump and bang around on their heads; they try to cushion the gear and the pack harness with sopping olive-drab towels draped around their necks. We notice one wiry figure humping the M-60 machine gun, with the big weapon crossways on his shoulders. With his arms up on either side steadying the weapon, he looks as if he is being crucified. Eventually we will realize it has been Elias, a sergeant, the platoon's senior squad leader, who would not be a machine gunner nor would be expected to do the physical work of carrying the heavy machine gun. The first time we see him he is, we later recall, giving one of his squad members some relief.

We hear accurate, vintage radio traffic: the familiar earphone hiss, squelch breaks when somebody keys the handset, communication checks, shackle codes being used to send grid coordinates, the captain riding the lead platoon leader's ass about moving too slowly. We focus in on Chris Taylor, the new guy we've seen disembarking from the plane, now humping the jungle, obviously unused to it, going through the last stages of heat exhaustion. He sees his first enemy body, a blackened, decaying corpse. He collapses, trying to puke, getting only stomach fluid and dry heaves. Elias quickly comes up with the medic. He offers to hump the excess gear that has gotten Chris in heat trouble, radiating concern, goodness, a kind of paternal indulgence. Barnes, the platoon sergeant, in pronounced contrast to Elias's sympathetic encouragement, thinks Chris is some kind of pussy. "You are one simple son of a bitch," he mutters in disgust. In a last touch, as Chris leans against a tree, trying to clear his head, a load of fire ants fall down his neck. The other new guy, a fatass, is sent forward to help him. We hear muttered voices calling them both "cherries": combat virgins, soldiers who haven't had their cherry busted yet, soldiers who haven't been blooded. Meanwhile, we are starting to learn the combat names of some of the more experienced members of the platoon. Save for Chris and the other new guy—overweight, goofy, uncomprehending, whose name, it turns out shortly, we will not need to remember save on the Vietnam Veterans' Memorial—nearly everybody else has only a last name, a nickname, or some kind of in-country name: Bunny, Tex, Junior, Ace, Big Harold, Manny, Rhah.

At a firebase later that day, the lieutenant holds a platoon command conference with his sergeants: Barnes, Elias, McNeil, and one black NCO, a silent, angry-looking man named Warren. Barnes and Elias already wear combat patches on their right shoulders from other units, suggesting extended service and/or multiple tours. The platoon sergeant, Barnes, is running the conference in a way that shows who is really commanding the platoon. Afterward, the lieutenant stages a wheedling, plaintive encounter with Barnes, requesting that the sergeant at least pretend to recognize his authority in front of the other NCOs. Barnes leans in his face and replies with murderous scorn: "Yes . . . Sir." The lieutenant is weak. Such will be dramatically necessary. He will stand by, eventually, when Barnes kills a villager in cold blood. He will crack in an ambush and call in the wrong grid coordinates. For his sins, he will eventually die, more or less cowardly and paralyzed, in the massive firebase defense with which the movie ends. At the moment, however, the pressing issue, as revealed in a shortly ensuing discussion among the NCOs, is whether to take the new guys on the night ambush that the platoon has been assigned. Elias again seems sympathetic to their inexperience, despite some in-country training they probably received on their arrival at the division. However, as revealed by Chris's ruminations in a voice-over, there would be the strong—and in this case, apparently decisive—motivation among the group to see them sacrificed as opposed to veteran members of the outfit.

For someone who remembers Vietnam combat, the ensuing night ambush, to which Chris and the other new guy are predictably assigned, in many ways tells a standard version of the story that in one form or another could pass for all the others: the rain; the black jungle darkness; the hypervigilant strain of alertness; the fog of sleep; the eerie, laborious process of coming on and going off guard duty. It is vintage III Corps in the monsoon. You are in a night position too dark to see, so you make all the effort you can to hear; between the drizzle and the incessant drips come the downpours. You already can't see anything. Now you know you can't hear anything. You realize that if somebody wants to come and get you, you're shit out of luck. In the middle of all this, Chris Taylor wakes up to the new guy's worst nightmare. The guy who has allegedly relieved him on watch has turned over and gone back to sleep. It is an incredible betrayal of trust, but he barely has time to think about it. The insects come, this time clouds of swarming, relentless mosquitoes, with the accompanying welts and maddening itch. As suddenly, the enemy comes. Chris tries to react according to SOP (standard operating procedure) by blowing claymore antipersonnel mines that have been placed on the ambush perimeter but forgets to unlock the safety on the handheld electrical detonators. Meanwhile, all hell has broken loose. The other FNG dies in the first minute of his first combat. Elias chastises Barnes for ignoring his sensible recommendations that the new men be given a break-in period before being committed to such dangerous missions. Chris is falsely accused of falling asleep on guard by the man actually guilty. Because the accuser has been with the platoon for a while, his version of the story carries weight. He is also a soul brother, so it's not just an old guy's word against a new guy's word; it's also a black guy's word against a white guy's. Nobody wants to go there. It signals a serious crisis that is never resolved. Here it is for the moment dramatically avoided by Chris's wounding. Later the black guy will get killed for the same kind of shamming and carelessness. But for now the war will go on. It has just been one more fucked-up ambush in one more fucked-up place during one more fucked-up night in the Nam.

The platoon will dust Chris off and send out the body of the other new guy with him.

Chris's return to the unit while it is on stand-down, a period when the platoon is removed from the jungle to rest and refit in the brigade or division base camp, is a very important inclusion. Among other things, it very accurately represents what units did when they got three or four days in a relatively secure base camp: drink cold beer, eat hot food, smoke dope, listen to music. With his wound, Chris is now part of the group. The rest period, to be certain, includes the petty harassments of rear-area life, such as the assignment to shit details, documented, quite literally, by the one moment in Vietnam film that pays homage to the indispensable base-camp memory, both visual and olfactory, for anyone who did time there—burning shit: that is, removing cut-down fifty-gallon drums of shit from field latrines, pouring diesel fuel in them, and then stirring and burning until all the shit and piss and toilet paper has turned to ashes and the smell has gotten into your nose for the rest of your life. Indeed, the scene in which Chris participates here is almost as archetypal of the in-country experience as the one that nearly claimed his life: burning shit against a glorious sunset.

Meanwhile, the rear area setting provides for other critical developments. Most pronounced is the bunker apartheid dividing the heads from the juicers. Chris has the luck to fall in with the nicely integrated group in the place called the hutch. The leader is Elias, who, according to his behavior in the rear, has clearly gone Asiatic in a distinctly countercultural way. Stoned out of his skull, smiling the biggest shit-eating grin in the world, he lounges blissfully suspended in a gook hammock. Behind him hangs a poster of Ho Chi Minh. He is eating a banana, enjoying every crumb of the primal moment. A kind of Roshi in all manner of things military and spiritual, he supervises Chris's initiation into Vietnamese marijuana. The technique is the one known to all experienced dope smokers, a way of setting up a vacuum pipe to trap and hold a blast of smoke and then shoot it right down into the lungs. It is called the shotgun. Here the instrument is, in fact, a shotgun.

Simultaneously, in a room more resembling a back-in-the-world barracks, the juicers get drunk and play cards. Barnes is in charge.

The lieutenant ambles through, trying to be one of the guys—he gets rebuffed. The film script calls for him to be furtive, rodentlike. He does a good job. Quite visibly, the only black guy in the juicer group is Junior, the ambush soldier who has falsely accused Chris of falling asleep on guard. The splits in the two locales are emphasized by the music. Back in the hutch, song cuts include Jefferson Airplane's "White Rabbit" and Smokey Robinson and the Miracles' "Tracks of My Tears." In the barracks, Merle Haggard sings "Okie from Muscogee." The divisions could not be more clear: on one hand, sturdy grunts, stoned warriors like Elias and Rhah, black superfly guys, and white college counterculture kids; on the other, white officers and lifer NCOs, redneck shitkickers and juicers, with one craven black turncoat in for good measure. One thing in all this stands out almost in spite of itself. Of the two NCOs soon to meet in a Manichaean death struggle, Elias, barely ambulatory, is a lot more stoned in his scene than Barnes is drunk. Barnes is just drunk enough to be his usual murderous redneck mean.

New Year's Day 1968 finds the platoon back humping the jungle. Portentously, in a voice-over, Chris suggests a sense of impending climax. There has been much enemy movement. The platoon tries to stay alive in what is increasingly death's gray landscape: "A lot of little firefights, ambushes, we drop a lot of bombs, then we walk through the napalm like ghosts in a landscape." The back of Chris's flak jacket now reads, "If I die bury me upside down so the whole world can kiss my ass." The platoon enters an enemy base camp and bunker complex. Elias spots the first tunnel and goes down, where he stalks and kills a Vietnamese stay-behind. Meanwhile, two platoon members get blown up handling a booby-trapped ammo can full of documents. Barnes fills with Ahab-like rage and violence. Like the *Pequod*'s crew, the GIs have begun to whisper of his scar, his branding in elemental combat, and the legend that he has seven bullets in him and he's still not dead. Shortly, a black guy, Manning, disappears from a post on perimeter security. Soon after, he is found tortured and executed.

Turning its collective frustration and rage on a nearby village, the platoon verges on a killing frenzy. Bunny, as if he's a kid on a visit to a farm, calling, "Here piggie piggie piggie," blows away a hog. Chris, cornering a likely VC suspect in his mother's hooch, goes wild with his M-16, firing at the man's feet, making him dance the way Jack Palance makes Stonewall dance in *Shane*. Bunny, who has caught up with him, proceeds to beat in the prisoner's skull with his rifle butt, blood and brains spattering all over the GIs. Meanwhile, outside, Barnes conducts an interrogation. Exasperated by an old woman who keeps screaming at him to stop beating her husband, without warning he shoots her dead. He threatens next to shoot a little girl. Elias manages to prevent him but provokes a brawl in which the lieutenant finally intervenes. As the village burns, Chris, somehow restored to his senses, prevents a rape. In a grand panorama-of-war moment, the screen fills with the scene of GIs evacuating the village, smoke and flame rising in the background. Some soldiers carry little children on their shoulders. One kid is wearing a helmet. Others are being led by the hand. A GI out in front of the procession turns back, snapping pictures.

It is as if a great geologic shift has taken place concerning film, message, and metaphor. Henceforth, the drama gives itself over to a grab bag of agenda-driven stylizations, political and artistic. Although the time is late 1967 and early 1968, scenes of dialogue are devoted to racial divisions between black and white that, as various conversations predict, will eventually tear the Vietnam army apart. Elias and Chris have a spiritualistic foxhole conversation on the war, on death, on time and eternity. Meanwhile, a new literary model makes its appearance, this time Melville's "Billy Budd." "Barnes got it in for you, don't he?" says Chris. "Barnes believes in what he's doing," Elias replies philosophically.

Accordingly, the Barnes/Elias struggle between good and evil now comes to dominate the drama in both action and symbology, with Chris the wandering, embattled soul up for grabs. Shortly, the platoon walks into an ambush. The increasingly demonic Barnes walks upright, unkillable in a hail of small arms, trying to establish discipline as to when the platoon fires its weaponry. The panicked lieutenant calls in fire on wrong coordinates and hits his own position. He comes apart when Barnes berates him, knocking the radio out of his hand. Meanwhile, Elias takes off on a flank movement and single-handedly routs an enemy force trying to come in from behind. Barnes goes looking for him. They come face-to-face in the final encounter. Elias matches the look of hate in Barnes's eyes with that great shit-eating grin. Barnes shoots Elias in cold blood, two ostensibly fatal rounds to the heart. As the platoon evacuates by helicopter, a final scene takes place on the ground: Elias, somehow having survived the bullets from Barnes, is hunted down by an enemy unit who can be seen pursuing him at close range. We watch as he is quite literally shot to pieces simultaneously by enemy small bullets and by rocket and machine-gun fire from strafing American gunships. To a reprise of Barber's *Adagio,* he dies with his arms flung heavenward in the signature crucifixion iconography rendered permanent in the movie ad, the theater poster, and the sound-track album cover, not to mention the words of anybody who has ever written a paragraph about the film.

On the way out, Chris looks at Barnes; Barnes looks at Chris. Chris knows. Barnes knows that Chris knows. In the dopehead bunker, almost as among the disciples bereft of their master, there is discussion about killing Barnes. As if in a preternatural summons, Barnes, the juicer extraordinaire, shows up swigging from a fifth of Jack Daniels Black. He delivers a sympathy-for-the-devil soliloquy. You smoke dope to escape reality, he says, but "I am reality." They are all part of the machine. "When the machine breaks down, we break down." "Go ahead and kill me," he partly dares, partly pleads. "I shit on all of you." He faces down the mob, cows the whole group. Chris erupts in fury. Barnes is barely restrained from killing him with a commando knife. With a last flourish, he flicks open a cut on Chris's cheek.

A conversation Chris has with a black buddy, King, a quiet, good guy from Mississippi, anticipates the final combat sequence of the movie. As grunts in a fucked-up war nobody cares about anyhow, Chris says, "We just don't add up to dry shit." King, playing a kind of Jim to Chris's Huck, dispensing mother-wit truth, replies wisely and sagely: "Does a chicken have lips? Whoever said we did, babe? Make it outta here, it's all gravy, every day of the rest of your life man—gravy." The exchange occurs just before a mission in which the grunts realize they are being hung out as bait for a major cross-border attack. At the last minute, King gets his orders to go home. "Jus 'member take it easy now," he urges; "don't think too much, don't be a fool, no such thing as a coward cause it don't mean nuthin. Jes keep on keepin' on. Okay my man." He and Chris exchange a big soul shake. Meanwhile, the bad black guy, Junior, is discovered trying to malinger by putting insect repellent on his feet. The fawning sergeant O'Neill, one of Barnes's hangers-on that the troops call "superlifer," turns craven, asking not to be sent on the mission. Barnes answers, "Everybody gotta die sometime, Red."

The last scenes open along the bunker line of a hastily established jungle perimeter. In final reflective moment, Bunny, of all people, the ultimate homicidal teenager, gets the climactic soliloquy: "Y' know some of the things we done, I don't feel like we done something wrong but sometimes y' know I get this bad feeling." Still, he confesses, repeating what he has earlier told the Chaplain, "The truth is I really like it here. You do what you want, nobody fucks with you. Only worry you got's dying and if dat happens you won't know it anyway. So what the fuck." Of all people, Junior gets to be his audience. Junior is incredulous. Already scared out of his wits, he is sharing his hole with a crazy man. Bunny concludes with a laugh, "Don't you worry 'bout a thing Junior, you with Audie Murphy here, my man." Quickly we see the captain on the radio. He's lost a listening post. An entire NVA assault regiment attacks. Chris, now seasoned, detonates his emplaced claymores expertly. He and a black guy, like Henry Fleming and Wilson at the end of *The Red Badge of Courage*, actually charge the attacking force. Bunny is killed. Junior runs in terror and dies by bayoneting. Superlifer O'Neill hides under a dead body. The command bunker is destroyed by a VC suicide bomber with a satchel charge. The captain, calmly informing his superiors that he's got zips in the wire, with a position being completely overrun, deliberately calls in an air strike on his own coordinates.

Barnes and Chris Taylor wind up in the middle of the battle on the hellish perimeter. Barnes, in a killing frenzy, turns on Chris, trying to beat him to death with a shattered M-16 rifle. He may mistake Chris for the enemy. He may be trying to silence him about Elias. He may be trying to kill Chris out of simple hate. He may be killing him in a pure frenzy. The final stroke is prevented when the concussion from an air strike slams Barnes away. The next thing we know, Chris is waking up. Barnes is crawling off into the bush like a wounded animal. Chris picks up an enemy AK-47 rifle and follows him. Barnes still tries to growl his defiance. "Get me a medic," he tells Chris. "Go on boy." It dawns on him what Chris is about to do. "Go on, do it," Barnes says. "Fuck you in hell." Chris kills him with short burst, three spaced rounds from the AK-47.

Sounds of armored vehicles fill the background. An ACAV with a Wehrmacht flag enters the clearing preceded by a scout with a tracker dog. The rescuers start cutting off ears from the dead enemy. One black guy, a survivor of the attack, stabs himself in the leg, making sure he'll get medevaced. Shortly, mounds of NVA bodies are being bulldozed into bomb craters. The captain, who has survived, looks down into faces of his wounded as they are carried by. Chris, having received his million-dollar wound, the one that will take him back to the world, is dusted off. Rhah, brandishing the barbed wire cudgel he carries everywhere in combat, salutes like some kind of jubilant rock ape. To the renewed strains of Barber's *Adagio,* Chris looks down on the battlefield and sheds his load of tears. A final voice-over attempts a redemptory message, a short gloss on Chris's awareness of the Barnes/Elias contest for his soul, followed by a resolve to try to teach others and to live meaningfully.

As even the radically abridged summation of plot and dialogue in the last several paragraphs makes clear, one could go on a good deal—as does much of the academic literature I've read over the years—about the degree to which the much-heralded combat realism of *Platoon* ultimately capitulates to the stylization of allegory, at the level of both Vietnam-era politics and of epic myth. Yet for the veteran, I suspect, the film breaks down in such a way, if at all, only at the end, when Chris, having completed his ritual enactment of the hero's journey—the descent into the world of death, the struggle with the preternaturally powerful foe, the rebirth into a new prize of wisdom—once again becomes a nineteen-year-old American boy, knowing he's probably lifting out of Vietnam for good, trying to honor the moment in language with some stumbling attempt at profundity of closure. And even then, I'm not sure *Platoon* breaks down the way it does for the movie critic or nonveteran viewer. I, for one, have systematically destroyed every letter I have found preserved from my time in Vietnam. The main reason is that I can't believe, having been in the middle of a war, that I could manage to sound, in every one I've ever seen, so stupidly portentous, vapid, self-dramatizing, and callow. Accordingly, that is what I hear at the end of *Platoon,* and I connect with it profoundly, just as I have connected with all the extremes of experience represented: fear, rage, boredom, horror, frustration, surreal amusement, astonished wonder.

Thus I suspect that many veterans' responses to *Platoon*—even if those veterans have neither read Joseph Campbell nor toiled through *Heart of Darkness, The Red Badge of Courage,* and the like—will be styled precisely according to the film's capacity to evoke both intensely personal recollection and a larger participation in corporate, ritual remembering. My own response parallels this because of what many veterans will also feel as a salutary sense of double anachronism now built into the film. First, of course, totally intentional, is the film's commitment to getting completely inside the Vietnam infantry experience: the focus on the small unit, the particularities of the mission, the leadership conflicts, the distinct personalities of the individual soldiers, the psychology of the friendships and group identifications within the unit. The film preserves the infantry war in the III Corps region of Vietnam at the height of the American military effort almost as an insect in amber. It has taken an experience mainly miserable, bloody, and confusing and fixed it before our eyes as something archaeological in the profoundest sense.

To this degree, with the exclusion of all but the most overt stylizations (the Barnes/Elias conflict, most notably) the film remains so scrupulously detailed as to the particular setting of the war, time, place, unit, and type of action that, when it compresses ideological content (the growing conflict between the white guys and the brothers, for instance, or dopers versus juicers, or draftees versus lifers; or issues of battlefield atrocities, like the murder of prisoners and civilians), it all still seems deeply continuous and integral. A lot happens to this platoon. Indeed, one could aver that the unit's experience is basically a gathering of Nam cliché, one of everything: the blown ambush, the booby-trap casualties, the tunnel-rat sequence; the tortured and murdered GI, the atrocities against civilians, the torching of the village, the cataclysmic firebase battle at the end. Then we add in the useless lieutenant, the light-and-dark struggle between Elias and Barnes, the cold-blooded murder scene, and the final passion of Elias's dying; then the reverse, as Chris coldly shoots Barnes and thus vanquishes the foe. At the same time, anyone who was there would admit that everything that happens surely did happen somewhere. It would likely not have all happened as the experience of one platoon over the course of less than one year. It could have.

The second kind of datedness, in retrospect, seems rather more fortuitous. It has to do with the political circumstances of the time in which the film appeared. And even here, I would propose, one might project at least a certain intentionality. To be specific, the film's date of release was 1986. After much controversy surrounding the creation of the Vietnam Veterans' Memorial, the monument had been unveiled to an outpouring of public approval that has to this day made it the most visited site in the nation's capital. Many veteran authors had published major works to both popular and critical acclaim. Others were beginning to achieve political prominence at the state and national level. To the American public, the Vietnam veteran had become like any other citizen, albeit one who had, while a very young person, been sent to fight an American war at a very particular time in a very particular place, but who had also returned to lead an average American life. And the assumption of this attitude had nothing to do with the fact that Reagan was president or that the mood of government was conservative revisionism. Somehow the film had managed to capture its own historical moment as the Vietnam soldier passed from pariah through victim through forgotten hero to middle-aged American with a mortgage, kids in college, and a retirement plan.

This sense of double distancing, for me at least, is reinforced by my corresponding sense of the indeterminate age of the soldiers on the screen. I must admit that I expected them to seem, with the exception of the occasional senior officer or NCO, as we were at the time: very, very young. In fact, many of them seem at once both young and old, as many of us may have seemed without knowing it. Or maybe the indeterminate age is the result of the memory of having been with young people who in some cases would wind up literally having lived to be as old as they were ever going to become. Maybe it is the casting. Stone, after all, had been there and knew the drill, the business of war–this war, any war–in putting old men's souls in young men's bodies. ("How do you feel," I once read in Michael Herr's work, with a pronounced jolt of recognition, "when a nineteen-year-old kid tells you from the bottom of his heart that he's gotten too old for this kind of shit?") In any event, there is Charlie Sheen, the college boy, old enough to know better, now reduced to the callow fucking new guy. There is Bunny, the boy-killer, as old and cold as murder itself. There is Rhah, with the king of the jungle headdress and staff, the guy who has become the war. The white guys and the black guys: in some cases, they are juvenile, loudmouthed, and childishly violent; in others, they are wise, reticent, and patiently enduring. They are too young to die. They are too old to go home. Even the NCOs inhabit the same midrange. Despite his empathy with the privates, Elias is not a shake-and-bake NCO–an enlisted man with extra training–but a professional busted down from more senior rank, a sergeant that just seems like a younger guy than he really is, a doper, a humanist, a closet intellectual, yet at the same time a tremendously adept fighter, a hunter, a tracker, a killer. I knew people like him. Barnes is likewise a definitive portrayal: in his mid- to late twenties or early thirties, a young lifer who has made his whole career on the battlefield. I never knew anybody exactly like him, but I knew some people who stepped pretty close to the edge.

Given my own background, I have some particular thoughts about the officers, both to age and conduct. First among these is that the captain is too old. To be sure, the time was late 1967 and early 1968, with a place for the rare older captain, frequently an up-from-the-ranks NCO. As to the portrayal in question, the actor was himself in fact a former marine company commander, retired at the rank of captain and doubling as the film's technical advisor. Still, by around Tet 1968 most of the captains would have been around twenty-five or so; the one in the film looks and sounds like most lieutenant colonels I knew. Likewise, even Stone, who inserts himself in a cameo as the ranking officer at the overrun firebase, a major who gets killed by a satchel charge in the command bunker, is by 1986 slightly too old for his role.

Then there's the lieutenant: hopelessly weak, incompetent, thoroughly scorned by his command from the NCOs down to the newest private. I never knew a lieutenant that bad in Vietnam. I did know a couple back in the world, including one, most notably, who at least had the good sense to weasel his way out of orders *to* Vietnam. *In* Vietnam the lieutenant would have gotten taken care of long before it happens in the movie. The company commander would have probably relieved him, although possibly, given Barnes's ruthless drive and expertise, the trade-off might have made it worthwhile for a captain to look the other way. In the alternative, his men would have simply killed him. To make that happen, of course, would have forced the whole Barnes/Elias structure to crumple like a house of cards. And it *is* a movie.

Still, I can't get out of my mind something described to me by one of my sergeants in the Sixth Cavalry, a recently returned Twenty-fifth Infantry Division veteran from exactly the period in question. He was a hot-tempered, mean little shit, who, knowing I was in the pipeline for Vietnam, for some reason liked me well enough to share his combat savvy when he got a chance. He told me one time of how he and his fellow platoon members had seized on the confusion of a firefight to execute a lieutenant they deemed dangerously incompetent. He told me he was the one chosen to do the killing, and he described how he did it. His voice was not only totally without remorse but also totally without emotion. The lieutenant had to go, he said. It was that simple. The story was so astonishing that I had trouble believing in the truth of it at the time. Interestingly, it took a movie where such an event *didn't* happen to make me see how real the story truly was.

How real the war truly was certainly applies to all the jungle stuff the movie brought back to me: the war of the patrol, the sweep, the ambush, the enemy base camp and/or bunker complex; the war of the triple canopy darkness, the wet and the heat, the stink and the sweat and the jungle slime; the nasty, crump-thump surprise of a mine or a booby trap and the rattling outbursts of automatic weapons fire; the oozy black color of a wounded man's blood; the eerie, menacing quiet of a base camp that has clearly been vacated within hours, perhaps even minutes. For most soldiers, I suspect, the cataclysmic firebase battle at the end, with the perimeter completely overrun and the calling in of an air strike on top of the American position, represents a scale of action infrequently seen. This one not only actually happened but also was in fact much bigger, taking place pretty much at the time and place depicted at a position named Firebase Burt, which was occupied by two full battalions of infantry: Stone's unit, Third Battalion, Twenty-second Infantry, and its mechanized counterpart, First Battalion, Twenty-second Infantry, a member of which happened to be the novelist Larry Heinemann, who describes his version of the event vividly in *Close Quarters*. The perimeter in question, then, was probably manned by as many as six or seven infantry companies, comprising fifteen to twenty platoons. Although not essentially wiped out as depicted, the firebase was overrun in a number of positions, with another mechanized unit actually rolling in during the attack. That the movie confines itself here, as elsewhere, to the single platoon position remains absolutely crucial to its realism. Although it is probably true for any soldier who ever fought, in Vietnam for certain, any single combat position or point of contact became completely your particular corner of the war. If you were lucky enough to lift out afterward, like Chris, maybe you would have had that rare strange moment when you got a look at the size of the perimeter, still smoking in the morning haze.

The movie also makes real again just about every bit of the firebase stuff: the booze and the dope, the music and the card games, the rear-area frictions and animosities, the lifer crap, right down to the haze of burning shit. On the would-be philosophical conversations and bunker profundities in the film, perhaps some of those were real too. I got an e-mail a year back or so from a friend I cared about a lot in Vietnam, an enlisted man who drove my jeep when I was the troop XO. He was my absolute sidekick. The two of us were a couple of young guys scared even more shitless sometimes than when we had been busting jungle with the platoon, scared because we were barreling alone in a jeep down roads that heavily armored convoys would travel only once a day on account of mines and ambushes. He thanked me for encouraging him one time when he thought he'd had enough. "You told me just to remember," he said, "that if we got out of here, everything else would be gravy."

Did I say that? Did one or the other of us hear it in a movie? It doesn't matter anymore. He went back to college and has spent his life as an educator. I'm grateful for the memory and the idea that I encouraged somebody.

Some of the particular movie conceits, however, ring false pretty much from start to finish. One is the continuously moralizing voice-over of the letters to grandma. Another is the Elias/Barnes allegory of good and evil. Most soldiers will also resent the representation of the killings in the village as a kind of mini–My Lai. I suspect that countless Vietnam veterans could tell stories of serving in a frustrated, vengeful, disorganized unit, poorly led, with conflicting leadership claims—perhaps a weak lieutenant, a hard-core sergeant, maybe a hippie sympathizer. Some may say they did the things the movie platoon does in the village. On one occasion, that produced a My Lai. My Lais did not happen all over Vietnam. However, too often comparable things probably did happen on an everyday basis in ways that many of us who came back would still just as soon not know about.

In any event, I think it is fair and truthful to say that what happens to Chris Taylor and the members of his platoon in one way or another happened to most of us who knew the war of the infantry brigades and battalions. Like Chris, we have been thinking, many of us, ever since about what a war like that does to a person and to a country and about what kind of closure we might bring to our memory of it. I suspect most of us would go for the closing that the last scene in *Platoon* doesn't give us. We would rewrite it: yes, the million-dollar wound; the helicopter ride out; popping smoke; Rhah, standing on the boulder below, brandishing his cudgel and roaring his farewell. But this time no voice-over. Just the Barber *Adagio*. And then silence. That would have gotten it: beauty, majesty, and eloquent closure. But it wouldn't have been true. Inside the frame, some yearning, self-dramatizing American mind would already be trying to stumble into words that would make wisdom out of it: Stephen Crane's Henry Fleming in *The Red Badge of Courage;* Tim O'Brien's Paul Berlin in *Going After Cacciato;* Larry Heinemann's Deadeye Dosier in *Close Quarters;* Oliver Stone's Chris Taylor in *Platoon;* or me.

The Music of the Nam

My guess would be that any Americans who served in-country during the Vietnamese war still have a personal sound-track album inside their head—a set of songs, titles, lyrics, that can flash them back to wherever they were thirty or thirty-five years ago, standing there now looking at their younger self in exactly the place they were when they heard some particular piece of the music of the Nam. It is said in this regard, with considerable aptness, that Vietnam was the first rock 'n' roll war. It is also said that, for Americans at least, Vietnam was not so much an eight- or ten-year war as a one-year war Americans fought eight or ten times or a war fought by 3.5 million individual American young men and women, each in his or her own personal way, going there, coming back, and then learning to live with it forever after, mainly alone. One thing that brings together the shifting frames of memory with the personal and cultural moment is the music. Once established and then gradually enlarged by accretion, the in-country playlist of the Nam's greatest hits came to chart the course of the American experience of Vietnam across a popular-culture continuum recognizable at once at home and abroad. Now, as then, the war lives on in the music of the Nam.

Moviemakers figured this out a good while ago. A set of representative sound tracks loops around like some ultimate audio rewind of history, bringing everything back for those who lived through the terrible years of the war both at home and abroad in a rush of strange, at times almost prurient, nostalgia. *Platoon,* for instance, anthologizes Smoky Robinson and the Miracles' "Tracks of My Tears," Merle Haggard's "Okie from Muskogee," the Doors' "Hello, I Love You," Jefferson Airplane's "White Rabbit," Aretha Franklin's "Respect," Otis Redding's "Sitting on the Dock of the Bay," Percy Sledge's "When a Man Loves a Woman," and the Young Rascals' "Groovin'." Against these, the filmmaker soberly juxtaposes Samuel Barber's "Adagio for Strings." In a similar strategy, *Full Metal Jacket* intersperses among its various tracks the Chiffons' "Chapel of Love," Sam the Sham and the Pharaohs' "Wooly Bully," Nancy Sinatra's "These Boots Are Made for Walking," Chris Kenner's "I Like It like That," and the Trashmen's "Surfin' Bird." Here, the notable juxtaposition is "The Marines' Hymn."

Popular music operates similarly in two films focused on the problems of returning veterans. The 1978 classic *Coming Home,* set during the height of the war a decade earlier, takes a California counterculture slant featuring the Beatles' "Hey, Jude" and "Strawberry Fields Forever," Buffalo Springfield's "Expecting to Fly" and "For What It's Worth," Janis Joplin's "Call on Me," Jefferson Airplane's "White Rabbit," Richie Havens's "Follow," Simon and Garfunkel's "Bookends," Aretha Franklin's "Save Me," Jimi Hendrix's "Manic Depression," the Chambers Brothers' "Time Has Come Today," Steppenwolf's "Born to Be Wild," Bob Dylan's "Just like a Woman," and Tim Buckley's "Once I Was a Soldier." The musical voices most pronounced, however, threading their way through the film like a period litany, are those of the Rolling Stones: "Out of Time," "No Expectations," "Ruby Tuesday," "Nineteenth Nervous Breakdown," "Jumping Jack Flash," "Sympathy for the Devil." In the more recent *In Country,* a teenage protagonist seeks to understand a father she never knew, killed in the war, and to comprehend concurrently the emotional struggles of an uncle who may suffer from both PTSD and Agent Orange poisoning. Reaching across history, the sound track juxtaposes their music with hers. A high-school friend wants to know who Country Joe and the Fish were. A veteran organizing a Vietnam reunion dance says he always liked that "White Rabbit" song. At the dance itself, the music includes the Mamas and Papas' "Dedicated to the One I Love," the Four Tops' "Baby, I Need Your Lovin'," Jackie DeShannon's "What the World Needs Now," and Martha and the Vandellas' "Dancin' in the Street." The dance ends with today's country: K. D. Lang's "Waltz Me One More Time around the Dance Floor" and a Hank Williams Jr. reprise of "Ain't Misbehavin'." A high-school boyfriend plays Dwight Yoakam and Webb Wilder on the radio. Meanwhile, when the dead Kentucky soldier's daughter goes out for a run with her earphones, the song is always, always Bruce Springsteen's "I'm on Fire."

Broadening the historical range to encase wartime music with prewar and postwar companion pieces, *Born on the Fourth of July* spotlights Creedence Clearwater Revival's "Born on the Bayou," Van Morrison's "Brown-Eyed Girl," and the Temptations' "My Girl." For fifties foregrounding it calls in the Shirelles' "Soldier Boy" and Frankie Avalon's "Venus." General post-Vietnam atmospherics include Don McLean's "American Pie" and an Edie Brickell version of Bob Dylan's "A Hard Rain's a Gonna Fall." (Absolutely astonishing in this connection is that somehow the movie misses the heartbreaking musical opportunity offered by Ron Kovic's book from which the movie is largely drawn: a concluding fifties scene of kids running on a summer evening, listening to a guy named Dell Shannon sing a song called "Runaway," and thinking they're going to live forever.) A similar kind of historical sweep distinguishes *Forrest Gump,* the sound track offering a full two volumes of period tracks, with vintage Nam pieces clustered at the center like some kind of nuclear-core matter. On a final army leave before Vietnam service, Forrest finds his beloved Jenny doing a counterculture novelty act in a strip joint, naked with a guitar, trying to perform "Blowin' in the Wind." In-country we are literally bombarded: Creedence Clearwater Revival's "Fortunate Son"; the Four Tops' "Sugar Pie Honey Bunch"; Aretha Franklin's "Respect"; the Beach Boys' "Sloop John B."; Jimi Hendrix's "All along the Watchtower"; the Doors' "Till the Music Ends," "Hello, I Love You," "People Are Strange," and "Break on Through (to the Other Side)"; the Mamas and the Papas' "California Dreamin'"; Buffalo Springfield's "For What It's Worth"; and Jackie DeShannon's "What the World Needs Now." Back home, the hero's adventures continue to period musical accompaniment. New entries, such as Simon and Garfunkel's "Mrs. Robinson," Jefferson Airplane's "Volunteers," Jimi Hendrix's "The Wind Cries Mary," and the Youngbloods' "Come Together," mix with classics like Peter, Paul, and Mary's "Where Have All the Flowers Gone," Scott McKenzie's "San Francisco (Be Sure to Wear Flowers in Your Hair)," and the Byrds' "Turn! Turn! Turn! (To Everything There Is a Season)." Forrest watches the moon landing to the Fifth Dimension's "Aquarius (Let the Sun Shine In)." He plays sports-ambassador ping pong in China to Three Dog Night's "Joy to the World." As the druggy sixties become the mellow seventies, the hits keep happening: the Doors' "Love Her Madly," B. J. Thomas's "Raindrops Keep Fallin' on My Head," Tony Orlando's "Tie a Yellow Ribbon 'round the Old Oak Tree," and Kool and the Gang's "Get Down Tonight."

The Robin Williams vehicle *Good Morning, Vietnam,* set fairly early in the American war and centered on the real-life attempts of an AFVN (Armed Forces Vietnam) disc jockey named Adrian Cronauer to revolutionize the playlist and give the soldiers their own music, includes mainly early and mid-1960s vintage selections like Martha and the Vandellas' "Nowhere to Run," the Beach Boys' "I Get Around" and "Walk with the Sun," Wayne Fontana and the Mindbenders' "Game of Love," the Searchers' "Sugar and Spice," the Castaways' "Liar, Liar," James Brown's "I Got You (I Feel Good)," Them's "Baby Please Don't Go," the Marvelettes' "Danger, Heartbreak Dead Ahead," the Vogues' "Five o'Clock World," and the Rivieras' "California Sun." Here again, as in *Platoon,* a melody is juxtaposed as an ironic sounding board—this time, Louis Armstrong's "What a Wonderful World."

Such in-country anthologizing in turn can be paired with the classic aftermath film *The Big Chill,* which features a parallel civilian greatest-hits reprise. Here, the Nam spectrum, given the twinned moods of nostalgia and recovery, divides itself into distinctly pre- and postwar. Included are Marvin Gaye's "Heard It through the Grapevine," the Temptations' "My Girl" and "Ain't Too Proud to Beg," the Rascals' "Good Lovin'," Smoky Robinson and the Miracles' "Tracks of My Tears" and "Second That Emotion," Three Dog Night's "Joy to the World," Aretha Franklin's "Natural Woman," Procul Harem's "A Whiter Shade of Pale," and the Exciters' "Tell Him."

Other movies restrict themselves to one or two representative selections, rendering them integral and thematic—even using them, as in the now classic case of *Apocalypse Now,* as great framing metaphors. There, in the extraordinary opening, helicopters dart to and fro across the sky as a napalm strike goes in against a distant treeline. The sound of their whacking blades merges into the sound of the helicopter rattling the windows of the seedy Saigon hotel room where the film's narrator-protagonist, a burnt-out American army captain, sleeps off a hallucinatory drunk. That sound merges into the whispering blades of a French-era ceiling fan. Presiding over the scene and then dying off into its own silence is the sound of Jim Morrison and the Doors singing "The End." Later, in one of the legendary moments in the film, an airmobile assault goes in with Wagner's "Ride of the Valkyries" blaring forth from helicopter speakers. In another moment, a Navy patrol-boat crewman water-skis to the Rolling Stones' "Satisfaction." Musical Nam atmospherics likewise brood over *Who Will Stop the Rain,* the movie version of Robert Stone's *Dog Soldiers,* with the movie's title and main theme taken from Creedence Clearwater Revival, a band that alone, as noted later, could supply its own greatest-hits anthology of the war. More recently, in *We Were Soldiers,* music of the era is used briefly but skillfully for dramatic-period effect. The year is 1965. The First Air Cavalry Division, the proud, new, high-tech heliborne unit on which the army has pinned its hopes for fighting a new kind of airmobile war, is about to deploy to Vietnam. At an officers' club dance, the two final songs played are Sam and Dave's "Hold On, I'm Comin'" and Mel Carter's "Hold Me, Kiss Me, Love Me." It is as if American pop on the eve of Vietnam has been caught in midsong.

Only two books, to my knowledge, make a comparable attempt to factor in the music of the Nam as part of the historical and cultural script. Presumably, because they were both published by larger commercial presses, with something like Hollywood-style funding, they remain two of the only books that have had permissions budgets big enough to bear the strain. For the music of the Nam, as will be discussed shortly, is among other things very expensive.

The first was Michael Herr's widely anticipated and much-heralded *Dispatches*. To this day, the first thing appearing in the book are two pages dedicated to permissions and acknowledgments. Herr's official list includes the Rolling Stones' "Two Thousand Light Years from Home" and "Citadel," Scott McKenzie's "San Francisco," Sonny Boy Williamson's "Good Morning, Little Schoolgirl," the Beatles' "Magical Mystery Tour," Archie Bell and the Drells' "Tighten Up," Buffalo Springfield's "For What It's Worth," Bob Dylan's "Visions of Johanna," Frank Zappa's "Trouble Comin' Everyday," Sam the Sham and the Pharaohs' "Little Red Riding Hood," Glenn Campbell's "Galveston," Junior Walker and the All Stars' "Shotgun," Johnny Cash's "Ring of Fire," Los Bravos' "Black Is Black," the Animals' "We Gotta Get Out of This Place" and "Hungry," and Jimi Hendrix's "Foxy Lady." Inside, lines sneak in other sources as diverse as Claude King's "Wolverton Mountain" and Wingy Manone's "Stop the War, These Cats Is Killin' Themselves." The lavish, extravagant, almost overwhelming array of lyrics proves deeply integral to a narrative strategy of relentless verbal, visual, and aural juxtapositions variously described as postmodern collage and/or mass-media montage. As it was for Herr, his fellow correspondents, the soldiers of the battalions and the base camps, and the support troops of the sprawling installations around Long Binh, Saigon, Bien Hoa, Da Nang, and Cam Ranh Bay, so it is for the reader: to hear the music of the Nam is in many ways to inhabit the country that was the war.

A second popular literary text suffused with the music of the era, serving as the basis of one of the films described earlier, is Bobbie Ann Mason's *In Country*. Here, as in the movie, the music of the Nam becomes important for its memory value, as well as crucial to the larger brand-name atmospherics for which Mason's assessments of the contemporary American mind and spirit have been famous. Accordingly, in the novel version, the teenage daughter of a father barely beyond his teens when he died in Vietnam goes through her mother's old sixties albums "the Beatles, the Kinks, the Stones, the Jefferson Airplane, Janis Joplin, Jimi Hendrix, Gerry and the Pacemakers, the Dave Clark Five." Later she plays yard-sale singles of " 'Wooly Bully' by Sam the Sham and the Pharaohs and 'Tutti Frutti' by Little Richard and 'Maybellene' by Chuck Berry." The Saturday oldies show at the local college plays the Doors' "Light My Fire." At the high-school reunion dance, Donovan sings "Sunshine Superman." But, as in the movie, the main music line is now Bruce Springsteen: "Born to Run," "Born in the USA," "Dancin' in the Dark."

These two textual examples, in their curious isolation, stand in eye-catching contrast to nearly all other novels, poems, plays, memoirs, oral histories, and works of journalism and reportage that have now become part of the academic and/or popular-culture canon of the literature of the war. Their isolation spotlights a feature at least until now peculiar to the cultural history of the music of the Nam in its relation to print discussions about American memory of the war. The reason is financial, a function of the unusual economic power exercised by the music industry over popular-culture history as far as the reproduction of musical materials is concerned. To put it directly, music publishers and trade organizations such as ASCAP (American Society of Composers, Authors, and Publishers) have generally charged staggering permissions fees for quotation of songs and lyrics. Accordingly, many of the works now regarded as Vietnam classics were frequently written and published before the authors were established with major presses or had acquired literary reputations sufficient to justify deep permissions pockets. Such now prominent figures include prose chroniclers of the war as diverse as Tim O'Brien, Philip Caputo, James Webb, Gustav Hasford, Winston Groom, Larry

Heinemann, Linda Van Devanter, Gloria Emerson, and David Halberstam; the dramatist David Rabe; and poets such as W. D. Ehhart, John Balaban, Michael Casey, Bruce Weigl, and Yusef Komunyakaa. In their works one will find frequent literary references, many of them drawn from the contemporary popular-culture scene: Joseph Heller, Kurt Vonnegut, Thomas Pynchon, Allen Ginsberg, Ken Kesey. Television and movie references abound: *Ozzie and Harriet, Get Smart,* Looney Tunes, the *Mickey Mouse Club, Sands of Iwo Jima, Fort Apache, The Green Berets.* But there are virtually no quotations of popular music. As noted, many of the figures named have now become established American authors, continuing to write on popular-culture themes. Almost uniformly, however, even today they all eschew popular music references, presumably as a strain on print publication budgets; or they wait, presumably, until the next stage of development, as in the case of Groom, Kovic, and, most recently, Harold G. Moore and Joseph L. Galloway of *We Were Soldiers Once . . . and Young,* for Hollywood to pick up the movie tab.

The prevalence of whopping permissions fees, frequently as much as thousands of dollars for the quotation of one or two lines, explains an equally pronounced paucity of discussion about the music of the Nam in critical and cultural-studies literature—academic authors and university presses the least able to support exorbitant permissions fees for lyrics and other source materials that continue to be more heavily guarded, as opposed to popular-culture print texts such as novels, poems, plays, memoirs, and the like, from the fair-use provisions of critical discourse, which allow citation for purposes of interpretive analysis and commentary.

After many years, one does now find the occasional Vietnam literature/popular-culture anthology with sections on the music, including a collection of songs reprinted in full for reading and critical comparison with accompanying literary selections. Bruce Franklin's *The Vietnam War in American Stories, Songs, and Poems* includes Barry Sadler's "Ballad of the Green Berets," Country Joe and the Fish's "I-Feel-Like-I'm-Fixin'-to-Die Rag," Crosby, Stills, Nash, and Young's "Ohio," Creedence Clearwater Revival's "Fortunate Son," and Bruce Springsteen's "Born in the USA." Stewart O'Nan's *Vietnam Reader* reprints the same Sadler, Country Joe and the Fish, Creedence Clearwater, and Springsteen selections and adds the Doors' "Unknown Soldier," Marvin Gaye's "What's Goin' On," Edwin Starr's "War," and Ten Thousand Maniacs' "The Big Parade."

Occasional overview essays on war-era popular music have appeared in scholarly collections. Interestingly, albeit not surprisingly, because the writers' backgrounds are most often academic, discussion tends to gravitate toward an antiwar protest list that, with a few exceptions, would have been almost totally unfamiliar to in-country listeners. Vietnam GIs knew enough about Peter, Paul, and Mary to call a gunship "Puff the Magic Dragon." They may have remembered Bob Dylan's early sixties protest stuff—"Blowin' in the Wind," "Masters of War," "A Hard Rain's Gonna Fall." But Phil Ochs, Joan Baez, Malvina Reynolds, or Buffy Sainte-Marie were basically off the GI scale. Even Country Joe and the Fish's "I-Feel-Like-I'm-Fixin'-to-Die Rag" was mostly a back-in-the-world favorite, with at best a cult following in-country. Likewise, late-stage antiwar statements such as John Lennon and Yoko Ono's "Give Peace a Chance" or Crosby, Stills, Nash, and Young's "Ohio" never attracted appreciable GI listenership. By that time GIs were too busy trying not to be the last one out of the tunnel.

This is not to say that the vast majority of the music of the Nam could not be heard playing simultaneously on Tu Do Street or at the Da Nang PX and in student bars in Madison or Boulder. GIs in Vietnam shared with counterculture audiences at home, for instance, a fondness for the psychedelic: the Rolling Stones' "Get Off of My Cloud," the Byrds' "Eight Miles High," the Beatles' "Magical Mystery Tour," Jefferson Airplane's "White Rabbit," Procul Harem's "A Whiter Shade of Pale." They also went, like their back-in-the-world counterparts, for the sixties apocalyptic: Barry McGuire's "The Eve of Destruction," Buffalo Springfield's "For What It's Worth," Edwin Starr's "War," Jimi Hendrix's "All along the Watchtower." Oddly in the case of the apocalyptic, "The End," chosen by Francis Ford Coppola as his opening theme for *Apocalypse Now,* was not a song particularly well known to GIs, whose choice from the Doors would more likely have been "Light My Fire" or "Riders on the Storm."

At the same time, as the latter comments suggest, while tapping into much of the popular scene at home, in-country the music of the era also took on its own peculiar contours. Most veterans, white *and* black, for instance, remember a tremendous amount of soul: Aretha Franklin's "Respect," Ray Charles's "Hit the Road, Jack," Sam and Dave's "Soul Man" and "Hold On, I'm Comin'," Percy Sledge's "When a Man Loves a Woman," Wilson Pickett's "Mustang Sally" and "Midnight Hour," Otis Redding's "Heard It through the Grapevine" and "Sitting on the Dock of the Bay," Marvin Gaye's "What's Goin' On." Motown was also ubiquitous, with the Temptations, the Miracles, the Marvelettes, the Impressions, Barbara Lewis, Mary Wells, Martha and the Vandellas, the Supremes, the Four Tops. One can argue forever about whether it was a black man's war; my own guess is that, because it was a grunt's war, it automatically became a black music war whether a GI was black or white. Similarly, crossing racial categories was an equal amount of seriously antisocial rock by a handful of groups and performers who will always hold their signature status. The Animals: "House of the Rising Sun," "We Gotta Get Out of This Place," "Hungry." The Doors: "Hello, I Love You," "Love Me Two Times," "Love Her Madly," "Light My Fire," "Riders on the Storm," "People Are Strange," "The Unknown Soldier," "Break on Through (to the Other Side)." Creedence Clearwater Revival: "Bad Moon Rising," "Proud Mary," "Run through the Jungle," "Have You Seen the Rain?," "Suzie Q," "Up around the Bend," "Fortunate Son." Jimi Hendrix: "Purple Haze," "Hey Joe," "Foxy Lady," "All along the Watch Tower," "The Star-Spangled Banner." The Rolling Stones: "Satisfaction," "Under My Thumb," "Nineteenth Nervous Breakdown," "Paint It Black," "Play with Fire," "Time Is on My Side," "Let's Spend the Night Together," "Ruby Tuesday," "Have You Seen Your Mother Standing in the Shadows," "Sympathy for the Devil." Especially the Rolling Stones.

For anyone who recalls Vietnam, it was definitely a Rolling Stones and not a Beatles War. One might have heard "Hey, Jude," "Strawberry Fields," "Nowhere Man," and a couple of others; or—as a joke, maybe— "All You Need Is Love." By then, the Beatles were already in their "Let It Be" phase—all the hokey words-of-wisdom and Mother Mary foolishness. The Stones knew better, well enough to write it in parody: "Let It Bleed." And so, in Vietnam, did the GIs. They may not have heard of Altamont, Monterrey pop, or any of the other big music scenes, but anyone who was there could agree with Michael Herr about all those moments in which the war really did seem to be the ultimate rock 'n' roll concert gone bad: sex, drugs, race, violence, cultural outlawry, and death right there in the front row; an army of stoned teenagers, making victory through firepower.

Oddly, the preferences for hard rock in Vietnam could often be matched by an incongruous fondness for the occasional piece of groovy nonsense, some peace-and-love favorite, all happiness and innocence. These were American young people, after all, listening, like their domestic counterparts, to the Youngbloods' "Come Together," the Rascals' "Good Lovin'" and "Groovin' on a Sunday Afternoon," the Fifth Dimension's "Aquarius," Jackie DeShannon's "What the World Needs Now," Scott McKenzie's "San Francisco (Be Sure to Wear Flowers in Your Hair)," the Animals' "Warm San Francisco Nights," Spanky and Our Gang's "I'd Like to Get to Know You," the Lovin' Spoonful's "Do You Believe in Magic" and "You Didn't Have to Be So Nice," the Turtles' "You Baby" and "Happy Together." For female sweetness, mixed with a kind of nostalgic sentimentalism, GIs tended to prefer British women: Jackie DeShannon's "Wishin' and Hopin'," Marianne Faithful's "As Tears Go By," Petula Clark's "Downtown" and "Don't Sleep on the Subway," Mary Hopkins's "Those Were the Days" and "Good-Bye." Similarly, one might also find the odd selection of British white soul— in the early days, Tom Jones's "It's Not Unusual," or later, Joe Cocker's "With a Little Help from My Friends."

There were also some decidedly well-defined Nam specialty genres. One was California music. Again, with the armed forces largely consisting of American teenagers, most of them male, some of the music naturally ran toward the subject of hot cars: Jan and Dean's "Dead Man's Curve" and "Little Old Lady from Pasadena," the Beach Boys' "Little Deuce Coupe" and "409." Most of the time, though—as honored by an otherwise strangely gratuitous interlude in *Apocalypse Now,* with Robert Duvall as a mad cavalry colonel looking for the perfect wave—the big California-music theme was surfing, often with hot cars thrown in for free: Jan and Dean's "Surf City"; the Rivieras' "Warm California Sun";

the Surfaris' "Wipeout"; and the whole Beach Boys' repertoire, "I Get Around," "California Girls," "Surfer Girl," "Surfin' USA," "Help Me, Rhonda," "Barbara Ann," "Good Vibrations," or, in a pensive interlude, "Wouldn't It Be Nice," "God Only Knows," and "In My Room." This was the California of the endless summer, the perfect wave, beautiful suntanned girls in tiny bikinis.

An alternative California was the home of loving mellow hippies, the world of the Mamas and Papas' "California Dreamin'," Dionne Warwick's "Do You Know the Way to San Jose," or the Animals' "Warm San Francisco Nights." This California featured a complete San Francisco subset: San Francisco, the epicenter of the counterculture scene–love, peace, sex, freedom; San Francisco, the place you passed through if you had the good fortune to be both sent home in one piece and simultaneously discharged from the military. There would be the landing at Travis Air Force Base, followed by the bus ride to Oakland Army Processing Station. Within hours, you could be on the street in San Francisco, forever remembered as the end of the pipeline, the way out of the tunnel, the exit from the green machine. For all these reasons, the name came to be something almost holy, like Jerusalem, Banaras, Mecca. Most prominent of all lyrical homages, of course, was Scott McKenzie's "San Francisco." But sometimes even a mention could be enough, as in Otis Redding's "Sitting on the Dock of the Bay." And then, of course, there was the ultimate San Francisco group, period, Jefferson Airplane.

Another decidedly Nam-specific genre was airplane music: the Boxtops' "The Letter," Peter, Paul, and Mary's "Leaving on a Jet Plane," Simon and Garfunkel's "Homeward Bound." Within that there was the ultimate subgenre–DEROS music. DEROS: in a world full of bad, ugly acronyms–WP (white phosphorus), HE (high explosive), RPG (rocket-propelled grenade); WIA (wounded in action); KIA (killed in action); MIA (missing in action)–it was the single sweetest sound in the whole Vietnam soldier's vocabulary. DEROS: Date of Eligibility for Return from Overseas, the day you get on the plane and go home. Here, crowning the music of the Nam, were always the three big ones: again, Scott McKenzie's "San Francisco"; the Boxtops' "The Letter," known alternately to most GIs by either its first line, "Gimme a Ticket for an Airplane," or its last, "My Baby Done Sent Me a Letter"; and finally, what most GIs would recognize to this day as the great in-country anthem, the Animals' "We Gotta Get Out of This Place."

Along with these were the other big uncategorizables—the signature songs, the odd great ones. The titles of some suggested a vague logic of inclusion: the Shirelles' "Soldier Boy," Fontella Bass's "Rescue Me," Little Anthony and the Imperials' "I Think I'm Going Out of My Head," the Platters' "Smoke Gets in Your Eyes." Others seemed a way of hanging on to happier memories: the Temptations' "Ain't Too Proud to Beg" and "My Girl," Mary Wells's "My Guy," the Four Tops' "Sugar Pie Honey Bunch" and "Reach out and I'll Be There," the Supremes' "Baby Love." Still others, to this day, strike one as simply fated, unerringly chosen for those strange times in that strange, terrible place: Question Mark and the Mysterians' "Ninety-six Tears," Headhunter and the Cannibals' "Land of a Thousand Dances," Sam the Sham and the Pharaohs' "Wooly Bully" and "Little Red Riding Hood," Janis Joplin's "Me and Bobby McGee," Tommy James and the Shondells' "Crimson and Clover," the Zombies' "Time of the Season." Did I read about Los Bravos' "Black Is Black" in Michael Herr's *Dispatches,* or did I hear it in Vietnam? Archie Bell and the Drells' "Tighten Up"? Junior Walker and the All Stars' "Shotgun"? After all these years I can't tell which anymore.

To be sure, as Michael Herr reports and moviemakers frequently make evident, in-country there was a definite politics to the music of the Nam. To borrow from the phrasing of the former, different pieces of information had different uses, and people made of them what they would: the GIs versus the lifers; the heads versus the juicers; the draftees versus the volunteers; the brothers versus the honkies; the hippies versus the straights. Merle Haggard and George Jones were for the boozers; the Stones and Jefferson Airplane were for the potheads. The classic gold Temptations and Supremes were for the white guys; the "Psychedelic Shack" Temptations and the "Love Child" Supremes were for the brothers. Thank God, at least, there wasn't much patriotic shit in the air to disagree with. Maybe at an NCO club you'd find a box with Merle Haggard's "Okie from Muskogee," Porter Wagoner's "Green, Green Grass of Home," Kenny Rogers's "Ruby," or Glen Campbell's "Galveston" but that was as far as it went. Nobody ever listened to Barry Sadler's "Ballad of the Green Berets," not even as a joke.

The last observation points to a major difference between the music of the Nam and the wartime music of other American military eras such as World War I and World War II, and that is a nearly complete disconnect of the former from any large sense of patriotic purpose. To be sure, much of this was a function not just of divisions over the war but of countless other conflicts–racial, political, generational–besetting the country during the era. Still, in the particular case of the music of the Nam, with the exception of the occasional country song, one remains struck by the absence of a contemporary musical tradition expressing public support for the war or its combatants: war songs that everybody listened to, that made people overseas think of home and people at home think of the troops overseas. World War I had "It's a Long Way to Tipperary" and "Over There." World War II likewise produced everything from "Praise the Lord and Pass the Ammunition" to "Don't Sit under the Apple Tree (with Anyone Else but Me)," romantic standards like "I'll Be Seeing You" or "White Cliffs of Dover," and familiar instrumentals like "String of Pearls" or "Chattanooga Choo Choo." The music of the Vietnam War, in contrast, played almost exclusively to the anger, the violence, and the radical cultural disruptions and divisions of the era. As with the befuddled lifer officers and NCOs in *Good Morning Vietnam,* the official culture couldn't seem to understand what was wrong with Mantovani and Percy Faith as opposed to Donovan and Percy Sledge or why a stoned GI might find it ironic that he was getting his ass shot off to the tune of the Stones' "Red Rooster" while Nixon sat in the White House watching *Patton* and listening to *Victory at Sea.*

The same distinction prevailed concerning Vietnam-era celebrity entertainment of the troops versus earlier USO shows, Victory Caravans, holiday extravaganzas, and comedy and musical reviews. In prior wars, a morale show was a piece of home, an expression of unity, congruence, and moral and social continuity, a fusion of values and commitments between the civilian culture and the fighting soldiers in far-flung locations of the earth. During World War II, popular musicians, comedians, and movie entertainers such as Bob Hope, Joe E. Brown, Betty

Grable, Marlene Dietrich, Frances Langford, the Andrews Sisters, Glenn Miller, and Harry James had girdled the globe in the war effort. Even in Korea, the GIs got Marilyn Monroe. In Vietnam, the USO show, its mold essentially unchanged, quickly came to look like an evolutionary throwback or a garishly preserved corpse. Visiting celebrities tended toward being grotesque, wizened, shrill Hollywood has-beens, mummified World War II leftovers like George Jessell and Martha Raye; Les Brown and His Band of Renown; and, of course, Bob Hope. Although the tour efforts extended into the seventies, the whole drill, especially the music, was late fifties and early sixties. The dancers in their lacquered bouffant hairdos and their pastel minidresses and white vinyl go-go boots were right off the latest Dean Martin or Perry Como special. For much the same reason, even the Playboy Bunny parody in *Apocalypse Now* doesn't work for a minute: the shows themselves were monuments of self-parody. So their idea of popular entertainers and musicians remained drearily consistent. In the early part of the war, Hope brought with him Janis Paige, Anna Maria Alberghetti, Jill St. John, and Anita Bryant. 1965 featured Jack Jones, Kaye Stevens, Joey Heatherton, Miss World Diana Lynn Batts, and the relentless Anita Bryant. 1967 brought Phil Crosby, Barbara McNair, Raquel Welch; 1968, Ann-Margret and Roosevelt Grier. Even after Tet and into the early seventies, Hope persevered, with Ursula Andress, Connie Stevens, Romy Schneider, astronaut Neil Armstrong, Jim Nabors, and Redd Foxx.

No one, to my knowledge, ever got to go to a Bob Hope show while I was in Vietnam. I never saw one. I never even heard of one. I don't think I know anybody who saw one—although there are plenty of photos to suggest that some people got to go whether they wanted to or not. More likely for us would have been a base-camp stand-down show with a stripper, a Vietnamese, a Thai, a Cambodian, a Filipina, with surgical silicone breasts and some kind of Asian backup band, or on a big night maybe an Australian band. The music would howl on endlessly in bad imitations of GI favorites, an excuse to wait around and get drunker, more stoned, or both, in honor of the moment when the stripper would take it all off, show the whole deal. Those are the kind of shows most of us still have playing in our heads. The scene was definitely *not* Les Brown. For that matter, in most cases, it wasn't even James Brown.

To this degree, *Good Morning, Vietnam*—a movie that I suspect many combat veterans otherwise may have trouble relating to because it is set so completely in Saigon and big back-in-the-world-style U.S. installations—really does work in those great visual and musical moments where Vietnam appears basically as a big set of speakers. The music was everywhere, they would agree, for grunts and REMFs (rear-echelon motherfuckers) alike: on portable radios or tape players, or on big component stereos that people who worked in a major installation could buy at the PX for next to nothing; from bands, loudspeakers, and jukeboxes in officer, NCO, and EM clubs; blaring from every moving vehicle, orderly room, barracks, mess hall, armory, supply depot, motor pool, maintenance shed, dispensary, or personnel or finance office. Not a single jeep, five-ton truck, or tracked vehicle didn't carry a portable radio or a tape cassette. Everywhere you rolled or flew, there was the panorama of GIs working, listening, waving, shooting the bird, flashing peace signs.

As might be expected—to borrow again from a Michael Herr phrase—like anyone else, I have my own mythopathic music moment from Vietnam, the place, as Herr would say, where all the vectors converged. Actually, like most people, I have a collection. The one I remember most vividly, where for a minute everything seemed to come together, was on a day in late 1969, around dawn, in a defensive position, a firebase east of Gia Ray, out toward the South China Sea, where we had a platoon of tracks guarding the berm for a couple of artillery batteries. I was doing my usual walk of the perimeter, checking on all the vehicles, making sure a guard was still up and alert. It must have been five or six o'clock, just at first light. Whatever time it was, it was something on the hour, because out of the back end of an ACAV on the perimeter, I could hear a radio deejay signing on for the day's programming. And yes, he actually was screaming, "Good Morning, Vietnam." The memory is vivid, I believe, because it was the only time, to my recollection, that I ever heard it.

Most mornings at first light, we were still ambushing or sitting in some night perimeter. Wherever we were, it was no time to be playing the radio. Not that we missed it. It was enough just to be alive, sitting on final two-hour watch, making sure the perimeter was secure, waiting until it was light enough to fire up a cigarette and, if there was time before moving out, to heat up a can of C-ration coffee. For these reasons, the particular moment I mention remains as vivid as today. The guy in Saigon was doing his voice-over, already into playing the first bars of a record by a black R&B group, the Delfonics' "Didn't I Blow Your Mind," featuring a really distinctive, big, French-horn opening with a bunch of whooping, soaring octaves that really did sound something like sunrise. Next was Merle Haggard's "Okie from Muskogee," with all its sour complaint about long hair and mara-ju-wana.

In that moment the whole surreal pointlessness of the war somehow came home to me with a clarity that I never experienced before or after. There we were, I saw; and there the music was, and there *it* was, as we used to say, already well on its way to being just another day in the Nam. I had other, modified versions of that moment, to be sure, while I was in Vietnam: sitting in a blocking position north of Xuan Loc, hearing for the first time Blood Sweat and Tears' "Spinning Wheel"; drunk as a rat in an Australian officers club in Vung Tau, waiting from my troops to get serviced in the U.S. Army–inspected whorehouses, the jukebox playing Neil Diamond's "Sweet Caroline" again and again; roaring down the road on a convoy run that had nasty premonitions written all over it, hearing above the roar of the engine somebody's tape deck playing Creedence Clearwater Revival's "Bad Moon Rising"; standing outside a part of our barracks in the rear called the Soul Shack, listening to the black guys playing the Temptations' "Ball of Confusion" over and over; drunk again, this time with a bunch of my sergeants at the NCO club, watching a Filipino band with a chunky little Cambodian lead singer in a fringed-gold minidress, with ball-bearing hips and a mouth doing some kind of strange lip synch, the words coming out as "Jummee Jummee Jummee I Got Rub in My Tummeee"; or sitting around near the end, after the general got shot, waiting for my orders to the Ninetieth Replacement Detachment and the flight home, listening to Simon and Garfunkel's "Bridge over Troubled Water." Above all, I see the recurrent officer's club scene: one more shitfaced lieutenant or captain going home the next day barely able to stand, obscenely saluting his buddies while the music plays one of the ultimate three big ones–Scott McKenzie's "San Francisco"; the Boxtops' "Gimme a Ticket for an Airplane"; or, most likely, the Animals' "We Gotta Get Out of this Place." The crowd roars the chorus in the background, thinking about going back to the field in the morning and aching for the day when they'll be the shitfaced DEROS guy. Three songs. To this day, for me, they're the big hits, the ones I hear in my head.

But even these, as I return to them in memory, blend in with everything else. And everything else in turn becomes part of the larger record of going and coming. A personal greatest-hits album, testament to the ubiquity and permanence of the music of the era: every single one of us has one, call it what you will, maybe the story of somebody's GI life, the sound track of before, during, and after. I remember a scalding day at Fort Bragg, returning at twilight to a hot barracks, hearing Sam the Sham and the Pharaohs' "Little Red Riding Hood" blaring across the lawn from a PX beer hall. Then, out in Kentucky, while I did the armor officers' basic course at Fort Knox, there were Kenny Rogers's "Ruby," Elvis's "In the Ghetto," B. J. Thomas's "I Just Can't Help Believin'," and "Otis Redding's "Sitting on the Dock of the Bay." At Fort Meade, with the Sixth Cavalry, doing riot-control duty for the military district of Washington, waiting for the orders for Vietnam, every morning on the car radio I heard the Fifth Dimension's "Aquarius" and the Doors' "Light My Fire." In jungle school in Panama, with two weeks to go before most of us were headed to the war, the cadre decided to bring us off the Chagres River at the end of a week for a Saturday afternoon's rest, herding us into a movie theater to see the Beatles in *Yellow Submarine.* I do not remember a thing except the title song. Most of us slipped out after fifteen minutes and spent the afternoon throwing down beers in a makeshift officer's club. What were they going to do? we asked, decidedly not for the first or last time. Send us to Vietnam?

Afterward, back in the world, a civilian again, a graduate student growing all the unauthorized hair I could possibly think of, I found rock 'n' roll wonderland. I had missed Woodstock completely, never even heard of it until I arrived home. Of course, in Vietnam, it took me a couple of weeks to find out that somebody had landed on the moon. I caught back up, playing the live album over and over again. I went to concerts: Steppenwolf, *Jesus Christ Superstar,* the Ike and Tina Turner Review. I listened nonstop to what were, to me, brand new albums by Cream; Janis Joplin; Blood Sweat and Tears; Crosby, Stills, Nash, and Young; the Jefferson Starship; the Grateful Dead. I got stuck on particular songs: happily stoned, albeit without the foggiest notion of what cocaine was, I got into the heavy pathos of Steppenwolf's "Snow Blind Friend"; at a party, I danced for a whole night in the hall with a stranger's wife to Delaney, Bonnie, and Friends' "Everlasting Love for You"; a Godard film, the worst movie I'd ever seen, at least took me back to the Stones' "Sympathy for the Devil" and dropped it on me again for life; I ruined a friend's Jefferson Airplane album by playing "Volunteers" over and over again while trying to drop the needle on the up-against-the-wall-motherfucker part. I kept on going until somewhere around Iron Butterfly and "Inna Gadda Da Vida," which I remember as sounding very Nam like, "in the Garden of Eden" and all, dark and Asian and menacing. I lost interest completely, however, after music started shifting into mid-1970s soft rock: James Taylor, Carol King, Three Dog Night, John Lennon and Yoko Ono, Paul McCartney and Wings, George Harrison and the Hare Krishnas, the Moody Blues with their London Philharmonic backgrounds and lyrics full of druggy profundities. Then, just when it couldn't get worse, came all the buzzy-bee-sounding, sensitive-guy shit–Dan Fogelberg, Loggins and Messina, Seals and Crofts. And *then* came disco, my God. The Bee Gees. Donna Summer. The Village People. Thank God, I remember thinking, I'll always have the Stones. And after the war, the Who. They're still my favorite all-time group from back then. Some people like *My Generation.* I prefer *Who's Next.* I especially like the single cut that I heard for the first time the summer I got back from Vietnam and that still says it all for me: "Won't Get Fooled Again."

Viet Pulp

Military history sections of big chain bookstores and the paperback buy-and-swaps now devote entire shelves to paperbacks about the war in Vietnam, books with titles like *LRRP Team Leader, Marine Sniper, Assault on Dak Pek, Death in the Delta, Death in the Jungle, Death in the A Shau Valley, Inside the LRRPs, Inside Force Recon, Inside the Crosshairs, Inside the VC and NVA.* On the lists of the big Internet marketers such offerings currently number around one hundred. More than forty years after the first American counterinsurgency warriors began arriving in Vietnam and more than twenty-five years after the last helicopter lifted off from Saigon, Viet pulp has become big business.

As a mass-market paperback phenomenon, Viet pulp, besides its abundance of titles and widespread availability, is distinguished by its relative uniformity of presentation and design: a cover illustration—frequently a personal photograph—of jungle fighters in camouflage, along with the title and a characteristic blurb in vintage-Vietnam, guts-and-glory style, about SEALs, LRRPs, SOGs (Special Operations Group), snipers, special forces, Rangers, or marine force recon. "Whether they were beating through razor-sharp elephant grass or spending all night soaked and shivering in the monsoon, walking into an ambush or getting caught in a hot LZ," the back cover of *First Recon—Second to None* breathlessly begins, "sudden death for the First Recon was never far away. Second lieutenant Paul Young had to be concerned not only with his own life but also with those of the men in his command. For Vietnam too often seemed like a monster with an insatiable appetite for blood." "Vietnam, 1968," another cover description reads, this one for *LRRP Team Leader:* "All of Sergeant John Burford's missions with F Company, 58th Infantry were deep in hostile territory. As leader of a six-man LRRP team, he found the enemy, staged ambushes, called in precision strikes, and rescued downed pilots. The lives of the entire team depended on his leadership and their combined skill and guts. A single mistake—a moment of panic—could mean death for everyone. Pictures."

Over the years, prices have remained low, even for mass-market paperbacks, usually between five and seven dollars. The current figure for most titles is $6.99.

At this writing, the market is increasingly dominated by a single publisher, Ivy, with a handful of titles from its parent company, Ballantine, and a scattering of other imprints—Avon, Bantam, Berkley, and Pocket. Virtually all texts are paperback originals. A few books are imported from mainstream publishing, such as Tom Mangold and John Penycate's *The Tunnels of Cu Chi,* reprinted by Berkley, or Lewis Puller Jr.'s *Fortunate Son,* picked up by Bantam. Three major oral histories—Al Santoli's *Everything We Had;* Wallace Terry's *Bloods: An Oral History of the Vietnam War by Black Veterans;* and Keith Walker's *A Piece of My Heart,* which features the narratives of twenty-six American women—were republished in the late eighties by Ballantine. There are also a scattering of reprints from two popular military publishers, Presidio and the Naval Institute Press, at present working increasingly in mainstream hardbound and paperback and themselves frequently given to such lurid titlings as *Hunters and Shooters* or *The Magnificent Bastards.*

Chronologically, one might be attempted to locate Viet pulp in certain ur-titles such as Robin Moore's *The Green Berets* (1965) or David Morrell's *First Blood* (1972), the genesis of the Rambo saga. One might also identify early counterparts in paperback lines as diverse as Barry Sadler's *Casca: The Eternal Mercenary* series or W. E. B. Griffin's *Brotherhood of War.* Viet pulp as described in the first paragraphs of this chapter, however, is almost exclusively a phenomenon of the last decade, beginning slowly in the late eighties and peaking in the last five years with the appearance of ten to fifteen new titles annually.

As a popular genre, it is distinguished by an emphasis on "authentic" combat narrative—invariably betokened, as noted earlier, by its signature "in-country" titling and cover copy—and, as importantly, by its nearly exclusive concentration on elite or special-operations units. Most texts present themselves as personal narratives by veterans, on occasion with collaborators. Most contain a photo section. Prominent descriptive terms in advertising and in subtitles include "diary," "journal," "true story," "firsthand account." Some comprise histories or extended accounts of operations in particular kinds of units. Conspicuously featured in these cases are the prepositions "with" or "inside." Yoking these appeals are often references to better-known works of literature and popular culture. With its creatively ambiguous entitling, Robert Hemphill's *Platoon: Bravo Company,* the narrative of an infantry company commander in the Twenty-fifth Infantry Division during late 1967 and early 1968, blazons the experiences described as simultaneously sharing some of those of unit member Oliver Stone, who made them the basis of the movie *Platoon.* With a cover blurb by Lieutenant General Hal Moore, former commanding officer of the First Battalion, Seventh Cavalry, Larry Gwin's *Baptism* likewise announces its status as an inside first-person narrative of the 1965 Ia Drang campaign described in Harold G. Moore and Joseph L. Galloway's *We Were Soldiers Once . . . And Young.* In this case, the book is by an actual First Cavalry platoon leader prominently featured in that widely read text, although he is not featured in the current movie, which concentrates solely on the battle of LZ X-Ray and not on the parallel action at LZ Albany in which Gwin's battalion, commanded by a far less competent lieutenant colonel, had the misfortune to be literally shot to pieces.

In numerous cases, veterans who became authors have emerged as veterans of the genre, producers of multiple titles with a considerable following. Michael Lee Lanning, for instance, began with a two-installment personal memoir, *The Only War We Had: A Platoon Leader's Journal of Vietnam* and *Vietnam 1969–1970: A Company Commander's Journal,* and has now moved on to popular-history titles, including the four "inside" books noted earlier: *Inside the Crosshairs, Inside Force Recon, Inside the LRRPs,* and *Inside the VC and NVA.* Similar is the career of Kregg P. J. Jorgenson, author of *Acceptable Loss, LRRP Company Command, Mia Rescue: Lrrps in Cambodia, The Ghosts of the Highlands: First Cav LRRPs in Vietnam 1966–67,* and, most recently, *Very Crazy, G.I.: Strange but True Stories of the Vietnam War.* There is also Gary A. Linderer, author of *Eyes of the Eagle, Eyes behind the Lines* and *Phantom Warriors,* books one and two; or Dennis Foley, author of two novels, *Night Work* and *Take Back the Night,* and two autobiographical narratives, *Special Men: A LRP's Reflections* and *Long Range Patrol,* with the latter blurbed for its authenticity by Gary A. Linderer. Alternatively, one may peruse single titles that have now enlarged into series, such as *Six Silent Men,* with book one written by Reynel Martinez; book two by Kenn Miller, author of a previous Ivy offering, *Tiger, the Lurp Dog;* and book three by, once more, the aforementioned Gary A. Linderer. The industry champion here for diversifying the model, however, has to be former Navy SEAL–and U.S. Federal Prison inmate, for defrauding the U.S. Navy on equipment contracts– Richard Marcinko. Coauthor, with prolific crime and adventure novelist John Weisman, of the eight-installment *Rogue Warrior* series, he has also become a prominent producer of best-selling business and leadership self-help guides, including *The Rogue Warrior's Strategies for Success: A Commando's Principles of Winning,* and *Leadership Secrets of the Rogue Warrior: A Commando's Guide to Success.*

In some cases, actual Vietnam veteran status, if not available, may be conveniently fudged. There is Charles W. Sasser, for instance, ubiquitous coauthor of such Viet pulp productions as *One Shot-One Kill* and *The Walking Dead* (both with Craig Roberts), *First Seal* (with Ray Boehm), *Taking Fire: The True Story of a Decorated Chopper Pilot* (with Ron Alexander), *Doc: Platoon Medic* (with Daniel E. Evans Jr.). Among a plethora of other titles, Sasser has written a novel of Vietnam, *The One Hundredth Kill,* and an allegedly autobiographical narrative, *Always a Warrior: The Memoir of a Six-War Soldier.* Internet reviewers have questioned the authenticity of the experience described by the primary narrator in several of Sasser's coauthored texts. One such respondent has termed Sasser's novel "phony, even for fiction." As to Sasser's Vietnam combat credentials, his biography is creatively ambiguous. One cover credit lists him as "a decorated Vietnam veteran and Green Beret . . . and one of today's most respected military and true crime writers." Another says, "Mr. Sasser served 29 years in the U.S. Navy, where he was a journalist, and in the U.S. Army as a Special Forces paratrooper (the Green Berets)." On a Web site sketch, the military record reads: "U.S. Navy, 1960–64; became journalist second class. U.S. Army, 1965–83, medic with U.S. Army Special Forces (Green Berets) in Southeast Asia and Central and South America; became sergeant first-class, U.S. Army reserve, 1983– combat tactics instructor. Military police company, first sergeant, 1991." In a personal synopsis, Sasser himself lists experiences as a "policeman, educator, airplane pilot, Golden Gloves boxer, paratrooper, sailor, rodeo bronco rider, rancher, fur trapper, newspaperman." He continues, "For stories I have parachuted into Korea's demilitarized zone, rode buses from the United States through Central America, chased after pirate treasure in the Caribbean, canoed 700 miles solo across the Yukon territory, chased wild mustangs, raft-floated the Mississippi River, solo-sailed the Caribbean in a 17-foot sailboat, searched for 'lost cities' in Central American jungles, hunted bear, caribou, and other big game." Amid all this, Vietnam service as a decorated Green Beret medic goes egregiously unmentioned.

Another author worth mentioning, apropos of authority and authenticity issues, is Shelby Stanton. *Rangers at War: LRRPs in Vietnam* was his first entry in the Ivy Viet pulp product line, although he had previously made his mark with a number of publishers as a popular historian of Vietnam combat with what was alleged to be substantive personal experience as a Green Beret combat veteran. In *The Rise and Fall of an American Army: U.S. Ground Forces in Vietnam, 1965–1973*, he allowed to go unchallenged, for instance, Colonel Harry G. Summers's description of him in the foreword as "a Vietnam combat veteran decorated for valor and now retired as a result of wounds suffered on the battlefield." Shortly after the Ivy issue of *Rangers at War*, Stanton was revealed to have falsified his combat credentials almost in their entirety. Nonetheless, Ballantine deemed his early "classic" *Green Berets at War* sufficiently saleable to reappear in a 1999 reprint. The cover copy is now carefully ambiguous about Stanton's combat record. Presumably to avoid resetting type, the Presidio paperback reissue of the hardbound *Rise and Fall of an American Army* reprints the Summers preface intact. The cover bio, on the other hand, carefully claims only that "Shelby Stanton was on active duty with the U.S. Army for six years."

The putatively first-person narratives in the genre sometimes rather conventionally begin with the protagonist's entry into military training or arrival in-country and then move into an extended presentation of the experience of combat. As often, however, the reader enters the text in the midst of a gripping mission with background information supplied along the way or developed in flashbacks. Sometimes, as in canonical texts, the 365-day format prevails. Frequently, however, as opposed to such well-known literary examples as Tim O'Brien's *If I Die in a Combat Zone* or Philip Caputo's *A Rumor of War* or such corresponding combat novels as James Webb's *Fields of Fire* or Larry Heinemann's *Close Quarters*, which depict the common infantry soldier—the enlisted man or junior officer of the line unit—the Viet pulp protagonist finds a home in some elite, specialized, highly trained formation. Accordingly, he often extends his time in the war zone or elects for multiple tours of duty, allowing the combat narrative—now extended beyond the standard initiation into warfare—to continue into the realm of more advanced and rare information as he becomes increasingly expert and professionalized at his dangerous task.

The popular-history texts, as noted earlier, likewise frequently bill themselves as the work of authors credentialed by their experience with elite formations, frequently involving multiple tours. They are replete with unit legends, campaign records, and detailed personal accounts of particular combat actions. Indeed, their reader popularity frequently depends on how quickly they move from historical overview to a close-combat focus. Like the Viet pulp personal narratives, they are detailed, specific, and extremely accurate as to the particulars of individual combat experiences and the use of Vietnam-era-soldier slang and military terminology. Many include glossaries.

In short, Viet pulp stakes its appeal on being authentic in every way, providing precise, you-are-there, minute-by-minute accounts of combat action, complete with the names and roles of fellow unit members, comrades dead and wounded, details of battlefield maneuvers, and individual acts of bravery, loyalty, and sacrifice, in many cases apparently vividly recalled and/or reconstructed from experiences decades earlier. Within a given text, one can find the particulars of every firefight, ambush, insertion, extraction, move-out, or stand-down. In some cases, source records are attributed. Michael Lee Lanning, for instance, in the two-volume memoir mentioned earlier, opens each chapter with journal entries. In other places, he notes his use of the letters he wrote during the period. Likewise Joseph T. Ward's *Dear Mom: A Sniper's Vietnam*—surely one of the strangest titles in the lot—announces its manner of documentation in its name. The book arises from information contained in 238 letters the boyish assassin wrote home to his mother. Other authors admit that they kept unauthorized diaries or journals or have likewise relied heavily on letters written in sufficient detail at the time to accurately reconstruct experience. In the case of unit histories, authors attest to the reliability of individual sources. Those sources, interestingly, now also frequently prove to be other works in the genre.

For all its precision and supposed authenticity, Viet pulp seems oddly innocuous and curiously generic—a vast number of texts with an incredible specificity frequently nonetheless reminding the reader mainly of each other. *Tan Phu* is a special forces book; *None Go Home Alone,* a marine book; *The Men Behind the Trident,* a SEAL book; *Diary of an Airborne Ranger,* an LRRP book; *Dead Center,* a sniper book. But in significant ways, they are the same book, a hotshot version of what the average GI remembers as the battle of the latest bunker complex or trail bend. There are helicopter insertions and helicopter extractions, firefights and ambushes, dustoffs and stand-downs, the occasional hot meal or cold beer. Radio exchanges, frequently rendered at great length, become tutorials in the phonetic alphabet and the identification of missions and grid coordinates, full of snappy call signs and vintage airwave slang. Radio-telephone procedure is carefully observed. Nobody says "roger" when he means "wilco." Nobody says "repeat" when he means "say again." And nobody *ever* says "over and out." (I am reminded here of the snotty marginal notation of an old college creative-writing teacher on one of my stories. "It may be real," he scribbled, "but it ain't writing.") In the case of personal narratives, a quick immersion into combat leads to an ongoing series of such experiences, eventually provoking a crisis of personal, and perhaps patriotic, purpose and commitment. A growth in military prowess and confidence ensues as loyalty to one's unit and close comrades deepens. Buddies die; platoon and company officers rotate. Frequently there is a personal wounding, followed by an evacuation, perhaps a hospital stay. On return to the unit, tension increases as a tour of duty approaches completion. The narrator-protagonist gets short. Eventually the magic word comes into focus: DEROS. The great moment of departure arrives, and some attempt is made at personal reflection on what the experience has meant. Only rarely, again as opposed to many canonical texts, is there any continuation of the story back in the world.

The structuring of narrative in virtually all these texts is largely sequential and fairly unselective. The voice is completely generic. Those narratives that derive from personal experience, with their frequent interpolations of anecdote and comment, read like popular history; those presenting themselves as popular history provide an idiosyncratic mix of the personal and the documentary.

The books are also cursorily edited. A moment after describing the completion of a successful ambush, a given narrator will expatiate on the relative merits of C-ration offerings or grouse about REMF bastards and their back-in-the-world comforts. What seem to be important details frequently wait for explanations that are never supplied. *Operation Tuscaloosa,* for instance, is subtitled *Second Battalion, Fifth Marines at An Hoa, 1967.* By marine veteran John J. Culbertson, also the author of *A Sniper in the Arizona,* the book details his participation in an early battle of the war in which a battalion of marines destroyed a comparable unit of main-force Viet Cong. Why is the book called Operation Tuscaloosa? Presumably because that was the name of the engagement described. In fact, at the end of the photo section of the book is a typographic copy of the headquarters mission order. As it happens, I have made my home for three decades in Tuscaloosa, Alabama. Was some officer a native of the place? Did someone at headquarters attend the University of Alabama? Was there a Crimson Tide football fan in the unit? Was there perhaps a devotee of early Alabama history who remembered a legendary Indian warrior of that name? The most likely answer is, of course, none of the above, but rather that *Operation Tuscaloosa: Second Battalion, Fifth Marines at An Hoa, 1967* is the kind of title needed for product recognition. It sounds like another good Ivy paperback, along with *Diary of an Airborne Ranger: A LRRP's Year in the Combat Zone* or *Team Sergeant: A Special Forces NCO at Lang Vei and Beyond.*

Where does one most frequently find the print product? As noted at the start of this chapter, entire shelves are now devoted to it in big chain bookstores. It also proves ubiquitous in paperback buy-and-swaps, frequently sold at secondhand prices of two to five dollars. The most significant sales venue of the moment, however, surely has to be that of the large Internet marketers—Amazon, Barnes and Noble, Books-a-Million, and the like. The Internet is also the site, as might be expected, of the most intensive marketing. A search for an author or title yields not only publication data on the text or texts in question but also related titles frequently bought by previous customers and other suggested reading. A click on a particular item yields an avalanche of further information, including enlargements of front and back covers, a paragraph of exciting description, usually reproducing the cover blurb, and as many as thirty sample pages of text. In a large majority of cases, compilations of as many as ten reader reviews follow.

The latter, as might be expected, in their large numbers and in the highly personalized nature of many responses, prove unusually revealing as to who buys and reads these texts. The largest audience seems to be male. Again, if shelf demographics are to be trusted, along with the Civil War and World War II, the Vietnamese war as a subject of popular military history now seems to account for a substantial audience of buffs. Some are Vietnam veterans, now in middle and late middle age, frequently using their reviews to connect with their own experiences in combat. In the main they write approvingly, offering factual corroboration, praising a given author for telling it like it was, or expressing gratitude for a book written from a perspective they feel to be mainly ignored or disparaged by cultural elites. The same is true of what seem to be male nonveteran readers, many of them Vietnam-era Americans, who frequently base their approval on a wide knowledge of the genre coupled with their own sense of appreciation for the veteran's sacrifice. Male responses also include the contributions of many young readers, who often identify themselves as teenagers or writers of book reports, avid to learn of Vietnam combat or of the experiences of fathers, uncles, and other family acquaintances.

At the same time, significant numbers of female reviewers also identify themselves. Frequently they too are members of households in which a husband, a father, an uncle, or some family friend has been a combat veteran of the war. Such respondents are distinguished by a particular interest in long-term veterans' problems having to do with combat stress disorders, drug and alcohol dependency, troubled interpersonal relationships, and associated ongoing difficulties with adjustment to the post-Vietnam civilian world.

Finally, during an era in which figures ranging from an eminent historian to the chief of naval operations have been revealed as falsely claiming Vietnam combat service—itself, I would propose, a phenomenon related to the extensive marketing and reading of the literature in question—a number of individual reviewers, describing themselves as veterans of multiple tours in various elite formations or as experts with a copious knowledge of the literature, have appointed themselves as authenticity police. Sometimes they single out exaggerations, inaccuracies, and outright falsehoods in the text; on other occasions they call into question not only the authenticity of certain particulars or the representation of a combat experience but also the author's claims of having encountered such action firsthand.

For a reader, such as myself, who served in the more conventional war of the brigades and battalions in Vietnam, however, or who is conversant with the general literature by and about Vietnam combat veterans, what remains most arresting about the genre is the demographics of the subject matter. An estimated 3.5 million Americans served in-country during the Vietnamese war. Of these, by my calculations (as opposed to those of others, which run as high as three-quarter million) a maximum of 350,000 probably had any extended combat experience in the field with a line-infantry, armor, or artillery unit. If the percentage of interest categories here were applied, let's say, to my numbers, just for the sake of illustration, fifty thousand would have been snipers, fifty thousand would have been SEALs, fifty thousand would have been special forces, fifty thousand would have been marine force recon, and fifty thousand would have been army LRRPs. The one hundred thousand left over would all have been either marines or members of the First Cavalry and/or 101st Airborne Divisions, except for maybe two helicopter pilots and a medic.

I spent my entire tour with an armored cavalry troop, first as a platoon leader and then as an executive officer, operating at one time or another with four different infantry battalions. I saw two snipers the whole time I was there. We had some transfers from the LRRPs, guys I realize in retrospect who must have quit or been dismissed. They were nothing but trouble. The Green Berets we met occasionally were expert scroungers and good to trade stuff with. SEALs? SOG? Never heard of them. Marines up north were good for making us feel better about our own lousy circumstances, as they were the saddest joke of all. Question: what's the basic difference between the marines and the boy scouts? Answer: the boy scouts have adult supervision. Everyone knew the marines had the lousiest food and equipment while getting their asses shot off on the worst missions. As for the airborne, most veterans know even today that there was only one combat jump during the whole war, by a battalion of the 173d Airborne, into a landing zone that had already been secured. As for the legendary units, under the standard Vietnam replacement system, the famous 101st Airborne Division quickly turned into a leg outfit just like everybody else. Ditto the First Cavalry: all they had more of was helicopters. The special-operations mystique may have gotten us into Vietnam, but from 1967 on, major U.S. combat units, army and marine, were all basically conventional infantry, army, and artillery. The war they fought was a dismally conventional, large-unit, mass-destruction, meat-grinder war, resulting in the deaths of more than fifty-eight thousand Americans, most of them members of standard combat formations, and an estimated two to four million Vietnamese, with a large proportion of those noncombatant civilians.

So what, then, does Viet pulp, as a relatively recent publishing phenomenon, tell us about evolving popular conceptions about America and the Vietnamese war? It is tempting initially to lament the degree to which a substantial body of literature has now brought us back around to the popular glorification of the elite special-operations warrior myth—Natty Bumppo in the central highlands, Batman in the Delta, John Wayne in the Iron Triangle, Chesty Puller in the DMZ—that got us foolishly involved in Vietnam in the first place. The same problem, in any event, pervades the more general literature, running the cultural gamut from Robin Moore's cartoonish *The Green Berets* to Michael Herr's highly praised *Dispatches*. Virtually ignored as well is any attempt at human representation of the Vietnamese, whether friend or foe. In this regard, all one can say is that it is, primarily, a combat literature, generally set in enemy territory, where there is little occasion, save for the odd return to some rear area, for contact with Vietnamese not identified unambiguously as VC or NVA.

Viet pulp sits uneasily with an equally copious literature of trauma and recovery. Without much apology, the soldiers in these narratives nonetheless come across then and now, to use Michael Herr's phrasing, as unapologetically high on war, proud of their service and their wartime prowess in dealing death to the enemy. If anything, one is struck by how closely these narratives parallel PTSD narratives: prolonged service in heavy combat, extended or multiple tours of duty, growing absorption in lethal ability and willingness to use it, voluntary participation in increasingly hazardous and secret and/or illegal operations. The only difference lies in the recurrent emphasis in traumatized veterans' narratives on indiscriminate killing and atrocity. A recent development in this regard is an increasing amount of literature of psychological and cultural imposterism—a problem originating from the tendency of early clinicians, deeply invested in the ideological aspects of treating troubled veterans, to accept stories from an unprofessionally small and statistically unreliable sample of multiple-tour veterans and activists involved in rap groups without checking service records for verification. VA hospitals now report an influx of Vietnam PTSD imitators touting an implausible history of multiple tours in specialized hunter-killer units, often claiming experience in multiple branches of service, coupled with numerous high-level combat decorations—multiple Purple Hearts, the Silver Star, the Distinguished Service Cross or Navy Cross, even the Medal of Honor—when in fact they served in Vietnam noncombat assignments or in some cases never left the United States. After all, the worst war stories bring the highest disability ratings and benefits. Nor does it pay to get well. As a result, decades later, common grunts become LRRPs; supply clerks become SOGs and paid assassins in the Phoenix program. To complicate matters, such well-known oral histories as Al Santoli's *Everything We Had* and Wallace Terry's *Bloods* have also been shown to include false claims of combat experience and ensuing psychological trauma. It is likewise no surprise that well-known public impostures frequently involve hair-raising tales of special-ops adventures. One of the first giveaways of the recent scandal involving historian Joseph Ellis's fabulation of autobiographical details, for most veterans at least, was his claim to have been a Vietnam paratrooper in the 101st Airborne when that unit did not conduct one jump during the entire war. As regards the literature at hand, the far more garish prevarications of the celebrated popular historian of Vietnam combat Shelby Stanton have already been discussed. One cannot at present pronounce any direct connection between Viet pulp and the false-claimant and wanna-be phenomena. The myth of the American soldier in Vietnam as stoned heavy killer has been around for a long time, as have cultural representations running the gamut from the literary and cinematic to the clinical. The stories are everywhere, walking the thin line between pathology and overheated imagination. Across the culture, it seems to be one of the ongoing problematic legacies of the war.

This literature also raises questions regarding other cherished cultural and academic commonplaces about the Vietnam soldier. If the soldiers in Viet pulp do not seem to suffer from long-term combat trauma, neither do they give the impression of being then or now particularly alienated from their culture, victimized, betrayed, or abandoned. Nor, as working-class soldiers—almost always the natives of rural areas, small towns, or blue-collar urban neighborhoods—do they prove to be particularly ideological. Frequently the authors express anger against the disparagement of military service and traditional notions of patriotic duty by antiwar intellectuals and political elites, but this is done without much overt class consciousness. Finally, as opposed to the prevailing academic theories about Vietnamese-war narrative, Viet pulp is invariably linear. Nor does Viet pulp create some sense of inevitable immersion into a world comprehensible only through complex strategies of imaginative experimentation. Vietnam may well have been America's heart-of-darkness trip, the first rock 'n' roll war, the first postmodern war, as it is variously tagged by theorists of literary and cultural representation. Viet pulp, however, if anything, depicts extended combat service, even among elite warriors, largely as many veterans, including me, remember it: laborious; fairly repetitious; mentally and physically exhausting; even in sporadic but inevitable contacts with the enemy, marked by a dreary punctuality; and in the endless vigilance and movement between engagements, downright boring.

Still, as with most popular-culture trends, in this case allegedly true-to-life representations of American soldiers in combat during a sad and strange Asian war taking place more than three decades ago, timing really does seem to be everything. The last ten years have certainly marked the continuing cultural rehabilitation of the Vietnam veteran. The wild swings in a cycle of figurations ranging from pariah to psychopath to victim to forgotten hero have stabilized as a generation reaching late middle age has become increasingly reflective about issues of individual circumstance and of choices made decades ago. The puffery attending the hit status of the recent movie *We Were Soldiers* as the "Saving Private Ryan of Vietnam" should be little surprise. (The movie, I am at pains to interject, is a good deal more than that.) In this same connection, the image of the Vietnam veteran has also profited from lavish valedictories being accorded the vanishing generation of World War II, with Vietnam veterans now entering their own later years seen increasingly as trying to live up to the example of their predecessors. As to the prestige of combat service, one may point to the nearly total rehabilitation of the post-Vietnam military generally. A series of late post-Vietnam immaculate interventions—Grenada, Panama, Haiti—largely carried out by special-operations units, have been crowned by the dazzling performance of specialized elite forces with larger conventional units of soldiers, sailors, airmen, and marines in Gulf Wars I and II and in the current war against terror. Nor has the image of the Vietnam combat veteran suffered by lavish media emphasis on a generation of commanders, in both the First Gulf War and the post–September 11 campaigns—Colin Powell, Norman Schwarzkopf, Walt Boomer, Barry McCaffrey, Wesley Clark, Hugh Shelton, Tommy Franks—who have reforged an innovative professionalism out of the memory of hard lessons learned as junior officers in Vietnam.

It is in this latter context, I believe, that we ought to see the current popularity of what I have called Viet pulp on balance as not a terribly alarming development. "Accentuate the Positive," goes the old World War II song, and that is the generation I grew up trying to emulate. The English professor in me likes that people are reading book-length writing, period. The Vietnam veteran in me likes that they are interested in reading stories about the personal experiences of American soldiers during the Vietnamese war as a way of knowing something about a troubled era in the national history now rapidly passing out of living memory. These, unquestionably, are war stories, frequently of a sort that various students and would-be arbiters of culture may deem pernicious. I myself, as a veteran, take offense at the dreary uniformity of the sensationalistic titling and cover copy. In an era when teenagers regularly execute commando plans to shoot up their high schools, I also recoil from the dreadful fascination conveyed in frequent reader reports, as in: "I've read all the sniper books, and this is the coolest." Nor, as a career academic and popular culture interpreter, does this particular emerging genre make me feel good about my inclination to give elite-force rock 'n' roll snake-eater romanticism pass as long as it's purveyed by postmodern virtuosos like Michael Herr. It sounded sexy in *Dispatches*: "Lurps, seals, recon-dos, Green-Beret bushmasters, redundant mutilators, heavy rapers, eye-shooters, widow-makers, nametakers, classic essential American types; point men, *isolatos* and outriders like they were programmed to do it, the first taste made them crazy for it, just like they knew it would." How-ever, the actual narratives sound dismally familiar when all the essential American types get around to telling their stories. Despite the garish titles and the overwrought cover blurbs, "High on war" just doesn't cut it here. If Viet pulp chronicles a war that was a season in hell, it doesn't read like Herr-Rimbaud; and if the inevitable popular progeny turned out to be *First Blood,* it doesn't read much like Morrell-Rambo either. As the texts flow into each other, the concentration on the mystique of the elite special-operations warrior, particularly in the vast majority devoted to the experiences of youthful soldier-protagonists, melds into the far more conventional structure of the Vietnam-initiation narrative. These are, in the end, disillusionnment narratives in that their murky epipha-nies mirror those of most of us who went there young: largely misin-formed, confused about our convictions, scared about our prospects, cu-rious about our prowess, somehow already sensing that what we would be fighting for while we were there was ultimately each other.

Viet pulp titles, inside the covers at least, ultimately do not really glamorize much about war. They do not go lightly on the bad stuff. Those who were there will acknowledge the sheer physical misery, the confusion, the terror, the ugly, graphic woundings and deaths, as the real thing. Nor do these texts romanticize violence or overplay heroism. The soldiers in these books are, again, mainly like the ones I remember: du-tiful; forbearing; incredibly loyal; humorous; poorly educated in many cases but plenty smart; competently brave, in a word, because they find it possible to fashion what is called bravery out of the content of average character.

Sorry, Mr. McNamara

When I first read Robert McNamara's *In Retrospect,* I almost went insane with grief and rage. The title of a review at the time, by Pat C. Hoy II, a former West Point officer of my generation, seemed to say it all: "They Died for Nothing, Did They Not?" Having read David Halberstam's *The Best and the Brightest* many years before, I knew the story was bad. However, until I read McNamara, compounding dismal policy rehash with the worst sort of mealymouthed apologia—a mea culpa, noted one editorialist, decidedly more mea than culpa—I didn't know how bad.

After picking the book up again recently to see if I could regard it with anything like dispassion, if not forbearance, I find myself more than ever wanting Robert McNamara to know that we still have his number—I mean us, the people who did the patrols, the sweeps, and the ambushes, the ones who pulled their buddies out of minefields and cleaned what was left of them out of tank turrets—and that we are not about to let him off the hook. Here was the guy who, more than any other figure, created and set in motion the death apparatus that wound up killing fifty-eight thousand Americans and between two and four million Vietnamese—indeed, who once allowed, early on, that if the press wanted to call the thing "McNamara's War," it would be fine with him. In retrospect, he tells us he's sorry it all turned out to be such a big corporate miscalculation.

Among other things, if I read correctly, apparently he, along with the best governmental minds of his generation, recognized from the outset the total futility of sending American military forces to prop up an intractable Vietnamese client regime unwilling or unable to mount its own military defense against a major communist insurgency. They then made a massive military commitment anyhow, meanwhile somehow failing to notice the defects of a command strategy yoking—oops!—two major operational premises *each already known in its own right to be fatally deficient as a formula for victory*. For these premises are what McNamara spends most of the book describing as the essential "two-pronged" American strategy: "The main prong—the ground war—was intended to show Hanoi and the Vietcong that they could not take the South by force. The ancillary prong—bombing the North—was intended both to reduce Hanoi's will and ability to support the Vietcong and to increase the cost of trying to do so." The only problem was that each "version" of the war was already understood by definition to be unwinnable.

As to ground action, it had been axiomatic from the outset that no amount of direct American military involvement in the South could prove successful in dissuading the communists from the pursuit of final victory as long as a South Vietnamese government existed as an American client state without the political loyalty of its people. All crucial intelligence estimates said exactly as much: if "the odds," as a 1964 report put it succinctly, were "against the emergence of a stable government capable of effectively prosecuting the war in Vietnam," report after report made equally clear that no amount of American commitment on the ground in South Vietnam was going to correct a military balance that was political at bottom. In McNamara's words, "military force—especially when wielded by an outside power—just cannot bring order in a country that cannot govern itself."

As to the air effort in the North, every single study had indicated from the outset that a strategic bombing campaign would be useless in persuading the communists to abandon their design for ultimate victory. The primitive northern technological infrastructure and economic base were simply not configured in terms of such a susceptibility. This fact is something McNamara himself would wind up explaining in late 1967 to Congress and everyone else. But again, it too was known as early as 1964, by which time it had already become recognized doctrine that "air attacks," as McNamara phrases it, "would neither break the will nor decisively reduce the ability of the North to continue supporting the insurgency in the South." Why, then, were such measures pursued when "data and analysis showed that such air attacks would not work"? In a brilliant recourse to the tactical passive, McNamara can only offer at this point that "there was such determination to do something, anything, to stop the Communists that discouraging reports were often ignored." Or, as perhaps put more succinctly in the title of a review, if all else failed, there was always the option of "Bombing for the Hell of It."

Whence, then, may we infer, arose the dreadful illogic of assumed complementarity between known no-win strategies? According to McNamara, its dates of origin can be reasonably identified as post-Diem and post-Kennedy—or, to put it more directly, when the Americans, as is their custom, could no longer resist taking the bull by the horns. Further, as to how the strategy emerged, McNamara shows that it could not have happened in more quintessential American fashion: in a smooth recasting of the old equations into a seamless circularity of relationship—at once beautiful and insane—that, like most bureaucratic lunacies, left no opening for human objection. With Nguyen Khanh installed in Saigon and Lyndon Johnson in Washington, it was decided, that because the situation in the South lacked political and military stability, suddenly the most effective strategy would be to strike the North. Of course, if this was to be done with maximum effectiveness—if I may use the term—new and enlarged U.S. air bases would also be needed in the South. And this, in turn, would naturally require commitment of ground troops in the South. Why? Because, given the instability of South Vietnamese affairs, someone, after all, would have to protect all those bases now needed to prosecute air operations against the North.

As if any debate was needed on the latter point, communist forces in the South shortly rendered it moot by obligingly attacking just such an installation at Pleiku, causing significant U.S. casualties. (Nor did it help matters, as Kai Bird documents, that McNamara's fire-breathing White House colleague, National Security Advisor McGeorge Bundy, was present in Vietnam when the attack came, running around head-quarters and barking retaliatory orders in a state described by no less an authority than William C. Westmoreland as "full field marshal psychosis.") In response, the first essentially freestanding U.S. ground forces, two marine battalions, were sent ashore at Da Nang, assuming perimeter responsibilities at first but quickly responding to increased communist pressure on their security role by enlarging their operations to include active patrolling. And this in turn suggested that such measures of enclave security combined with active interdiction might be profitably undertaken by more substantial U.S. forces distributed countrywide, with placements of further units near major infiltration points and major population and government centers such as Saigon.

What had changed, McNamara asks, to alter the strategic givens? If only efforts by the South Vietnamese themselves could win the war on the ground, why now did U.S. forces in the South suddenly become effective if supported by a U.S. air war in the North? If all studies showed the North Vietnamese absorbing indefinitely the punishment of an air war, why now did such operations suddenly become effective if supported by a U.S. ground war in the South? Sadly, the answers to those questions remain as stupid and gratuitous as we have always imagined them to be. The strategic givens had changed because apparently, somewhere around the last day of 1964, Lyndon Johnson wanted that change and because apparently, out of a sizeable collection of the most astonishingly powerful adult males on the planet, no one felt obliged to disagree.

Indeed, almost instantly, everyone bought in, sagely assembling the old information in the new synthesis. The joint chiefs, McNamara records, now went on record as generously sharing a belief "that bombing, by itself, would not force a change. Bombing would only work, they agreed, if accompanied by actions in the South that convinced the Vietcong and North Vietnamese they could not win. Doing that would require increasing numbers of U.S. ground troops to supplement the South Vietnamese Army's flagging efforts." McGeorge Bundy, cabling back from Saigon, was similarly at pains to confirm the newly prevailing wisdom: "We should . . . make very clear that we do not believe that any feasible amount of bombing is of itself likely to cause the DRV to cease and desist its actions in the South. Such a change in DRV attitudes can probably be brought about only when . . . there is a conviction on their part that the tide has turned or soon will turn against them in the South." As the ground troops began to arrive in force, the dreadful logic began to exercise its own impeccable circularity. Take two separate enterprises, both known to be no-win enterprises, and put them together on the assumption that, if engaged in concurrently, they will become one winning enterprise, or at least one no-lose enterprise, or at the very least an enterprise with each part possessing the brilliant virtue of defining the other's necessity. The American war had become its own justification.

Yet now would come one more great Dr. Strangelove twist, perhaps the most bizarre piece of information revealed by McNamara in the entire book. And that would involve the administration's further response to the message of a Pentagon war game, Sigma II-65, which duplicated the conclusions provided above, down to the most minute specifics of concept and phrasing. As to the ground war, the top-level exercise confirmed "considerable feeling among participants that Viet Cong adoption of the strategy of avoiding major engagements with U.S. forces would make it extremely difficult to find and fix enemy units. . . . Viet Cong experience in the jungles [and] guerilla warfare . . . would pose serious problems, even for well-equipped and highly mobile U.S. regulars." Similarly, as for bombing, the report continued, "there was considerable feeling . . . that [the] punishment being imposed could and would be absorbed by the Hanoi leadership . . . based on the fact that the country is basically a subsistence economy . . . centering on the self-sustaining village. . . . Industrial activities constitute such a limited portion of the total economy that even [its] disruption seemed an acceptable price" to pay. To put it another way, to the truest believers in the hegemony of objective knowledge, the ultimate objective model, Sigma II-65, had now also spoken. To be sure, the experts tried switching things around some, one side playing with the other side's players and so on, and the predictions came out a little better. But by now no one had the courage or honest objectivity to listen.

There is a truly insane elegance to this, coming, as it does, from a figure who, as A. J. Langguth records, once made technocratic quotation history by averring to Neil Sheehan during an early visit to the war zone that "every quantitative measure we have shows that we're winning this war" and who now continues to profess faith in "quantification as a language to add precision about the world," even if it is still deficient, he generously adds, in reckoning "issues of morality, beauty, . . . love," and the like. For what these comments finally tell us is that when the mathematical models, either real *or* simulated, did not lie to the administration's satisfaction, telling war planners instead that they were getting enormous numbers of Americans and Vietnamese killed for next to no purpose, the people reading them simply elected to fudge in their own technocratic calculus of willed blindness and mendacity. Experts who admit they are wrong, after all, lose their powerful jobs to better experts who are more skilled at pleasing the boss and not admitting they are wrong; not better experts, that is—just better liars.

Trying to play with numbers as if they were the truth but refusing to accept the numbers when they don't add up to the truth desired is a hoary political game, not to mention an economic one that has lately brought the nation and the world close to financial ruin. Not for nothing did Benjamin Disraeli, a British prime minister in the Victorian age of empire and an accomplished fiction writer, once observe, "There are lies, there are damnable lies, and there are statistics." The quote has become a bureaucratic cliché, sounding so American that it is frequently attributed to Mark Twain. The computer age has predictably replaced it with a shorter, more efficient one: garbage in, garbage out. I suspect

McNamara is familiar with both of them. If he is like most people, how-ever, he forgot the first lesson about clichés, and that is that they always begin by being true. Accordingly, when his own statistical and bureau-cratic lying on Vietnam came up completely on the wrong side of his-torical reality, he acted as if he did not know what hit him. David Hal-berstam records the definitive moment: "I didn't think these people had the capacity to fight this way," McNamara is cited as shakenly confessing to a journalist friend. "If I thought they could take this punishment and fight this well, enjoy fighting like this, I would have thought differently at the start."

McNamara bailed, leaving others to deal with the task of crunch-ing statistics on the only numbers that eventually came to matter: the number of Americans and Vietnamese still to be killed in the war that would go on for another eight years. Meanwhile he was rewarded with the presidency of the World Bank. After that, he received a series of book contracts, going the McGeorge Bundy–Dean Rusk–Walt Rostow publishing route of the post-Vietnam geopolitical sage prophetically con-templating the big picture. In 1986 he published *Blundering into Disaster: Surviving the First Century of the Nuclear Age;* in 1989, *Out of the Cold: New Thinking for American Foreign and Defense Policy in the Twenty-first Century;* and in 1992, getting riskily close to a subject he had theretofore carefully eschewed, *The Changing Nature of Global Security and Its Impact on Southeast Asia.* In 1995, with *In Retrospect,* he allegedly faced the music on Vietnam. God knows, it also sold him a gazillion books. In addition, it allowed him a second public career of traveling around, semiapologizing for the war and semirecanting his role in its conduct, a sort of "The Best and the Brightest II: Sackcloth and Ashes." Graciously, he extended the act by padding out a paperback reissue of *In Retrospect* with long passages from reviews and editorials in which people said awful things about him and his book. He followed the performance with another slapped-together volume, *Argument without End,* basically the report of a "lessons-learned" conference he staged in Hanoi with many of his old Vietnamese coun-terparts, in which they got to do their Ho Chi Minh act—"you Americans are an impatient people; you never understood how long we could fight, how determined we were"—while he and some of his old policy people tried to reconstruct the latest version of the Gulf of Tonkin incident. Most recently, sufficiently rehabilitated from Vietnam, *per se,* he's back to big books. The latest is *Wilson's Ghost: Reducing the Risk of Conflict, Killing, and Catastrophe in the Twenty-first Century.* In it he plots new courses for permanent world peace. As evident in his subtitles, he's wanted to get on with the twenty-first century for a long while: enough of *The Tragedy and Lessons of Vietnam* and *In Search of Answers to the Vietnam Tragedy*—the subtitles, respectively, of *In Retrospect* and *Argument without End.* Agreeably, we let McNamara slide and pretend that he's okay. If we can rehabilitate Nixon and live with finding out what a sleazeball Kennedy really was, God knows we can handle Bob McNamara.

Or by now, it may be, that in reading and writing on matters related to the subject described in the Library of Congress Index as Vietnamese Conflict, 1961–1975, we have just gotten worn out on the latest instance of catch-22 trying to keep up with catch-22. As to the text at hand, at the policy-content level, at least, such resignation seemed to be the dominant sentiment of much review and commentary at the time the book was published. The current mood continues to be much the same. There remain so many awful things to know about the self-consuming madness of the war at the highest levels of policy that the obviousness of this bottom line is at this late date too much to handle: that, thanks to McCarthy-era purges of the State Department, in the early stages of commitment, no Asian specialists remained in the higher levels of government to give reasonable advice on the nature and history of Vietnamese nationalism and its cultural tradition of resistance to outside neighbors in the region, especially China; that, once the war was launched, Johnson and his advisors did everything possible to conceal the magnitude of the commitment in ways guaranteed to make the disaster exponentially worse; that, for instance, to protect Great Society legislation, they misrepresented the war's financial burden, which skyrocketed the national debt, which fueled inflation, which increased the misery of the poor, which led to explosive racial and economic tensions, which frequently manifested themselves in civil upheavals on the part of those who were the focus of Great Society legislation, and so on; or, that, to avoid having to seek congressional authority in the traditional domain of war powers, they elected not to call up the reserves, which generated massive draft inequities, which led to widespread conditions of disturbance and resistance, which contributed further to the problems of a largely conscript military already significantly diminished in its abilities to fight the war in Vietnam, and so on. These things in turn are so bad that other things that might have once been considered major admissions almost go by the board: that near the beginning, for instance, out of the crucial sequence of two naval clashes alleged to have formed the Gulf of Tonkin incident, the first was the direct result of a South Vietnamese–U.S. provocation, and the second, as confirmed later by a meeting between McNamara and General Vo Nguyen Giap, just plain never happened; or that toward the end, as command and control problems got completely out of hand, on several occasions, including one extremely important contact involving French go-betweens, negotiations leading to peace talks were broken off because the people working on the negotiations could not control the people doing the bombing.

By the time the narrative breaks off with McNamara's departure from the scene, leaving us still the agony of the late Lyndon Johnson and new Richard Nixon–Henry Kissinger war to come, this has become an old, mad story; maybe by now it's only natural we'd be tired of hearing about it. What remains, however, perhaps most uniquely appalling and catch-22-like about McNamara's particular account is the relentlessly ingratiating and totalitarian mindset of the policy intellectual–cum-technocrat through which the horrifying information is filtered. To steal an image from Lawrence Ferlinghetti's iconic poem of the era, here indeed is the face of the smiling mortician. Or to invoke Joseph Heller himself, it is like allowing a postmortem on *Catch-22* to be written by the war managers, Peckem and Dreedle, Cathcart and Korn—in this case, an after-action report on Vietnam by a guy telling us that he and well-meaning buddies like McGeorge Bundy may have been bad, but at least they were not as bad as Curtis LeMay or the bombing freak even the hawks referred to derisively as Air Marshal Rostow. (All you have to do to get sent back to the States, I hear the colonels, Cathcart and Korn, telling Yossarian near the end, in the most chilling passage in Heller's book, is "like us." You know, "like us," "be our pal.")

For that, finally, on first read and since, is the thing that still moves me to almost insane fury about McNamara's *In Retrospect* in its recital of the conduct of the war. It's the totally unconscious, transparent–I hesitate to use "innocent," but it's close to that–reproduction of the spirit of manic collegiality in which the horrific decision-making all seems to have been pursued. Indeed, on the basis of his narrative, I am tempted to envision the entire U.S. command effort, in its vast circuitry of bad-idea overload–the White House, Saigon, the Pentagon, the State Department, the Defense Department, the CIA, the NSC, the Wise Men, and all the various other advisory groupings–as some enormous collocation of feckless, self-important college deans, each required to generate a memo or briefing paper on a hard-ass tenure and promotion policy with the express design of rendering any rival document unintelligible. This is not to mention the even worse atmospherics of a truly horrific chumminess. Nearly everyone seems to have a Rover-Boy nickname: "Max" Taylor, "Westy" Westmoreland, "Bus" Wheeler, "Oley" Sharp, "Andy" Goodpaster, "Bill" Bundy, "Mac" Bundy. And, of course, "Bob" McNamara. How, one is invited to ask, could such swell guys possibly have meant badly? Or maybe it really is true: generals, admirals, cabinet secretaries, presidential advisors, and the like *are* only human.

If only. For in the case of "Bob" especially, this continues to be the thing that most disturbs and appalls, something even worse than moral abdication or denial, the strange kink of technocratic personality that leads him even now to create a memoir purporting to be at once candid and even brave while continuing to evince the barest seeming grasp of the corpse-horror engendered by the events it describes: he simply seems congenitally unable, that is, even after three decades, to cut himself loose of such dreadful Orwellian bonhomie to suggest that so long a period of pain and loss have brought him even a modicum of moral self-awareness. It is as if he is saying, to put this another way, that after all these years, being a whiz kid still means never really having to say you're sorry.

For this, indeed, is the dispiriting message that continues to be delivered by McNamara's book from the jacket onward. There is the cover photo, showing the author in solitary reflection, briefcase open, sitting quietly, studying some official-looking sheaf of typescript, in a deserted White House briefing room, for God's sake, complete with riser, podium, and flip chart. There is the design layout, that dreadful, ball-bearing smooth, staff-study title, the cover document for the quintessential big-time after-action report after the big-time action in question has been a colossal fuckup: *"In Retrospect: The Tragedy and Lessons of Vietnam."* ("Whose tragedy?" one nearly wishes to scream. "What lessons?") There is the mind-numbing five-page table of contents, itself set up like a briefing summary, with more phonily dramatic titles attended by chapter sketches suggesting some dreadful hybrid of Dickensian novel and NSC cover memorandum.

And then, shortly into the first chapter, come those celebrated lines that everyone, including myself, became familiar with through advertisements and review and comment, where they were endlessly cited: " . . . we were wrong, terribly wrong. We owe it to future generations to explain why." Yes, these were the very phrasings, the ones that had been seized on eagerly as McNamara's opening to a long-delayed, but somehow grand and worthy, contribution to the healing of America in the long aftermath of the Vietnam War, a brave mea culpa by one of the major architects of that war at last weighed into the balance of history as part of the burden of national self-reflection. The problem, I discovered, as suggested by my punctuation in attempting to reproduce them accurately here, is that, like a lot of other good lines about Vietnam, they had been quoted endlessly out of context. Had indeed anyone besides me noticed that a crucial qualifying antecedent had been lopped off? That the sentence in question began with "Yet"? As in, "Yet we were wrong, terribly wrong . . . ." And that its clear implication in connection to the foregoing paragraph, about intention and motive and full of words like "principles," "traditions," and "values," is that, nevertheless after all these years, *you must still understand that we meant well*? As in, it was a good cause in which we meant well and tried to act honorably, and "Yet . . ."?

Yet, indeed. The little words never lie. Or as McNamara has phrased it on the first page, how could such right-minded people have managed so badly to "get it wrong in Vietnam"? If anything, then, what's here is something even more bleak than the delusional lying asserted in a properly scathing review by David Halberstam. For, to put it baldly, one cannot be morally mendacious about something of which one is morally unaware, puffing up managerial arrogance to the status of "tragic" hubris and then talking about the result as if it were a flawed management-school case study, a botched staff report, or somebody's sloppy math homework. "Robert McNamara's state of mind," one might call it, after Frances Fitzgerald's brilliant figure in *Fire in the Lake:* the quantum difference in understanding that had to be traversed between American and Vietnamese ways of looking at the world, an abyss that had to be crossed to arrive at the idea that *human thinking itself* just might have categories besides reason and emotion, mind and spirit, body and soul. Then and now, McNamara's state of mind remains a true politics of Western consciousness in the fullest sense, here further engrafted on the policy mentality of the modern, technological, bureaucratic nation-state. It remains the politics of faith in reason, science, and objective knowledge—the politics of value-free technology—as opposed to any politics of a larger physical or spiritual connection, of a whole in relation to the world.

This, then, remains Robert McNamara's state of mind: he still cannot see, beyond some general quality of rueful admission, that some problems are simply insoluble, that some problems become insoluble precisely because of their structural relation to states of mind, of which the twentieth-century, western, technocratic, managerial is only one of many. And so even now, he traverses the world, conducting symposia on problem solving about past mistakes, a kind of road-show version of what is done at the big foundations and institutes: used-up college presidents, diplomats, politicians, and retired assistant deputy secretaries of something or other, all sitting around in nice paneled conference rooms after big expense-account lunches bullshitting about public policy. He pursues and records his journey of atonement with more self-serving and mealymouthed prose, not realizing for a moment that the structural approach is itself the problem, that—then *and* now—the method itself was the madness. *In Retrospect: The Tragedy and Lessons of Vietnam* begets *Argument without End: In Search of Answers to the Vietnam Tragedy.*

Tragedy: the word in Robert McNamara's mouth disgraces language and humanity. Vietnam *was* a tragedy, predicated on the overweening assumption by the most proud, rich, and powerful military nation in the history of the world that a three-thousand-year-old Asian culture, with a fierce tradition of independence and a legacy of millennia of conflict with would-be imperialist masters, could be forced to abandon its own, peculiar, intensely Vietnamese dynamic of historical evolution, exchanging overnight deeply seated traditional values of social harmony for American-style ideas of expansion, progress, mobility. The cost of America's fall into history and the resultant laying waste to a small Asian nation was commensurately stunning: deaths in the millions, with the civilian vastly exceeding the military, and two nations still trying to clean up the human and political wreckage several generations later. But Robert McNamara wouldn't understand the word if it bit him on the ass. The problem still has to have a rational, corporate, managerial solution.

Given McNamara's mindset, it is a shame that we have probably seen Bob McNamara come as close as he will ever get to saying he's sorry, because his "apology" really only makes things worse, confounding the "solution" with the kind of thinking that created the "problem." The fellow with the sta-comb hair, as Lyndon Johnson memorably described him, and the ball-bearing mind for detail still doesn't get it. In any event, from the veteran's perspective, McNamara's "apology" is at least appreciated, an attempt at personal confession as a form of atonement. If nothing else, it's something we never saw a Rusk or a Rostow or a Bundy (take a pick) trying to get off his soul. (Actually, a McGeorge Bundy manuscript on the war is supposed to exist, allegedly in press now for more than five years. Meanwhile Rostow, only recently departed, lived out his placid last years down in Austin at the Lyndon Johnson Center, smiling all the way.) No matter, for most of us, it has largely been a moot issue all these years, the idea that the incompetents who sent us out on the ass end of nowhere to die would ever apologize to us; or that, if they did, it would do us any good. It was something we ourselves had long ago learned to handle with "sorry" itself as the operative word.

Calley's Ghost

Bizarre as it may seem, as recently as a year ago, an Internet search for the name "William Calley" led you directly to his alumni association Web page at Miami Edison High School in Florida. The first thing you saw was his graduation picture, class of 1962, in which he already wore the look of goofy vacuity made familiar during his army court-martial and brief period of public notoriety. A short, upbeat paragraph followed about what he did in the years immediately after high school. Only then did the narrative turn to his involvement in the My Lai massacre and his subsequent prosecution for the mass murder of Vietnamese civilians. The tone was mildly sympathetic, although the narrative provided links to a My Lai Web site giving an account of the incident based on testimony presented at trial. An illustration accompanied these paragraphs. It was the famous Alfred E. Neuman caricature of Calley in uniform from the cover of the *National Lampoon*. That the site designers did not choose the equally famous *Esquire* cover photo in which he is shown with a lapful of cute Asian children is a measure of the casual horror involved. The *National Lampoon* illustration had the odd merit at least of looking very much like the graduation picture. The entry then concluded, as if the subject had spent his life as an accountant or a plumbing contractor, with a brief account of his subsequent attempts to live anonymously in Columbus, Georgia, as a manager of his father-in-law's jewelry store.

Thus Miami Edison High School, his alma mater, preserved the memory of William L. Calley Jr., the former U.S. Army second lieutenant who, on the morning of March 16, 1968, entered the village of My Lai 4 with a platoon of infantry and initiated the slaughter of between four hundred and five hundred Vietnamese civilians, using automatic weapons, grenades, knives, and bayonets. The killing rampage, eventually involving all three platoons of C Company, 1/20th Infantry, Eleventh Infantry Brigade, Americal Division, included countless individual acts of rape, torture, murder, and mutilation.

Let us be clear what happened. A heavily armed combat unit of roughly one hundred American soldiers in the space of a few hours killed between four and five times their number of unarmed Vietnamese civilians. Not a single Viet Cong soldier was found. One U.S. soldier was wounded, taken out by a medical-evacuation helicopter in the midst of the killing, after accidentally shooting himself in the foot while trying to clear a jammed .45-caliber pistol. The pistol had been borrowed by a squad mate to finish off a small boy he saw moving in a pile of wounded. He shot the boy in the neck. Bleeding heavily, the child crawled to his feet and stumbled forward two or three steps trying to escape. As he fell, the GI with the .45 tried to shoot him again, jamming the weapon. He returned it disgustedly to the owner, who then managed to shoot himself while attending to the malfunction.

The Vietnamese victims of the massacre were nearly all women and children with a sprinkling of old men. Even as they died by the hundreds, they died individually in astonishingly violent, painful, and terrifying ways. Some were herded into cowering groups and blown apart piece by piece with rounds from grenade launchers. Others were mowed down at point-blank range by machine-gun and automatic-weapons fire, with Calley personally involved in two such mass executions. Numerous women were raped and forced to perform oral sex. Then they were killed at close range and their bodies mutilated. One was beheaded. One was killed by rounds fired from an M-16 rifle after the barrel had been rammed up her vagina. A child, barely old enough to walk, tried to crawl out of a ditch where its mother had just been executed. Calley personally pushed it back down into the pile of bodies, shot it, and returned to beating an old man he had been in the process of interrogating. When it was all done, the slaughter was too immense even for the body count sweepstakes that had become the measure of combat performance in Vietnam. The division operations journal revised the figure of Vietnamese dead down to what was deemed a suitably modest 128 killed, with an alleged recapture of three U.S. weapons from enemy hands thrown in as some idiotic stab at corroboration.

I don't remember when I first heard about My Lai. It is hard to imagine that I did not read something in Vietnam during late 1969, at the time of the first journalistic revelations, when I was an armored cavalry platoon leader in a separate light infantry brigade not unlike the three, including Calley's, that had been slapped together to form the Americal. Down in III Corps, relatively near Saigon, we had at least intermittent access to *Pacific Stars and Stripes*. I've looked at the files for that paper, and the story seems to have been all over the place. When it came to national headlines, however, we didn't talk about home as being back in the world for nothing. I remember finding out about the moon landing around two weeks after it happened. To this day, hearing about news events of 1969 strikes me as not unlike having been in a coma.

After Vietnam I went to graduate school and spent four years reading a lot of books and staying to myself. Then I went on to my first job. I didn't have a television during the seventies, nor did I read a newspaper regularly, so I missed most of the reports of the official inquiry conducted by a U.S. Army commission under Lieutenant General

William G. Peers; of the court proceedings eventuating in the conviction of Calley, the acquittal of his company commander Ernest Medina, and the dropping of cases against all the other defendants charged with complicity in the massacre or subsequent cover-up, most notably the brigade and division commanders, Colonel Oran K. Henderson and Major General Samuel W. Koster; and of the successive revisions of Calley's sentence from life imprisonment to ten years to house arrest to parole—all of which, as far as I can discern, were swallowed up by the Cambodian and Laotian invasions, the 1972 Christmas bombing raids, the Paris peace talks, and eventually Nixon and Watergate. Only in the last year did I feel impelled to read about it in detail. Maybe I thought that getting older and more generally accepting of experience and memory would help, not to mention having witnessed the dying throes of one century of blood and the beginning horrors of another. Maybe I thought that a career as a university researcher with a long interest in personal and cultural representations of the Vietnamese war would provide some kind of analytic or intellectual insulation. What I have found, instead, is that My Lai remains the Vietnam nightmare story worse than any human mind could invent. For those of us who knew the everyday war of the battalions and brigades, it is the visitation from which memory can never allow itself to find release, continuing to beggar every instinct of moral accountability, then or now.

Some historians have alleged that the massacre arose more or less spontaneously out of a collective psychological breakdown by a significant number of C Company soldiers, including both enlisted men and officers. Specifically, the massacre has been yoked to rage over the deaths of several members of the company killed by an unseen enemy, the first shot by a sniper, another blown apart by a booby trap, with a memorial service for the most recent victim held on the day before the mission and thus bearing direct connection to the tone of bloodthirsty vengeance that saturated a briefing by the company commander, Captain Ernest Medina, about the operation to be conducted at My Lai 4 the next morning. Proponents of the collective-psychological-breakdown theory frequently buttress it with an emphasis on the stress of the peculiar combat dangers faced by American troops operating in

Quang Ngai province: a maddeningly invisible military enemy, persistently evading detection, yet claiming victory day after day through U.S. victims of sniper rounds and mines and booby traps studding the landscape; and a likewise largely uncooperative and hostile civilian population, too fearful or hate filled to yield assistance or information, and in many cases probably complicit in the campaign of attrition.

Measure against this, however, the fact that the vast majority of American combatants in the field faced such circumstances of fear, frustration, and horror, in one combination or another, for up to a year, whereas the Eleventh Brigade, in contrast, had been in Vietnam for three months, deploying there as a unit after a training period in Hawaii. Further, Charlie Company had spent fully half of its early period in-country in various rear-area activities. This is to say that it had been in combat for six weeks. It had experienced its first American death a month earlier. As noted previously, another had occurred just one day before the My Lai operation. In between, three men had been killed in a minefield incident. Over the period in question, twenty-eight had been wounded. Actual contacts with the enemy amounted to one or two at most. Meanwhile, for all its relative combat inexperience, it had already forged the habit of raping, torturing, and killing. On a prior operation, after a First Platoon radio operator angrily threw an old man down a well, Calley himself shot the man in cold blood. The Second Platoon had already become known as accomplished rapists, with the platoon leader on at least one occasion allegedly a participant. Nor was the Third Platoon by March 16 apparently a stranger to brutality. On the morning of My Lai, its just-arrived lieutenant, a replacement officer, watched with horror as his new command moved through in the wake of the others finishing off anyone or anything that moved. "Is it always like this?" he asked.

My Lai was not just Calley and a handful of renegades then. At My Lai 4 alone, three platoons were on the ground that morning, in excess of one hundred armed infantrymen, with significant numbers of all three taking part in the slaughter over a period of several hours. Also present, and in the first two cases actively torturing and killing people, were three commissioned officers. Furthermore, accompanying the Third Platoon was the commanding officer of the entire unit, Ernest Medina.

Throughout the day, *he* responded evasively to radioed inquiries about civilian casualties with vague reports about a number possibly killed by supporting air and artillery strikes but would later profess ignorance of the killing by the platoons. As to personal actions, he admitted only to shooting, in instinctive self-defense, as he described it, one mortally wounded Vietnamese woman whose movement he caught out of his peripheral vision as his command group moved through the village. As to his briefing the night before, witnesses agree that he actively presented the impending mission to the company as a chance to get even for their dead and wounded buddies. Testimony splits on whether he actually authorized in advance the killing of civilians but generally agrees that, if he did not tell the soldiers of C Company to kill anyone they saw the next day, he at least gave them the firm impression that anyone they saw the next day could be considered the enemy and killed. Hordes of investigators and lawyers could debate endlessly over the fine legal points of such ambiguity in the message but not its results. It had primed a large number of men to commit mass murder.

But even now the larger massacre story is incompletely told. Another full company of infantry was on the ground elsewhere in the My Lai complex that morning, getting off helicopters within sound of Charlie Company's rampage already in progress. B Company of the 1/20th was the second main component that day of Task Force Barker, commanded by a lieutenant colonel of that name who had been running it as an independent unit for several weeks. It too had gotten a briefing the night before similar to Medina's from its commander, a captain named Earl Ray Michles, with the message that any Vietnamese encountered the next day could be considered the enemy; and it too, once on the ground, quickly began murdering large numbers of Vietnamese civilians. Some have claimed that its part of the massacre began with shooting at Vietnamese under the impression that the Charlie Company gunfire was part of an enemy attack. More certain is the fact that one of its platoons, after witnessing the death of a nearby platoon leader and several of his men in a booby-trap explosion, shortly undertook, under the active direction of its lieutenant, an additional campaign of murder, adding at least a hundred civilians to the day's total. Ironically, then, we come closest to any picture of collective psychological breakdown in the lesser-known mass murders at My Lai. Nevertheless, testimony about the premission briefing again suggests a unit being prepared to kill people on sight. "There was a general conception," recalled Michles's personal radio operator, speaking to reporter Seymour Hersh, "that we were going to destroy everything."

If there was a "breakdown," then, at My Lai, somehow it encompassed not just one but two full companies of infantry, commanded by captains, as part of a task force commanded by a lieutenant colonel, with substantial numbers of soldiers slaughtering unarmed women, children, and old men during a period of several hours in which they did not receive a single round of enemy fire. Accordingly, the emphasis on mob identification and common outlawry here leads to a second major hypothesis frequently ventured about the My Lai massacre as largely attributable to a failure of leadership at every level from the platoon up to the division and back. This idea contains perhaps a greater amount of truth. To understand it fully, however, one has to return to the ranks. One point everyone agrees on is that there seems to have been close to a vacuum of traditional, professionalized noncommissioned officer leadership–in itself a death sentence for discipline in any unit facing combat. Medina had a first sergeant with eighteen years experience; but in accord with fairly common practice in Vietnam, he seems not to have been in the field. In contrast, the other NCOs with the platoons, few in number and relatively young and inexperienced, seem to have partaken of the disastrously common unit mentality in a way that made them fairly indistinguishable from their enlisted counterparts. To be sure, the absence of experienced senior NCOs was a problem common to the Vietnam army by early 1968, particularly in the infantry, where professional cadres had already experienced the attrition of death, wounds, age, and multiple tours of service. Here, that absence proved uniquely catastrophic. For in the newly arrived Eleventh Infantry Brigade, not only were most of the handful of NCOs with the two companies unsure and untested, so were *all* the enlisted men.

Many leveled reproach at the time and later at an in-country replacement system in Vietnam whereby units were regularly replenished after losses and rotations by men totally new to combat, thrown into the field after minimal in-country training with the hope that they would survive long enough to learn from their experienced squad and platoon mates. Here, ironically, that maligned system might have supplied at least minimal leadership in the ranks, with a cohort sufficiently acquainted with the fears and frustrations of combat over a period of time to provide an example of experienced restraint. Instead, to a man, one of the least combat-ready formations imaginable for the kind of fighting generally encountered by Americans throughout Vietnam was cast into arguably one of the most difficult areas of wartime operation.

As to the officers of the units involved on the ground, to a man, they weren't just bad; they were terrible. To be sure, Calley led the list. He was the laughingstock of Charlie Company. In the platoon, his men didn't know whether to ignore him or kill him. He was an incompetent and a pariah, under attack from above and below, who tried to mask his insecurities with unconvincing explosions of rage. The resultant buffoonery was further packaged into the blustering and strutting often characteristic of the little man in the military, the proverbial shortround. Nor was any of this helped by the company commander's unrelenting mockery of him in front of his men, who consistently heard him addressed as "Young Thing," "Sweetheart," or "Lieutenant Shithead."

If Calley led the officer disaster list, however, he did so just barely. In lieutenants, as suggested earlier, C Company could count only degrees of bad. Meanwhile, the company commander, Captain Ernest Medina, compounded his officer-subordinates' weaknesses by treating them as incompetent fools and foils, while frequently buddying around with the enlisted men. A former enlisted soldier and NCO himself, he performed well in officer candidate school and had a good training record with the company in Hawaii. In Vietnam, however, he quickly reaped the consequences of running all three platoons like a gang lord. With their own lieutenants in charge, they invariably performed poorly. When all discipline vanished among the lead platoons during the first few minutes that morning in My Lai 4, the meltdown was uncontrollable.

We know less about B Company, except to say that the commander,

Earl Ray Michles, on the basis of the parallel mission briefings and the subsequent conduct of the unit on the ground, seems to have been of Medina's sort. B Company was also, since joining Task Force Barker, a unit with a history of brutality. This was the testimony of another captain, the commander of the third unit initially assigned to the ad hoc formation, A Company, 1/20th, who a month before My Lai found himself alarmed by Medina's loose discipline and by Michles's tendency to fire indiscriminately at Vietnamese to increase body count. A West Pointer, by his own accounting considered "uptight" by his troops, amid the endless "dirty" war of sniping and booby traps waged by the enemy, as commander of A Company he insisted on strict rules of engagement and restrained the unit from abusing Vietnamese in search of information or as a way of venting their fear and anger. Accordingly, he testified, in contrast to Medina and Michles, he gained a reputation for "not looking after his men." In Lieutenant Colonel Frank Barker's eyes, he also earned a reputation for hesitation and uncooperativeness, with a result that A Company became increasingly distanced from the task-force core operations. For his pains, the third captain got a bullet in the back during a firefight in mid-February. The general assumption was that one of his own soldiers shot him. Whatever the caliber of his leadership or the manner of his wounding, any veteran of A Company who was alive a month later must surely reverence their brief association with him. When Barker planned and executed the new task-force mission for March 16, he made sure the less than reliable A Company was left behind.

In fact, then, we know now the only thing that differentiated the two companies present at My Lai by the end of the killing on March 16 was the sheer volume of the murders committed by the runaway Calley platoon. What prevents us from knowing too much more is that the C Company killings were so egregious that "the other massacre," as it came to be called, failed to receive much attention even after later investigations brought it to light. Michles was killed a few months later in a helicopter crash. Also killed was Barker, by then promoted to command of a full battalion, with the former B Company commander chosen by Barker to serve as his intelligence officer.

As for that higher-ranking officer, remembered now to history for commanding the infamous task force bearing his name, at the time of My Lai he was an unassigned lieutenant colonel trying to make good in a war where literally hundreds of counterparts of the same rank were scrambling to earn command time with official line battalions, let alone odd, off-the-wall formations like this. In gaining such an assignment, he seems to have enjoyed the particular favor of the Americal Division commander, a two-star general named Samuel Koster, with the 1/20th Infantry elements of the task force—more than half the battalion—summarily snatched from the official unit commander, Lieutenant Colonel Edwin Beers, who was reduced to operating with one line company and a recon-heavy weapons unit. Barker quickly created his own war as well, racking up body counts that became the envy of the division.

On the afternoon before My Lai, he too met with his staff and subordinates, including, most crucially, the two ground-company commanders, for a briefing about their newest mission. Again, there is no evidence that his exhortations to "neutralize" the objective included authorization to kill any Vietnamese in sight. Notably, however, at this particular meeting, the task-force intelligence officer assured that all civilians would be out of My Lai by seven o'clock in the morning, allowing the two captains conducting the ground assault to infer—and presumably to convey the inference to their troops—that anyone left there should be considered the military enemy. As to his immediate superior's approval of the mission, Barker could not have been more sure of the support of the new brigade commander, a full colonel named Oran K. Henderson. Henderson had in fact flown personally to Task Force Barker headquarters that day and honored the briefing group with a prefatory pep talk urging increased aggressiveness in closing with the enemy and destroying his capacity to operate any longer as a military threat. By gross mischance, he had taken command of the brigade a few hours earlier, determined to prove himself worthy of Koster's confidence in the high-level command assignment that during three years' previous service in Vietnam he had been frustratingly denied.

Meanwhile, Koster, a major general, ran his division, in existence as a unit for only five months, as if it had a traditional, well-established identification and command structure like that of such veteran Vietnam counterparts as the First Infantry, the Twenty-fifth Infantry, the 101st Airborne, or the First Air Cavalry, when the Americal—the name itself resurrected from World War II Pacific lore—was in fact a field expedient, a grab bag parading as a fusion of three separate, light infantry brigades, all of them rushed into existence for service in Vietnam and of uneven, disparate leadership and experience. An ambitious careerist, with a high opinion of his aptitude for Olympian overviews, on one hand, he ran his headquarters at an unusual distance from subordinate commands. On the other hand, when he felt like it—most disastrously in the case of Task Force Barker—he too fractured the chain of command to facilitate personal projects, overleaping the conventional brigade structure to allow Barker independent command, just as the task-force organization would take Medina and Michles out of the traditional battalion command structure, as Medina would take his lieutenants out of the traditional company command organization, and so forth down the line to the rampaging mob of rapists and murderers on the ground.

For anyone who remembers how quickly any combat action in Vietnam from the squad level up could turn into a command and communications nightmare both on the ground and above, there can be little surprise at how the hot-wired arrangement of March 16 began acting itself out with grim predictability as the slaughter began. Echelons of helicopters hovered above the battlefield, with a progression of officers—the task-force executive officer, the task-force commander, the brigade commander—micromanaging in the air above, demanding reports, shouting orders, insuring in the customary squad-leader-in-the-sky fashion that command radio frequencies would be filled with confused and frequently conflicting information. The killing of civilians was a repeated subject of radio traffic, with Barker landing in one case to engage Medina in a shouted argument on the topic. As is known to readers of the historical literature, in another instance a heroic helicopter pilot from an aviation unit flying in support of the operation, Warrant Officer Hugh Thompson, also reported over the air about what looked to him like a massacre, actually landing at one point to rescue wounded Vietnamese and threatening to have his door gunners open fire on U.S. soldiers if they continued killing unarmed people.

Meanwhile, over the infantry channels, from the platoon and company level up to brigade and division and then back down again, confusion locked in like a fire wall so that truthful reporting could be avoided and responsibility, then and later, suitably befuddled. Some perfunctory inquiries were made at the brigade and division level about civilian casualties. Flying over Medina's position as he returned to division headquarters on the night of March 16, Koster, taking the unusual step for a division commander of radioing an individual company commander on the ground, tried to draw him out on the precise number of civilian casualties. Medina stuck to his earlier story of twenty to twenty-five mistakenly killed by air and artillery support. Koster replied, "That seems about right." A day or so later, Henderson was on the ground as C Company returned to brigade base camp, anxiously walking to and fro and questioning individual soldiers disembarking from helicopters about any unusual killing of civilians. Thompson, the helicopter pilot, registered an official protest about of the killings he had witnessed. It went through the aviation chain of command. By this time, at brigade and division level, the "investigation" had retooled itself as a cover-up. Thompson's account arrived nowhere.

If anything, the days and months following My Lai saw its primary command participants actively prospering in the army rewards system. As noted, at the time of their deaths three months later, Barker had received his own battalion, and Michles, the B Company commander, had been selected to join him as his intelligence officer. Medina returned to Fort Benning for the infantry officers' career course, a necessary step toward promotion to major. Calley went on to other positions, actually being allowed to extend his combat tour for assignments including, of all things, a civil-affairs staff position and some long-range patrol duty–the latter usually reserved for only the most expert and reliable field soldiers. Henderson joined the headquarters staff at Schofield Barracks in Hawaii, pending his assignment to the faculty of the Armed Forces Staff College in Norfolk, Virginia. And for his Americal duty, Koster was rewarded by his superiors with the prize position of superintendent of West Point, in the tradition of Douglas MacArthur, William Westmoreland, and others, almost a sure preliminary to ultimate selection as chief of staff.

This spectacle of actual reward for a war-crime atrocity and cover-up leads to the largest supposition ventured about the massacre and its continuing moral centrality to the American memory of the Vietnamese war: that, despite its astonishing and horrifying magnitude, the My Lai horror was in many ways a microcosm, an abstract or epitome, of the American way of war in Vietnam. And in many respects this may be the one closest to the truth: that, in a guerrilla war, where an indigenous enemy hid itself among a civilian population of dubious loyalty to a U.S.-supported government, the employment of massive firepower, including the indiscriminate use of artillery and air strikes, coupled with body count as a measure of combat success, had ultimately led to My Lai over a trail of years in which every day of the war yielded a record of civilian deaths ranging from the individual to the many. The press openly reported about high-ranking officers going "gook hunting" in their command helicopters, about pilots and door gunners shooting people on the ground because they tried to run, about commanders destroying villages in order to "save" them. Only the rare personal narrative of the war does not involve some particular moment of confrontation with the sufferings and deaths of civilians. Almost every Vietnam novel contains a core of atrocity—some distinct, specifiable scene of horror: a rape, a murder, the torture of prisoners, or the abandonment of them to the South Vietnamese Army, the ARVN, which was the moral equivalent. To be sure, throughout the war, no matter what the area of operation, Americans in combat tried to honor rules of engagement, in many cases even to rescue civilians, sometimes paying with their bodies and their lives for the effort. The fact remains, however, that, according to what now seem to be reliable figures, of the possibly four million Vietnamese north and south who died in the war, at least one million were South Vietnamese civilians—wounded and killed at the rate of one hundred thousand per year.

Despite all this, we still struggle hopelessly to comprehend what a particular unit of American soldiers did to a particular population of unarmed Vietnamese civilians in the My Lai village complex on March

16, 1968. Indeed, we do so to the degree that we would be almost relieved to find in it some dreadful convergence of the fates, *everything* that was wrong with the American conduct of the war somehow achieving critical mass in one concentrated horror. One version of the story would then go like this: Frustrated and enraged by the deaths and mutilations of comrades by sniper bullets and booby traps, an ill-disciplined, trigger-happy task force of two infantry companies from probably the worst brigade of the worst division in Vietnam is given a mission where the soldiers are led to believe they will finally get revenge on the unseen enemy. One company, going in by air assault amid preparatory air and artillery strikes, by gross mischance is spearheaded by a platoon led by the worst lieutenant in the army; by equally gross mischance, the other company, landing a short distance away, immediately loses an officer and several men to yet another booby trap. Encountering in both cases no enemy but only the usual sullen civilians, significant numbers of soldiers snap, going wild with torture, rape, and killing on a scale that even the most inspired antiwar activist could not have dreamed.

But there is also a parallel version equally proximate, markedly cynical, and, if possible, even more ghastly. That story would go like this: The newly formed Americal Division is given the mission of eliminating Viet Cong domination in Quang Ngai province, for decades a notorious communist stronghold. The division commander, a major general on the career fast track, understands that he has been given the opportunity to solve a problem that has defied his American predecessors and, for that matter, the French before them. Unfortunately, one of his brigades is making no progress toward the mission because of a civilian-infestation problem of VC sympathizers in a crucial cluster of hamlets. He finds a possible solution in a task force he has previously authorized as an operational command for a favorite younger officer, a protégé with an already endearing trait of combining flashy results with dubious methods. Although fairly inexperienced, elements of the new command have been posting significant body count, albeit with a notable absence of enemy weapons and material recovered on the battlefield. The clear implication must be, then, that the task-force commander has imbued his unit with an attitude of killing fairly indiscriminately on the basis that "mistakes" can always be added to body count. Accordingly, the general realizes he has found just the people to take care of the infestation problem—"neutralization" is the operative term—with substantial confidence that whatever they do will never be questioned, let alone investigated.

The problem with both of these stories is that they are the same story. One emphasizes a systemic "psychological" hypothesis, denying much command responsibility. Given a certain way of waging war, with a certain kind of unit, no matter who was in charge, something like this was bound to happen. The other does just the opposite, investing the butchering mob with the status of hapless pawns, scapegoats, even victims. As will be seen, both versions locked quickly into effect during subsequent investigations and the few legal proceedings that eventually took place.

As to the cover-up, about the only response possible for someone with any knowledge of the infantry war in Vietnam is angry incredulity that anyone could have thought it would work. I lived in that world for a year, and I know. For every small-unit commander on the ground, the chain of command on any given day operated through literal echelons of rank above the battlefield with radios blaring in every direction. Within minutes of possible combat, the airspace above could be filled with helicopters: a major orbiting below a lieutenant colonel orbiting below a colonel orbiting below a general, with each on company and/or platoon radio frequencies contending for the direction of captains, lieutenants, sergeants, and privates. The name of the war, particularly in the body-count sweepstakes, was micromanagement. As to the men at the top of the immediate micromanagement combine that day, we know definitively that Henderson, Barker, Barker's executive officer, and various artillery, aviation, and staff-liaison officers were on station above the massacre area more or less continuously, jamming the air with their own radio transmissions and listening to those of others, not a few of them, it turns out, directly concerning civilian casualties. We do not know what Koster heard. It doesn't matter. What matters is that everyone else from the division near a radio in the immediate vicinity could not *not* have

heard what was going on, listening on innumerable handsets and head-
sets or monitoring the speakers filling every command bunker and radio
room within miles.

A person remembers many things about combat in Vietnam. One
of the most unforgettable is the cacophonous rush, no matter where one
was or what one was doing at the time, of nonstop radio traffic. Especially
in combat, everybody is trying to talk to everybody else. Everybody carrying an infantry radio on the ground or riding a tank or armored personnel carrier hears it; artillery support people hear it; helicopter pilots
and door gunners hear it; tactical-operations center duty officers, NCOs,
and enlisted staff hear it; orderly-room clerks hear it. One may surmise
that hundreds of people heard something about what was happening at
My Lai that morning while it was happening–including, most notably
mentioned by those interviewed afterward, something about American
troops threatening to kill other American troops if they didn't stop killing
Vietnamese civilians.

Whatever went into the battalion, brigade, or division log that night,
a thousand people thus had their own version. As to the GI information
network itself, I can also say this: soldiers wearing the patch of a particular unit know what is happening and what has previously happened in
that unit; they hear about it, and they talk about it, and they pass it on
to the soldiers who come after them. One of the first things pointed out
to me when I assumed command of my platoon was the hole in the gun
shield from the rocket-propelled grenade that killed a predecessor of
mine several lieutenants back in the battle for Saigon during Tet. That
was more than a year earlier. The same people knew that the grunts
who fought beside the troop in the Cholon racetrack that day had been
the 3/7th Infantry. They could also tell me what was happening with the
same battalion now even though it was detached and operating with the
Ninth Division down in the Delta. Soldiers know. Soldiers remember.
And soldiers talk.

It is no surprise to any veteran that it was a relatively low-ranking enlisted man, a specialist fourth class from another unit in the division, after
hearing endless talk about what he called the "dark deeds" of Task Force
Barker, who sent the letters that commenced the congressional investiga-

tion that in turn launched the army inquiry and judicial proceedings that made the My Lai massacre public knowledge. Colin Powell alleges in his memoirs that, as the acting Americal division G-3 in mid-1969–himself a hot young major plucked by the commanding general from a backwater assignment as executive officer of the notorious 1/20th–it was he who first encountered mysterious investigators requesting access to divisional combat records for March 1968. He says that only when pointed queries led him back through the operations log for specific dates did the March 16 figure of 128 "jump out at him." If that was true, all I can say is that he should have been talking to more of the spec fours and the PFCs. They would have known.

And so, with a massive new official investigation, this time headed by a lieutenant general and a staff of hundreds, did the history of the massacre at My Lai run all the way up the chain of the command one last time and then all the way back down, with fourteen officers initially charged. Absolutely providential for virtually everyone involved, of course, was the death of Barker in June 1968. Thereby both Koster and Henderson could blame others for false reporting at the time of the massacre and self-protective cover-up in the aftermath. Charges against midlevel staff officers likewise could be foisted on the deceased colonel. The death of Michles in the same helicopter crash with Barker further obscured whatever communications he had had with his subordinates and his role on the ground at My Lai 1. Barker's death also protected Medina to some degree, although much evidence still existed to connect him with the much more widely publicized atrocities committed by C Company. Medina managed to sneak by for several reasons. First, he could say that he was only repeating Barker's somewhat ambiguous instructions. Second, his long service as an NCO had trained him in a cardinal rule of reporting: once you have lied to a superior, do not change your story. The twenty-to-twenty-five "estimate" of civilians allegedly killed by air and artillery stuck. Third and most important for Medina was the legal and public relations advantage he shared with all the other junior officers, NCOs, and enlisted men implicated in the murders. They all had Calley, despised and ridiculous, the lieutenant without a clue.

Of all the Americans involved in My Lai, only the feckless First Platoon leader of C Company was convicted in court. Found guilty of the deaths of nineteen Vietnamese, he spent roughly four years under house arrest. Along the way he found a kind of absurd celebrity. He became a hero of the diehard right, honored by patriotic organizations and a personal visit from George Wallace. He drove around in a white Mercedes provided by a supporter and had a brief stint on the lecture circuit. Human interest stories about his girlfriend and his gentle way with pets appeared in periodicals. There was the *National Lampoon* caricature, not to mention the truly appalling *Esquire* cover shot with the smiling Asiatic children. Eventually he was paroled by the president of the United States. The country let the lieutenant slide into domestic obscurity. Everyone hoped that he would take the massacre with him.

For a time, the general wish for amnesia was forestalled by the ongoing visibility of a substantial literature of investigation. This had begun with the journalistic inquiries of Seymour Hersh and others who had first brought the massacre to light and continued, with considerable media coverage, through the official investigation and trial. Hersh eventually wrote two books on the subject, the first on the massacre and the second on the cover-up. The official findings of the Peers commission followed, with a text of sixty-five hundred pages. These were summarized, along with the history of the court-martial proceedings and eventual disposition of individual cases, in a 1976 volume, *The My Lai Massacre and Its Cover-Up: Beyond the Reach of Law?* More than a decade then ensued, however, before an important 1992 text, *Four Hours in My Lai,* originating from a BBC documentary shown in the United States in 1989, undertook a significant reevaluation and updating of the previous information. A symposium was held at Tulane University in 1994—followed by a 1998 volume of the proceedings, titled *Facing My Lai*—involving major figures ranging from GI Ron Ridenour and journalist Seymour Hersh, who first brought the massacre to official attention, to historians George Herring, Marilyn Young, and Harry Summers Jr. to such seasoned authorities on the war as David Halberstam, author of *The Best and the Brightest,* and Robert Jay Lifton, who formulated the concept of traumatic stress disorder. Of particular interest to veterans were the reflections of the writer

Tim O'Brien, himself a combat infantry veteran of the Americal Division in Quang Ngai province, who has dealt with My Lai extensively in his writing, including his most disturbing novel, *In the Lake of the Woods.* Uncannily prophetic of the subsequent revelations by medal-of-honor winner Robert Kerry that he had participated in a mission where civilians were murdered, it concerns the mysterious disappearance of a candidate for the U.S. Senate, an unhinged Vietnam veteran, who may or may not have brutally murdered his spouse and disposed of her corpse at a remote cabin in the North Woods in the wake of his shattering election defeat. The mystery is deepened by the reason for his loss of the election: he has been revealed to have airbrushed his history, including his official army records, so as to eliminate evidence of his presence at the My Lai massacre.

The opening of official diplomatic relations between the United States and the Republic of Vietnam in the last decade has further helped to keep the memory of My Lai alive. The site itself, maintained by the Vietnamese government as a memorial, has become a kind of requisite station of the cross for everyone from returning veterans and journalists to travel writers. More important, new possibilities for historical reporting and documentation now include access to numerous Vietnamese accounts of the massacre, at last supplying in sorrowful detail individual names and life histories to accompany those *Life* magazine photos of three decades ago. Ironically, thirty-five years after the mass killing, individual Vietnamese still have names, faces, families, and village histories while their executioners now fade further and further into old age and common cultural obloquy. At the same time, however, one must remember that such a particular idea of communing with the individual dead is also something very Vietnamese. We have no English word for *xa,* the Vietnamese term that comes closest to village. As Frances Fitzgerald revealed to us in *Fire in the Lake,* the nearest translation would be "the place where people come together to worship the spirits."

As for the American lieutenant whose surname eventually became synonymous with the massacre, he is a short, fat, bald guy in his late fifties. In a recent picture I've seen, he scuttles along like a little old man. I am told he has since grown a gray mustache. It must have the odd effect of some strange theatrical disguise, something he puts on in the morning so that no one will notice he is William Calley. For a long time, as I went through the months of reading and writing it took to produce a text I had decided to call "Calley's Ghost," I wrestled with a strange instinct that told me I would finally have to get closure on all this by tracking him down and finding him, probably at the V. V. Vick Jewelry Store at the Cross Plaza Shopping Mall in Columbus, Georgia, around three hours by car from where I live. It was something I had to do, I kept telling myself. I had to go and see that he existed, that I could actually look at him and remember after all these years that he was real. I had to see Calley and remember that the terrible things he and his platoon did, along with the rest of Task Force Barker, were real.

I did not do that. Perhaps I could have given a nice melodramatic bump to the connection between experience and memory here, an auto-biographical moment at last conflating personal and cultural reflection. For just that reason, I saw the idea finally for what it was: a waste. I did not have enough time left in the life that has been vouchsafed to me since I came home from Vietnam to spend even a day driving somewhere to stalk William Calley. More important, I did not have enough time left in my life to spend a single day away from my family, my friends, and my students, stalking William Calley.

My business was not with Calley in any event. It was with Calley's ghost. To put this another way, the person I was looking for was not William Calley. It was me. If I changed Calley from a specter into a person so much the better. But what I was really trying to find was my way of facing it, this problem of Calley's ghost that I finally share with every other Vietnamese-war veteran who once served in any kind of leadership role with a platoon or company-sized unit in combat. He is forever identified with us, and we are forever identified with him. We can say that he should never have been an officer; that he should never have been given responsibility for a platoon; that he should have received the most severe sentence possible under the law for his crimes; that he should never have been pardoned, let alone by Nixon of all people. Along with Vietnam combatants generally, although we probably do not say it, we also resent the fact that, in public memory, he and others participating in the massacre and cover-up are now considered more or less ordinary veterans, that, as far as anyone knows or cares after all these years, one of them could just as easily be one of us. That, however, is not the thought that really haunts us.

The thought that haunts us forever, of course, is that we could once have been them, participants in a horror that now stands as a byword with Wounded Knee, Lidice, Babi Yar. For our sanity, we say no to that thought. We say no even to *listening* for the whisper that says we could have been part of such a thing. We try not to go back and feel for even the possibility of what Tim O'Brien calls "the sizzle in the blood." It isn't there, we say. It was never there, we tell ourselves: I know I was never, ever, while there, like that. Our parents, wives, children, aunts and uncles, friends and lovers, all want to believe this. We who served in combat want to believe this with all our hearts. Meanwhile, stalking death again, we find ourselves in our fifties and sixties, beginning to get old, partaking of the general invisibility.

Wanting to Be John Balaban

This is a story of parallel lives. The time lines they follow are almost

exactly contemporary. You might call the narrative accounts twinned

moral and political autobiographies. The first is that of the poet John

Balaban. The second is mine. They both center initially on our expe-

rience with the Vietnamese war during an intense period of personal

involvement in the late 1960s. They then turn to the life of writing and

the effort, extending over several decades, to come to an understand-

ing of that experience in terms of both personal memory and cultural

reflection.

In many respects, the two lifelines, as they relate to our particular experience of the war, could not seem more different. On the one hand, Balaban was a conscientious objector to the Vietnam-era military draft who gave up his student deferment to express his opposition to the war and who did alternative service in Vietnam first at the University of Can Tho in the Delta as a teacher of linguistics and later in the regions around Saigon as a medical relief worker for war-injured children. I was U.S. Army lieutenant, with a college ROTC commission, who engaged in combat missions in an armored cavalry unit, mainly between Saigon and the South China Sea, as a platoon leader and later as an executive officer. On the other hand, when we came home, we both found careers as university professors of English. We also, in response to our experience of the Vietnamese war, have written and published widely on the subject—Balaban as a poet, translator, essayist, novelist, and memoirist; me as a critic and interpreter of literary and popular-culture representations of the war. Apace, our lifelines have converged in ways that neither of us might have expected. Literally, this is so.

At a first meeting, during a 1985 Asia Society symposium marking the tenth anniversary of the final American evacuation of Saigon, we formed a friendship that periodic correspondence and reunions have cemented over the years. Intellectually, we also stay close. I read what he writes, and he reads what I write. A long time ago, somehow, we determined that we were making the same journey. On the basis of what we did in Vietnam and on the basis of what happened to us there, we understood that we would spend much of the remainder of our lives trying to make as much sense as we could, both personal and cultural, of that pointless and terrible war. We would talk about what happened to the Americans and the Vietnamese there; we would trace whatever directions we could toward understanding and recovery for both nations; we would never let our country forget what we did there; and we would do our best to keep Americans from ever doing anything like that again.

But what I mainly want to do here, as expressed in my title, is pay homage to a lopsided moral friendship. The real story I want to tell is of two lifelines that, when they have converged, have always found one, my own, greatly enlarged at its intersection with the other, his. Call my titling what you will: a tribute to the power of moral example, a testament of modest hope concerning the possibility of moral education, or maybe just a fatuous wish. I am not so foolish as to think we can live lives other than the ones we are dealt. I can't go back and change the terms of political consciousness—or, in my case, the lack thereof—whereby I was led to make the callow and deeply conventional choices that took me to Vietnam as an American soldier any more than I can change those whereby John Balaban was led to make the deeply principled choices that took him to Vietnam as a conscientious objector and relief worker. I can't change what either of us did there. I can't change the years I spent after the war getting over it in solitude and silence any more than I can change his unbroken years of commitment to speaking out about ending the horror.

At the same time, I would like to think that a kind of moral wishing here may in some small way have come true. I am, as a result of our friendship, at least less myself where I am now more like him. Accordingly, I can tell a moral fable by recounting his story and my story about a time when we were both young and put in the position to make certain choices about our country and our participation in its policies and its history. I can write this, if nothing else, in testimony to my hope that other Americans someday, especially young people, when they are forced to make choices about peace and war, about the uses of U.S. political and military power in the world, can be granted the political awareness to know that they have choices, and that, when they make them, they ought to understand why.

Here, then, are the stories.

In spring 1967, as part of a Harvard University visit made by Secretary of Defense Robert McNamara to meet with undergraduate classes at Harvard's new John F. Kennedy School of Public Policy, John Balaban, a graduate student in literature, walking back to his apartment after a long afternoon in the library, found himself part of a crowd of anti–Vietnam War demonstrators who trapped the defense secretary in his car behind Lowell House. Balaban, the first member of his Romanian immigrant family to receive a college degree, had also won a prestigious Woodrow Wilson graduate fellowship. Although he had been actively involved in antiwar politics as an undergraduate at Penn State and before that in the civil rights movement, at Harvard he had spent most of his time heavily invested in his new program of advanced studies. Something changed that day in 1967 not simply to put him back into the antiwar struggle for good but to effect a political radicalization that would change the course of his life forever. It was McNamara's "astounding arrogance," he would recall later, "and his refusal to acknowledge American responsibility for civilian casualties—or even that *there were* significant numbers of civilian casualties"—that made him choose to become, as he puts it, the patriotic enemy of his own government. To make the point clear—that he was in fact acting "in the spirit of the Federalist Papers," wherein a citizen is encouraged to take action when his government becomes "odious"—he officially surrendered his student deferment, petitioned his draft board to have him reclassified as a conscientious objector, and volunteered to go to Vietnam to do his alternative service.

Balaban's experiences there were recorded in a memoir, *Remembering Heaven's Face.* He taught linguistics until his university was bombed during the 1968 Tet Offensive. After a brief convalescence in the United States following his wounding during the battle for Can Tho, he returned to Vietnam to work with severely war-injured children—"a boy whose chin was melted to his chest by a white phosphorus shell, a teen-aged girl who had been scalped in a canal by propeller blades, a 3-year old girl shot through the face, a little boy who had so many gunshot wounds he was dying of protein loss, a boy deafened and blinded by a hand grenade, another little boy, and orphan, who had touched his tongue to a Dragon's Jaw landmine that blew away his lower face, etc." Meanwhile, he discovered a language and a culture, and he came to love a people. After being released from his conscientious-objector obligation in 1969—in a letter from Lewis Hershey, no less—and, ironically, having spent two years in Vietnam, as opposed to the standard one-year military tour, he returned once more to the war zone a year later, this time as a writer. Eventually joined by his wife, he roamed the country, collecting the folk poems called ca dao, which he would eventually publish in translation.

When Balaban came home, he quickly became a distinguished poet in his own right. His first book, *After Our War,* won the Lamont Prize, one of the most prestigious awards in American poetry. Other volumes over the years continued to earn him major recognition. Eventually the ca dao collections became a book, as did more recently, under the title of *Spring Essence,* translations of the work of Ho Xuan Huong, an eighteenth-century Vietnamese woman of astonishing poetic eroticism and political wit. In his academic career, Balaban advanced through the ranks to professor at Pennsylvania State University before going on to direct the program in creative writing and translation at the University of Miami and, most recently, to become poet in residence at North Carolina State University. Anthologies and surveys, as well as books and numerous scholarly articles, attest to his status as one of the major Vietnamese-war poets of his generation, on one hand ranked with war veterans, such as W. D. Ehrhart, Bruce Weigl, and Yusef Komunyakaa, and on the other with major poets of the anti-Vietnamese-war literary canon, including Alan Ginsberg, Robert Lowell, Robert Bly, Galway Kinnell, and Denise Levertov.

In spring 1967, I too was a graduate student and likewise the winner of a Woodrow Wilson fellowship, finishing a master's degree in English, albeit far to the south at Thomas Jefferson's University of Virginia. In comparison to Cambridge, Charlottesville was a moral and ideological world away. It wasn't so much that anyone at the university was in favor of the war. There was just this academic atmosphere of almost willful incomprehension. I can't remember anyone I knew talking about it much, let alone getting into a political argument over it. One imagines it would have been deemed ungentlemanly. Nor can I remember a single anti-war meeting or public demonstration. To compound matters, I could not have been more politically or intellectually unaware at the time. People in Charlottesville still wore jackets and ties to class—it was a university tradition—although a few graduate students in my cohort were flaunting beards and flannel shirts in a kind of trendy bohemianism. I was on a prestigious fellowship that I had been pressured into applying for by my undergraduate mentors and had won in spite of myself—for the final cut, I badly overslept, drove two hours like a maniac, with a blistering hangover, and barely managed to make a late-morning interview. (For the record, Balaban has an analogous interview story. "I arrived early," he writes, "was incredibly ill at ease, went down to the hotel bar, and had a boilermaker [2, actually], realized I was now *late,* and barely managed to get upstairs for the interview on time. I smelled of whiskey and beer.")

I was young and married, like most of my classmates, to someone I had met and dated during college. A barely overgrown undergraduate, completely directionless, I walked the path of preppy conventionality.

I also had a military obligation, having been commissioned a second lieutenant in the armor branch of the U.S. Army out of college at Davidson in North Carolina but granted a delay from entering into active duty because of what even the government seemed to consider the intellectual heft and importance of the Woodrow Wilson. Even the reserve officer's commission was a story of how clueless I was. Originally I had endured two years of freshman and sophomore ROTC, required under some obscure land-grant requirement at my otherwise deeply elitist private undergraduate school, as a member of a ragtag military marching band—its members, like me, dragooned from the ranks of hapless former high-school musicians foolish enough to have included such a qualification on their admissions records. Meanwhile, having entered school as a premed—what bright young idealist didn't in those days?—I was having the typical romantic identity crisis. Sophomores aren't called sophomoric for nothing. Attracted to English, I had become the kind of vaguely literary undergraduate who takes creative-writing classes and thinks someday he might have a novel in him. I debated changing majors, for the moment drifting along on a double academic track as an excuse for not making up my mind. Oddly, I also drifted into advanced ROTC. There was money in it. You were paid for both semesters of your junior and senior years but only had to attend classes and drills during one. A war was heating up in Vietnam. I can't remember thinking very much about whether I'd have to go. At least I would be an officer. For the English major envisioning a senior thesis on the World War I literary expatriates, Hemingway, Fitzgerald, Dos Passos, E. E. Cummings, and the like, war held the vague promise of material. Who had even written a good novel, after all, without the big *experience?* And then there were the more recent examples of James Jones, Norman Mailer, Herman Wouk, Leon Uris, and Irwin Shaw. Who could be said to have had the experience of an American generation without its including an American war?

est notion that I could easily have pursued a Ph.D. and probably taught out my military hitch at West Point, as did a contemporary of the era, the now infamous historian Joseph Ellis? I never asked. Consulting no one, I gave up my induction-deferred status and wrote a letter to the Department of Defense saying that I was ready to go on active duty. Even the army seems to have been shocked that I was presenting myself for active service. I was informed that an open slot couldn't be found for me in the Armor Officer's Basic Course, a mandatory training program of several months' duration, until nearly a year later, in May 1968. I was to find other work.

A young husband, with a spouse finishing her undergraduate degree, I spent a summer working in a children's shoe store. I then got a job teaching high-school English for the year, albeit with the understanding that I would be leaving a month early. In February I watched Lyndon Johnson's surprise announcement on television that he was not running for another term as president. A military reprieve may have crossed my mind, but it took no more hold on my understanding of the reality of the war than any other part of the news in those days. As wrapped up as I was in my high-school teaching—without an iota of professional preparation or experience, I had been thrust into a total 1960s educational integration laboratory, a new high school in Greensboro, North Carolina, built on the fault line between the blue-collar white part of town and the black ghetto—I can't recall that even news of the Tet Offensive, for example, made much of an impression on me. Martin Luther King's assassination was another story. But even then I didn't make the connection between the fire in the streets over race and the anger of the antiwar movement that would ignite Chicago and other places during that year's political campaigns.

Meanwhile, my orders to report arrived. In a military code unknown to me, they already specified what the army called an MOS—a military occupational specialty. If you knew how to read the administrative cipher, my working destiny was identifiable as 1204—armored cavalry reconnaissance platoon leader. The more common one for entering officers in my branch was 1203—tank platoon leader. 1203 meant you were probably going to Germany, to one of the big tank divisions. 1204 meant that you were almost certainly going to Vietnam. The handwriting was on the wall and everywhere else.

I still didn't believe it, I suppose. Assigned after the basic course to troop duty with the Sixth Armored Cavalry, an old-line regiment quartered at Fort Meade, Maryland, I prepared for riot-control duty for the military district of Washington while I continued with my conventional field training. Tet may have gone off in Vietnam, but at home was the incendiary 1968 summer of race, with riots, triggered by the King and Kennedy assassinations, as well as a succession of other events, in cities across the nation. My unit, depending on which of the three squadrons, or battalion-sized units, had the highest readiness designation, was on two-, four-, or six-hour alert. A flotilla of armored vehicles was loaded on flatcars at a railhead in suburban Maryland. If the city had gone up again, as it had in April, troops riding armored personnel carriers and tanks would have been on K Street in two hours.

Aside from a few weeks of tank firing and other big field exercises in Virginia, the long period of alert status must have helped me cultivate resignation. Even though I had not officially received the expected orders for Vietnam, in retrospect, riot duty actually rehearsed the emotional patterns of combat: long, long periods of tense vigilance, punctuated by sudden alarms, musters, and troop movements. All that was missing was the live ammunition. And we had that loaded in trucks riding with the tanks and APCs. Actually, in the case of the Nixon inauguration, where the regiment was detailed to perimeter security, we also had it in the basement of the U.S. Capitol, right next to row upon row of racked weapons, disposed at the ready for squad and platoon. In field-training stints, I tried to learn what I could of Vietnam from people who had been there—NCOs, enlisted combat veterans serving out a few last months, the troop executive officer, an infantry first lieutenant still recovering from being shot on the first day of Tet. When my Vietnam orders came, assigning me to the Ninetieth Replacement Detachment at Long Binh, they could not have been more clear about my ultimate fate. They said USARV. U.S. Army, Vietnam. Long Binh. To that end, I was not to be an "advisor." My assignment would be with an American combat unit in the field. I got three miserable weeks at a jungle-operations training course in Panama. The entire process became a blur. Even when I wound up in the Vietnam jungle of III Corps around Saigon leading an armored cavalry platoon, I could never quite think of it as really happening to me. Combat duty in the field mercifully spared me—and, more importantly, the people in my platoon—anything too big to handle, given my limited experience. Service as the troop executive officer, allegedly safer duty, ironically brought me into my heaviest combat, as well as into long months of confrontation with racial strife and disintegrating morale as the army fell into disarray.

When I came home I was numb. I returned to graduate school because I couldn't think of anything else to do. I got divorced. I lived in seclusion, a good bit of the time in places in the country. I anesthetized myself daily with alcohol, beginning a long marriage with booze that I would break only with a treatment program nearly two decades later and a subsequent commitment to abstinence. I barnstormed through a long series of relationships with women, occasional pretenses of serious commitment punctuated by boozy sexual adventuring. I stayed away from people generally. Certainly I stayed away from the war. I knew a couple of vets. One was a West Pointer, an artillery captain, studying for a master's so that he could teach at the academy. Another, in a garish coincidence, was a former artillery forward observer, whose command group I had picked up on my tracks after the group's infantry company had gotten pinned down and shot up in a bunker complex near Xuan Loc. I wrote a dissertation, on colonial and classic American literature, everything before 1865, which carried me into academe on a groundswell of awakening interest in early American studies. I got a good job at a flagship state university and settled down to teaching American literature and making a research career on the likes of Benjamin Franklin and Washington Irving, William Bradford and Charles Brockden Brown.

I read nothing about the war. The first thing I got handed that had anything to do with Vietnam was ironically David Morrell's novel *First Blood,* the origin of the Rambo saga. I read it because it was recommended by a smart, beautiful graduate student I was in love with. It got me started. Not long after, I read part of Ron Kovic's *Born on the Fourth of*

July when it came out in *Playboy.* I called Chicago to find out more about him. Other remarkable memoirs appeared, most notably Tim O'Brien's *If I Die in a Combat Zone* and Philip Caputo's *A Rumor of War.* I started looking around: the university library, the public library, chain book-stores, paperback buy-and-swaps. I found strange early novels: William Eastlake's *The Bamboo Bed,* Victor Kolpacoff's *The Prisoners of Quai Dong,* Daniel Ford's *Incident at Muc Wa.* I discovered that David Halberstam had written a novel, still one of the best to come from the war, *One Very Hot Day.* Others I found, among the earliest produced by actual veteran-authors, included Josiah Bunting's *The Lionheads* and Charles Durden's *No Bugles, No Drums.* An antiwar veterans' collective called the First Casualty Press published volumes of poetry and short fiction in-cluding *Free Fire Zone* and *Winning Hearts and Minds.* A collection of po-ems by an army veteran, Michael Casey's *Obscenities,* won the Yale Prize for Younger Poets. On Broadway, considerable attention was paid to plays such as *The Basic Training of Pavlo Hummel* and *Sticks and Bones* by David Rabe, also a veteran of the war. While doing my duty as an early Americanist, publishing in scholarly journals on Franklin, Crèvecoeur, Melville, Clemens, and the like, I wrote a couple of essays on early nov-els about the Vietnamese war when no one was talking much about it, let alone writing on the subject and suggesting that it had produced a major literature. When they were accepted for publication, I decided that I would write a book surveying the field.

It was while I was casting about for texts by what we then called Vietnam authors–making the easy metonymy, as most of us did in those days, of "Vietnam" as a generic adjective for a fundamentally American experience–that I first heard of John Balaban, and his book *After Our War,* from a friend who had also won the Lamont Prize. Some of the poems in the First Casualty Press collections had certainly moved me, but I was in no way prepared to be as moved and stunned as I was by Balaban's poems. Political anger was armed with the visceral bite of experience. Poetic virtuosity combined with the clarity and fierceness of moral understanding. Here was a soldier poet who had soldiered on the side of conscience, resistance, compassion, care, and humanity. Here was an antiwar poet who cared enough about the Vietnamese to become a translator of their poetry. Speaking both a metaphorical and a literal language of cultural difference, this poet opened me to the understanding of how much suffering and destruction had arisen from my countrymen's stupid, arrogant incomprehension of the power of cultural difference—an arrogance enforced by an infantile energy of massive destructiveness. I had experienced this view of the Vietnamese and the Americans in Vietnam only in rare texts such as Frances Fitzgerald's *Fire in the Lake* and Gloria Emerson's *Winners and Losers.* Now I found it in a poetry of the highest order of cultural achievement. I had found, I truly believed at the time and continue to believe now, the great poet of the war.

Of the poems over my life that have dazed me into awareness, I can but assemble here a handful of representative fragments.

From "Along the Mekong"

>   But what if I said,
> Simply suggested, that all this blood fleck,
> muscle rot, earth root and earth leaf, scraps
> of glittery scales, fine white grains, fast talk,
> gut grime, crab claws, sweetest smells
> —Said: a human self; a mirror held up before.

From "Graveyard at Bald Eagle Ridge"

> Looking out, the dead—the Shirks,
> Browns, Gingerys, and Rines—
> find their children green-haired,
> socket blind, and lying beside them.
> In this year of our Lord, 1969,
> a sparse generation tills the land.

From "Words for my Daughter"

> If you're reading this, I hope you will think,
> Well, my dad had it rough as a kid, so what?

If you're reading this, you can read the news
and you know that children suffer worse.

Worse for me is a cloud of memories
still drifting off the South China Sea,
like the 9-year-old boy, naked and lacerated,
thrashing in his pee on a steel operating table
and yelling, *"Dau, Dau,"* while I, trying to translate
in the mayhem of Tet for surgeons who didn't know
who this boy was or what happened to him, kept asking
"Where? Where's the pain?" until a surgeon
said, "Forget it, His ears are blown."

My memory of the war, however, turns primarily on two poems—
actually, two poems that are same poem, the one fierce, horrific poem
of the war that keeps rewriting itself.

From "Carcanet: After Our War"

Spontaneous Generation: the Bore-Flies sang,
"Every wound has two lips, so give us a kiss."
Then a two-headed cow jumped over the moon,
kicked over its lantern. Fire caught Straw.
The cow burst like a 500-lb. Bomb. Everyone
came running—all the old folks—Slit Eye
and Spilled Guts, Fried Face and little Missy Stumps.
They plaited a daisy chain. This necklace. For you.

From "After Our War"

So, now, one can sometimes see a friend or a famous man talking
with an extra pair of lips glued and yammering on his cheek,
and this is why handshakes are often unpleasant,
why it is better, sometimes, not to look another in the eye,
why, at your daughter's breast thickens a hard keloidal scar.
After the war, with such Cheshire cats grinning in our trees,

will the ancient tales still tell us new truths?
Will the myriad world surrender new metaphor?
After our war, how will love speak?

Meanwhile, on an especially bad day after the war, there can also seem at least the chastened promise of a modest hope:

From "In Celebration of Spring"

Swear by the locust, by dragonflies on ferns,
by the minnow's flash, the tremble of a breast,
by the new earth spongy under our feet:
that as we grow old, we will not grow evil,
that although our garden seeps with sewage,
and our elders think it's up for auction—swear
by this dazzle that does not wish to leave us—
that we will be keepers of a garden, nonetheless.

I keep many things by John Balaban close to me: an early article of wry self-assessment he once sent me called "Doing Good"; a beautiful, eloquent documentary volume with the photographer Geoffrey Clifford, *Vietnam: The Land We Never Knew;* the aforementioned memoir, *Remembering Heaven's Face*—to my thinking one of the great veteran-autobiographies of the Vietnamese war, ranking with those of Philip Caputo, Ron Kovic, Tim O'Brien, if not one of the great ones of all time, right there with Robert Graves, Vera Brittain, and Siegfried Sassoon. As a work of testimony on the Vietnamese and Americans in Vietnam, it is surely of a stature with Frances Fitzgerald's *Fire in the Lake.* From the latter, for instance, we find this trenchant encapsulation of the Vietnamese worldview: "More than a 'religion' in any western sense, it was the authority for, and the confirmation of, an entire way of life—an agriculture, a social structure, a political system." Here is the phrasing of the analogous discovery made by Balaban in the Vietnamese countryside, a characteristic merging of the political and the poetic: "I began to see that Vietnamese lives were lived not on a Spenglerian trash heap of history but, rather, in a dense spiritual and physical continuum in which ancestors guided them and history reflected destinies cast in heaven." Characteristic of John Balaban is that he would subtitled *Remembering Heaven's Face,* without apology, *A Moral Witness in Vietnam.* For John Balaban, only one kind of witness is possible in the world, and that is moral witness.

I do not want to get too solemn about this. John Balaban, for one, would find it morally pretentious. Many of the wisest passages in his autobiographical texts involve great moments of moral self-deflation. There is his incredible disappointment, recorded in the opening chapter of *Remembering Heaven's Face,* that he does not get to give a diligently rehearsed politico-religious lecture to his draft board. "The hearing was about as long as McNamara's baiting of the crowd outside Lowell House," he writes. "I was crushed. I had prepared answers regarding the sanctity of life. I was ready to state that the supreme Deity, which the Selective Service Act required me to believe in, was a kind of goodly energy permeating the universe. I was ready to quote Martin Luther King, Mahatma Gandhi, and George Fox's declaration of 1660 to Charles II ('we utterly deny all outward wars and strife'), but they didn't ask me anything except if I would agree to serve my alternative service in Vietnam." There is likewise, in "Story" from *Locusts at the Edge of Summer,* a 1997 mixture of new and selected poems, the record of the westward-faring singer of tales, the hitchhiker poet earnestly taking in the echt-narrative of a great American truck driver.

"What about your kids?" I asked. "What do they do?"
"My daughter runs our store. My son is dead."
He studied a distant peak and didn't continue.
"What did he die of?"

                    "He died of suicide.
No, that's not right . . . Nixon killed him.
My son was a sweet kid, hated guns and violence
and then, during that fucking war, he hijacked a plane
and flew it to Cuba. He shot himself in Havana."

He watched the peak, then grinned and said,
"Brave little fucker wasn't he?"

Thus, in putting John Balaban's life next to mine after our war, I find with relief that, if he remains a role model, a kind of political gold standard, he wisely gives no quarter to moral or literary self-dramatization. That being acknowledged, whatever serious Vietnamese-war veteranitis is, he still has a lifetime case of it and I do too. There is plenty to go around. There is survivor guilt. There is complicity guilt. There are all the amorphous, inexplicable, dark days and dark nights that remain the portion of a lot of us who just live with the war every minute of our lives. In a phrase brought into ironic currency by high-profile journalistic figures such as Christopher Buckley and James Fallows, there is now even the "Viet guilt" of a generational cohort who *didn't go*. More recently, considerable attention has been devoted to the Vietnam wannabe business, most notably via the scandal provoked by revelations that Pulitzer Prize–winning historian Joseph Ellis regularly salted his lectures with completely falsified tales of in-country combat experience. Meanwhile, on the other side of memory and regret are the scourings of the VA wards, the PTSD counseling groups, and the alcohol and drug treatment programs. Somewhere keeping company with the father of the kid in Cuba is that graduate student of mine whose father shot himself on the thirtieth anniversary of the Tet Offensive. He left behind a photo of himself and a buddy, with a cryptic inscription about loyalty and rescue suggesting that he owed somebody a life.

If a profile exists of whatever there is in me of Viet second-guessing, as one might call it, it probably corresponds to the political awareness of middle-American retrospection I find in another contemporary, Tim O'Brien. How I could have possibly accepted service in the Vietnam-era army, let alone served in combat in a war that was by every standard of international law undeclared and immoral? "I was a coward," a character in one of his stories says. "I went to the war." If only. The words I cite appear in a story about a draftee, on orders to Vietnam, on a lake in northern Michigan, looking across at the Canadian border, trying one last time to decide what to do. I can't even claim that modicum of awareness, or the awareness of the O'Brien character in *If I Die in a Combat Zone,* who, after a feckless evening of trying to find a University of Washington sorority girl to go out with him on his last night in the States, almost deserts before catching the plane. I was not even *that kind* of coward. I felt no moral struggle. I just went, for reasons that seem as muddled today as they were then, reasons that because of that muddling, in retrospect, were reprehensible.

I can say, along with Tim O'Brien, that "I grew out of one war and into another . . . the offspring of the great campaign of the tyrants of the 1940s." I can say that I was the kind of model high-school kid who came within an ace of getting a service-academy appointment and who, once there, would undoubtedly have seen the whole Duty-Honor-Country thing through with as much earnest American passion as I embraced Ernest Hemingway and F. Scott Fitzgerald as a college English major. But can I say I just went? Even worse, can I say that I went to a war out of curiosity? About war? About my ability to perform as a military officer in battle? About extreme experience? Because I thought someday I would write about it? Because I thought I might be a writer, and for a writer, especially an American male, war is the great crucible of American manhood, the ultimate material? Could I have known that I would wind up writing about people writing about war, making a big academic reputation, pretty good money for an English teacher, a reduced course load for writing, invitations to come and be a big-shot lecturer?

At the very least, I get to read John Balaban on salary. I also get to go somewhere every so often where John Balaban is going to be. I get to hear him read from his texts of moral witness, for which he still does not apologize. At the same time I watch him humbly interact with Americans who come to hear him—academics, leftover antiwar activists, messed-up vets—as well as with Vietnamese who are invariably a part of the gathering. The last time we were together, he read from the *Spring Essence* translations. He did the best he could with the pronunciation, he said, the accent, the nuances of political wit and bawdy feminist humor. Then he did something typically John Balaban. He asked a beautiful Vietnamese woman of roughly our age to read the last selection. He knew where the voice belonged—with a language, a poetry, a people, a culture.

He also exercises his own distinctly more assertive opinions about the relationship between a radical poetics and an activist poetics. If we are going to make choices about peace and war, he says everywhere he gets a chance, let us do so from a position of informed knowledge about cultural difference. The son of immigrant Romanians who fell in with Quakers on his way to spending a lifetime immersing himself in Vietnamese language and culture, John Balaban tells us that the duty of every citizen—whether of a country or of a world—is to keep him- or herself politically aware and to encourage others to be as well. We have to resist any political idea that requires uncritical acceptance. We have to talk back to our government when it tries to talk us into such ideas. If necessary, we have to find a position of principled opposition when it does something odious.

This is where wanting to be John Balaban, at least for someone like me, can still be something other than a fatuous wish. I cannot change who I was as a young person or what I did as a consequence in making decisions about peace and war. However, I have a daughter about to grow into the age I was when I made my choices about my country and the war; I have students almost exactly that age passing through my classes by the hundreds each year; I have people who read what I write. And I do, finally, have myself. None of us may have the power to change how we have become who we are, but every one of us has the power of choosing who we want to be.

John Balaban wrote his own moral epitaph all the way back during Tet in Can Tho. With a characteristic mixture of fatal resignation and comic drama, he says he decided to carry it in his rear hip pocket. If he got hit in the ass, he reasoned, the note would be least likely to get covered up with blood.

The story and the epitaph are as good now as they were then. The note reads:

TO WHOM IT MAY CONCERN:
"I, John Balaban, have no regrets for what I have done. I wish the world well. Stop the goddamn war."

The Years

Forty years ago, Bernard Fall published an interview with Ho Chi Minh that began with some of the North Vietnamese leader's observations on an impending war between the People's Republic of Vietnam and the United States of America. "It took us eight years of bitter fighting to defeat you French in Indochina," he said. "Now the South Vietnamese regime of Ngo Dinh Diem is well armed and helped by ten thousand Americans. The Americans are much stronger than the French, though they know us less well. It may perhaps take ten years to do it, but our heroic compatriots in the South will defeat them in the end." He paused. "I think the Americans greatly underestimate the determination of the

Vietnamese people. The Vietnamese people always have shown great determination when they were faced with a foreign invader."

In a PBS retrospective televised last spring, a Vietnamese veteran reflected on his nation's ultimately victorious struggle in what is now called there the American War and spoke as simply. "We fought the Chinese for a thousand years," he said. "We fought the French for a hundred years. You were here for ten years. You are a blip in this history of a proud nation."

For a recent assembly at her school commemorating the anniversary of the September 11, 2001, terrorist attacks, my nine-year-old daughter insisted on completing her red, white, and blue outfit with the unit crest of my infantry brigade from Vietnam. Somebody had given it to me at a reunion ten or fifteen years earlier. I threw it in a box, where my daughter found it, thought it was pretty, and made it part of her pin collection. Ten or fifteen years earlier, it took everything a bunch of my old army friends could do to get me to a unit reunion. Today my daughter wears an emblem of her father's long-ago military service in Vietnam while she grows up in an America that now, as the nation decidedly did not as recently as ten or fifteen years ago, finds such service worthy of commemoration and even honor.

I wish I could find a lesson about memory and acceptance embedded in this chronological anecdote. A nice one might go something like this: If the Vietnamese, as is their custom, tend to think in centuries and millennia, we at least are beginning to think in generations. But I can't find such a lesson. All I can think of is the years. It is now about fifty years since the end of the French War. It is over thirty-five years since the Tet Offensive. It is nearly as long since I served with an armored cavalry unit in the jungles of III Corps. It is now more than twenty-five years since the last U.S. helicopter lifted off from Saigon. We have had thousands of books, hundreds of movies, God knows how many articles, reviews, editorials, and documentaries, and all I can think about is the ease, over a relatively short space of years, with which Americans have again proven capable of making history—as in, oh yes, but that's history—out of a war in which the nearly incomprehensible violence and destruction visited by us upon a small Asian nation has been equaled only by the ignominy of our failure to this day to come to terms with what we did there.

I hear a lot of talk about the healing of America. Endless accounts exist about the astonishing generosity and forgiveness displayed by the Vietnamese to Americans, including many veterans, who now travel there. Notable policy texts in recent years have suggested that Vietnam was, if not a good war, a necessary war, a war in which Americans may have hastened the breakdown of world communism. Some people have expressed the hope that the war may have taught us something about the relationship between national power and geopolitical responsibility. But the years will take care of this. Actually, the work of historical amnesia here is nearly finished even as I write. Nobody does the years better than Americans. El Salvador may have been Spanish for Vietnam. But after Grenada, Panama, Haiti, Kuwait, Bosnia, Somalia, and Afghanistan, Iraq has basically turned out to be American for Son of Desert Storm, this time without the United Nations and, save the British, minus the support of much of an international coalition.

As a veteran and a teacher and writer who has spent much of his career talking about the war and American memory, I must admit to having once possessed a certain hopefulness that things would not turn out this way. It seemed to me possible that the pain and waste of the Vietnamese war both as a military debacle and as a source of domestic upheaval unprecedented in the nation's history would come to be remembered by Americans as a version of the fall into history, an end to the myth of national chosenness. That certainly seemed to be the claim of a body of literature that had generated numerous best-sellers and on several occasions had won both the Pulitzer Prize and the National Book Award—works as diverse and celebrated as David Halberstam's *The Best and the Brightest,* Frances Fitzgerald's *Fire in the Lake,* Gloria Emerson's *Winners and Losers,* Michael Herr's *Dispatches,* Tim O'Brien's *Going after Cacciato,* Larry Heinemann's *Paco's Story,* and Neil Sheehan's *A Bright Shining Lie.* On numerous occasions I advanced such an argument in print, winning in the process my own share of recognition and reward. Now I see that I have committed a customary academic mistake. I have confused my reading and writing and thinking with the way the world works.

In March 2002, I went to a movie theater to see *We Were Soldiers,* depicting the large-scale battles of late 1965 between the U.S. First Air Cavalry Division and several regiments of North Vietnamese regulars in the ghostly, rugged Central Highlands of Vietnam—the first engagement of the war between major American forces and opposing communist formations. I went by myself, because I didn't know how I would react. I was ready to take offense, especially with all the drumbeating about how this was the *Saving Private Ryan* of Vietnam, the great post-9/11 hymn to the boys of 1965 saved for release until after the dust of the 2001 terrorist attacks had cleared. (Albeit sufficiently patriotic, it had apparently been deemed for the moment too graphic in the amount of American death.) "Let's roll," I imagined some handsome, fresh-faced squad leader saying to his boyish cohorts, and of course Mel Gibson was going to play the lead role of an American lieutenant colonel, with Sam Elliot as his crusty sergeant major. Oh boy, I thought, *Braveheart* and *Lonesome Dove* do the Ia Drang.

Instead, for all the nonstop Hollywood combat carnage, I found an austere dignity in the presentation. Angry at myself for being swindled by emotion, I shed some silent tears for the defenders of LZ X-Ray at the end. Those tears had to do, I believe, not so much with the movie as with the recognition it provoked about how young we once were back in the war of the battalions and brigades. That is in fact the title of the book by Harold G. Moore and Joseph L. Galloway from which the movie was adapted: *We Were Soldiers Once . . . And Young.*

I found I couldn't get angry about a movie that was half the book and half the battle totally ignoring a whole other battalion of roughly four hundred men who had marched out of X-Ray and got shot to shit in a landing zone a few kilometers away. Moore's losses had been 79 men killed and 121 wounded. Such bloodletting alone had been enough to invoke comparisons with Custer. The battle at the other LZ, Albany, was an absolute catastrophe, with a battalion of the same number suffering 121 killed, 151 wounded, and 4 missing—or roughly 75 percent casualties.

To put this into perspective, a figure frequently cited as one of the most disastrous instances of unit annihilation in the American Civil War is the 82 percent casualty rate suffered by the First Minnesota Regiment on the second day at Gettysburg. The Dieppe Raid, rightly considered one of the great allied bloodlettings of World War II, resulted in 65 percent casualties to the Canadians who made the assault. The same figure is usually applied to the July 1, 1916, British slaughter on the first day of the Battle of the Somme. I tried to think this through. It took my going to an academic conference, of all places, to get myself disabused of such absent reflection. There, a fellow speaker reminded me that movies are made for eighteen-year-olds who go to Cineplexes in New Jersey. Keeping that in mind has been helpful.

During summer 2002, I read two new books about the war. One was David Hackworth's *Steel My Soldiers' Hearts,* about his command of a battalion of the Ninth Infantry Division in the Delta during 1969. Much in the spirit of *We Were Soldiers,* it too takes a revisionary look at the infantry war in Vietnam, this time in its later stages. Against the stereotypical vision of a post-Tet 1968 army of drug-addled killers and misfits, it chronicles the shaping up of a dispirited mob of forgotten soldiers in a lost war into a unit that finds a kind of purpose in its military professionalism and unit solidarity and that fights with resolve and discipline against both the shadowy enemy opposing them in the paddy swamp of the Delta and the ticket-punching careerists so frequently committing them to useless, bloody missions. In this respect, it jibes with an important early novel of the war, by another respected military professional, Josiah Bunting's *The Lionheads.* It also tallies with my experience as an armored cavalry officer with an infantry brigade in nearby III Corps during the same period, where the conduct of the members of my platoon gave me an admiration for the common American soldier that I carry with me to this day.

Yet buried in Hackworth's book as well is the alternative scenario that unravels it all—the record of a 1969 conversation in Vietnam between the author and John Paul Vann, the legendary Vietnam soldier-advisor whose life and career, as shown by Neil Sheehan in *A Bright Shining Lie,* can be seen in many ways as a parable of the egregiously failed heroism of the American cause. In the course of the meeting, Vann, a friend of Hackworth's from the old army and from multiple tours in Vietnam, notes ruefully that during the period in question, Hackworth's division commander, Julian Ewell, had not earned his epithet as the Butcher of the Mekong Delta for nothing. Ewell claimed to have killed twenty-two thousand of the enemy in his divisional area of operations in a single year, Vann observes, but his captured-weapons ratio was only two hundred to one. The only reasonable conclusion is that, even allowing for the formidable enemy discipline in not abandoning weapons on the battlefield, the U.S. Ninth Infantry Division, more than a year after the Tet Offensive, and during an alleged process of steady American military disengagement, was killing a horrendous number of Vietnamese civilians.

The second book I read during the summer also concerned bloody events involving Vietnamese civilians in the Delta during 1969. It was former senator Bob Kerrey's memoir, *When I Was a Young Man,* published after a flurry of news reporting and editorializing earlier in the year over revelations that Kerrey, a Vietnamese-war veteran awarded the Congressional Medal of Honor for his service as a Navy SEAL, may have participated during his first mission in the massacre of more than twenty unarmed people, clearly noncombatants. No one denies that the Vietnamese in question—old men, women, and children, residents of a village called Thanh Phong—were killed as part of a botched raid. The conflicting testimony in the case is over how they died. One member has said they were simply executed, shot down in cold blood, to prevent their raising an alarm while the SEAL team tried to escape. Kerrey, along with the remainder of the participants, insisted that the civilians were caught in a mysterious crossfire. Kerrey's version of the incident in the latter form is the one that appears in the book. Although admitting that the printed version differs in some details from his original recounting, he attests in an afterword that he has written to the best of his memory. Interviewed for the television news program *Sixty Minutes,* he stuck to the crossfire story and came off as what a judge would call a credible witness. He did admit further that, for the mission on which the civilians were killed, he had been issued a Bronze Star citation for valor. But he somewhat legalistically insisted that in his conscience, at least, he had refused to accept the award.

I don't know what to think about Kerrey and all the versions of what happened at Thanh Phong given the tricks—revealed on occasion after I've talked with people who were in Vietnam with me—that the war seems to have played on my own memory. I'm not sure he knows what to think anymore either. I must say I am astonished—both regarding the mission in which the civilian killings occurred and the next mission, in which Kerrey lost part of his leg and won the Medal of Honor—at what appears to have been the staggering tactical incompetence of the Navy SEALs, allegedly our most elite fighters. They may have been great at swimming, paddling rubber boats, scaling cliffs, and infiltrating, but at least in these two instances their intelligence was lousy and their plans quickly fell apart. The bottom line, however, is those twenty Vietnamese civilians. Sometimes it seems to me that, increasingly, everywhere I look after all these years, all I see are more civilian Vietnamese bodies.

Two more books came out in fall 2002. One, titled *War Torn* and edited by Gloria Emerson among others, consisted of retrospective attempts by several well-known women correspondents of the era to document their coverage of the American war and its aftermath, frequently involving their concurrent protest of the war and of their second-class journalistic citizenship. Given especially my respect for Emerson—the author of *Winners and Losers* and one of the great pioneering writers of the war—it seemed yet another version of the story just waiting to be read. Instead, I could not have been less compelled. In essay after essay, I now found confirmed what I confess I had been thinking for a long time about journalists period: what REMF bastards they *all* were, civilians to the core, commuters on helicopters, combat war junkies off on a spree. They may have risked their lives—or in the case of the women even struggled against a relentlessly sexist structure of authority, both military and civilian, to get official permission to risk their lives—to cover the war. The GIs they covered, however, stayed there day after day and night after night in the mud, the heat, and the fear, doing what GIs have always done, which is basically eat shit and die. Meanwhile, back in Saigon or Da Nang or Cam Ranh, there the journalists were, male and female alike, drinking and fucking and lying under the air conditioners after they had showered and telexed their pictures and stories back to the States. For all my admiration of the great American journalism that came out of Vietnam, David Halberstam, Gloria Emerson, Neil Sheehan, Michael Herr—even with the latter's *Dispatches,* in many ways to me, still the book that captures so much of the dreadful, frantic energy of the American war—after all these years, it now turned out to be a story that I just couldn't, as the saying goes, relate to.

The other fall book I read about the war, *Heart of a Soldier,* managed, of all things, to connect the 1965 Vietnam combat depicted in *We Were Soldiers* with the events of the September 11, 2001, terrorist attacks on the twin towers of the New York City World Trade Center by centering on the fate of Rick Rescorla, one of the participants in the former who ultimately became one of the victims of the latter. A former First Cavalry officer renowned for his heroism in the Ia Drang battles of Landing Zones X-Ray and Albany, Rescorla died with equal courage more than thirty-five years later while trying to rescue people from the upper floors of one of the towers in the minutes after the attack that would shortly plunge it to the ground. Both ends of the story are more than documentably true. In the Ia Drang, helicoptered in as part of a reinforcement unit, Rescorla had been a bona fide hero of X-Ray. Lifted out with his platoon after that action, he went back into Albany with what was left of them and did it all over. It's a photograph of a grimy, resolute Rescorla at X-Ray, in fact, that emblazons the original cover of the best-selling book *We Were Soldiers Once . . . and Young.* The actions of Rescorla's last heroic moments on earth turn out to be equally well verifiable. Countless people testified to his cool resolve and effectiveness in helping thousands of people to escape, refusing at the last moment his own evacuation so that he could return to the burning upper stories to look for more survivors. As if to cement the uncanny parallels, further included in *Heart of a Soldier* is yet another photograph of Rescorla in action. It is taken inside the burning tower on September 11, 2001. Rick Rescorla stands with a security aide, holding a portable microphone as he calmly instructs people in how to descend from the upper floors of the building.

The book in question involves a number of compelling features about the life of this brave, complex, and interesting man. It recounts a tale of lifelong loyalty and friendship with a fellow former soldier. It also includes an account of autumnal love and marriage. Rick Rescorla's life story turns out to be full of deep human interest, and I was moved by it. But at least as far as the Vietnam part of it is concerned, I am determined to resist sentimentality. Rescorla, it turns out, was a native of Wales, an army OCS graduate with previous military service in the British army in Cyprus and as a colonial police officer in Zimbabwe. In Vietnam, however bravely he may have fought, he was basically a mercenary, a soldier of fortune. Likewise, when he died working in the World Trade Center, he was a director of security for a large investment firm, a corporate cop. Throughout his life, he was exactly what his line of work required him to be. He was a hard man.

As for the book on the journalists, I feel much the same way an old friend, ex–Vietnam marine Bill Ehrhart, does, as documented in his recent writing about his own encounters during and after the war with reporters and correspondents. Looking back at this distance, I don't feel sorry for any of them either, women or men. They can protest all they want about getting the story or telling the truth in the face of official lying. They went to cover the war, as Michael Herr admitted long ago, and the war covered them. The fact remains, as Ehrhart says, regarding his experiences of 1967 at the deadly, beleaguered marine outpost of Con Thien, that "after I left Con Thien, I and the rest of my battalion did not repair to the air-conditioned bar of the Caravelle Hotel, there to drink gin and tonics and tell green reporters how tough it was at Con Thien; we merely took up new positions south of Quang Tri." Robert Capa, Bernard Fall, Larry Burrows, Dickey Chappelle, and a bunch of other really brave and talented people got killed. Sean Flynn's and Dana Stone's bodies are still out there buried somewhere in Cambodia. Tim Page is missing part of his brain. A handsome coffee-table book titled *Requiem* now serves as a memorial to the sacrifice of those who died. Meanwhile, as an ex-marine, Ehrhart still pretty much says it for me too from the grunt's eye view, albeit putting into printed words what we are only supposed to think: "Am I really supposed to give a rat's ass?"

We may truly feel sorry for Bob Kerrey in his present anguish. I do. Every single one of us, I dare say, especially if we had a similar tactical command responsibility in the war, wonders deep inside what we would have done in the circumstances. Kerrey is a manifestly thoughtful person and a dedicated public servant, a man who resigned from a seat in the U.S. Senate he could have probably held indefinitely to begin a late-life career as an educator. He is also clearly tortured, to the point of believing that his mutilated body is a kind of retribution for the events of the Thanh Phong Raid. Let us remember, though, that in Vietnam he too was a hard man, a Navy SEAL, a unit commander in an elite force that prides itself on winnowing out all but born survivors, trained to fight silently and remorselessly to the limits of human endurance. As the navy lieutenant leading the team into the village of Thanh Phong that night, he may have been a lot of things, but he was no wide-eyed kid from Nebraska doing some kind of Henry Fleming–*Red Badge of Courage* number.

As for Hackworth, I admire just about everything he has written over the years as a memoirist and military commentator. He is a think-ing person's soldier. During multiple command assignments in Vietnam, he was a legendary warrior and troop leader, who at the end terminated his career with public pronouncements about the futility of American operational thinking and particularly about the needless butchery of common soldiers at the hands of ticket-punching incompetents seeking professional advancement. In *Steel My Soldiers' Hearts,* he clearly wants to memorialize the bravery and sacrifice of the infantrymen he person-ally led in nearly impossible circumstances during late 1969. Given the similar loyalty I feel and a respect that now borders on reverence for the people who spent a year in the shit with me down around Xuan Loc in 1969, I find it hard not to identify with his wish to honor his troops. At the same time, he still has to know what his old friend and Vietnam cohort John Vann told him that day in the Delta: that, while the men of his battalion may have been conducting themselves with military discipline and restraint, the U.S. infantry brigade and division to which they belonged, as late as 1969, presumably with approval at the highest levels of command, were still padding out the grim statistics of body count by killing unconscionable numbers of noncombatant Vietnamese.

I don't want to sentimentalize anything about this war. It was a war of hard people on both sides. It was savage. It was hateful. It was a war of the patrol, the ambush, the bunker complex, the land mine, the booby trap, the rocket attack. Combat was always a nasty surprise. It was literally take-no-prisoners. Everybody was prepared to live or die, to go down fighting, no in-between. In ground action at least, the idea of being captured never entered an American infantryman's mind. Nobody planned to be taken alive, and once the shooting was done, no one expected to see the semblance of a live enemy soldier either.

Meanwhile, lest we become too sappy about the Vietnamese, we should note the current difficulties of Don Duong, the actor who played Mel Gibson's communist opposite number in *We Were Soldiers*. Among the features the movie was praised for was its "human" and "informed" depiction of the opposing NVA soldiers in the events depicted—as opposed to the traditional faceless, black pajama-clad Charlies, the charging AK-47 toting hordes. For his pains, Duong was recently declared "a national traitor" by the official Vietnamese press, with a recommended punishment that he be banned from acting in any movie for ten years. There is also the writer Duong Thu Huong, who spent seven years at the front as part of a traveling entertainment-propaganda troop with communist combat forces. The author of *Novel without a Name,* one of the greatest accounts of the endless terror and deprivation experienced by the common soldier of the North Vietnamese forces fighting in the South, she followed it with *Paradise of the Blind,* a novel critical of the postwar regime. She now lives in internal exile, forbidden to leave Vietnam. In the country where she fought for independence as commander of a youth brigade of forty members, three of whom survived, her works are banned.

In fact, the last thing we want to do is sentimentalize the Vietnamese. They don't need us. They are a hard people. We may be moved by the astonishing generosity they show to Americans, their former enemies, the national spirit of forgive and forget. Well, forget that. They can afford it, because they paid so much for it: more than a decade of indiscriminate artillery and bombing; defoliation of enormous tracts of forest, with flotillas of bulldozers and burning and chemical agents; long-term environmental damage, including pollution and birth defects; assassination programs; mass relocations and resettlements to refugee camps and urban slums. We turned a blind eye as their leaders grew rich and fat on their corruption and our money, as we turned their men into cripples and beggars, their women into prostitutes, and their children into con artists and pimps. Meanwhile, we dropped eight million tons of bombs on the country—more than twice the total expended in the European and Pacific theaters in World War II. We dropped half of it on South Vietnam. And the better part of that, along with virtually unlimited artillery fire and air-to-ground gunfire and rocketry, seems to have landed on the people we were supposedly trying to protect, with most of them noncombatants. Recording his work as a conscientious objector with nonmilitary Vietnamese casualties of the war, John Balaban notes in a recent interview, "almost every child I encountered had been wounded by Americans or American firepower." His informed figures on overall civilian deaths and injuries suggest that American military forces were responsible for "100,000 *South* Vietnamese casualties per year of our ten-year war, most of whom were children under 16."

For their part, the North Vietnamese were invaders. Following the international windings of the Ho Chi Minh Trail, they carried out mass infiltrations of soldiers, weaponry, and supplies in the South and fought from sanctuaries across the border in Laos and Cambodia. In Hanoi and elsewhere, they mercilessly tortured and killed American POWs. In the South, the NLF were terrorists, torturing and killing countless numbers of their own people. Meanwhile, even as they heralded their great brotherly battles of liberation, Vietnamese communists North and South did not spare each other. The leadership in the North, mistrusting the National Liberation Force from its rise in the South during the early 1960s, did not blink at its utter decimation in the Tet Offensive. Rather, they seized the opportunity to replace major figures killed in the countrywide assault with northern cadres so as to make ideological solidarity less of a problem after eventual reunification. As to deaths of average, noncombatant Vietnamese, they planned and executed campaigns guaranteed to result in civilian casualties and then looked on with a grisly resoluteness bordering on Stalinesque cynicism, betting–quite correctly–that the Americans would be the first to sicken and turn away in shame from the killing.

Such, precisely, was the meaning of Tet, realized Tobias Wolff, author of *In Pharaoh's Army*, a special-forces lieutenant serving in the Delta, as he surveyed the bodies splayed out in the destroyed streets of My Tho. More than anything else, Tet had finished the Americans for good, he saw, although only a few people saw exactly how. As the communists had forced the South Vietnamese regime to return terror for terror, repression for repression, so they also would now force the Americans to return plain killing for plain killing. "As a military project, Tet failed," wrote Wolff; "as a lesson it succeeded. The VC came into My Tho and all the other towns knowing what would happen. They knew that once they were among the people we would abandon our pretense of distinguishing between them. We would kill them all to get at one. In this way they taught the people that we did not love them and would not protect them; that for all our talk of partnership and brotherhood we disliked and mistrusted them, and that we would kill every last one of them to save our own skins. To believe otherwise was self-deception."

And that was exactly how it worked out. We know with some accuracy how many of our own people we lost before we withdrew. The number was around fifty-eight thousand–about the same, curiously, as that estimated by the French for their own forces. We will never really know how many Vietnamese we killed, nor will the French before us. Estimates for the American war alone run between two and four million, to which we might compare, for instance, the total of three million Japanese military and civilian deaths recorded in World War II. In the end, we simply did not know how to kill enough of them to make them quit fighting us: a very serious policy consideration in the final decision to withdraw seems to have been that our military killing power would never exceed the annual birthrate of North Vietnam. So we gave up and went home.

The number of Vietnamese killed is now mainly what I think of when I have late thoughts on an old war. Of course, I also think about the Americans who fought and gave so much for each other, especially the people I knew and served with. It still seems oddly quaint and melodramatic to me after all these years to turn back in contemplation of terms I would have certainly thought foolish at the time such as "comrades" or "brothers in arms," but that is literally and truly what we were. *Cameradas* are people who learn to share the same four walls. Ours were made of olive-drab metal and impenetrable jungle. We grabbed the odd hour or two of sleep huddled up together in our stinking fatigues and dripping ponchos while we trusted others of our number to stay awake and watch over us; we went out every day and every night to do close combat with a clearly defined, highly disciplined, and extraordinarily skilled military enemy; we smoked wet cigarettes, ate lousy food, and were ready to die for each other. The fact remains that I spent the worst year of my life with many of the best people I will ever know. The word "brothers" does not even begin to describe how close some of us got to each other. To this day I can name every single one of my track commanders from First Platoon, Delta Troop, Seventeenth Armored Cavalry, and most of their crews.

I also know where to find all the familiar names on the wall, somewhere well up in the double figures from my unit alone. These lead me to the others I know I'll see. A guy from my confirmation class in the Presbyterian Church is up there, a marine corporal who died in I Corps. A high-school kid my sister double-dated with on prom night is up there. When he died in Quang Tri Province, he still wasn't old enough to buy a drink. There's a guy from my officer's basic course, somebody I remember as having an almost goofy sweetness to him. He did his field time in the Americal and then got blown away on the division helipad as an escort officer waiting for an Australian rock band. My general is up there. As a young captain, he went in with William Darby at Salerno and held out to the end at Cisterna. The Rangers still talk about the battle at Cisterna today. Badly wounded and taken prisoner by the Germans, he eventually escaped and in spring 1945 was walking back across Poland when the war ended. Twenty-five years later, in April 1970, he was shot down a hundred yards from me on a strip of dusty road in Binh Thuy

Province where so many people had been killed that everyone called it Ambush Alley.

At least these soldiers have names written down somewhere, as opposed to the others who have followed them in new American wars in strange places that most people would just as soon not hear about: Panama, Grenada, Haiti, Kuwait, Bosnia, Somalia, Afghanistan, Iraq. Who's worried about Tora Bora or Tikrit when maybe five people in the country even know where to look up the number of Americans killed in the first Persian Gulf War of more than a decade ago, let alone their names? (For the record, the combat figure quoted is usually 148, with another 242 attributed to other causes.) Nor, save on fugitive Web sites, will one find a single available image of the estimated 100 to 150 thousand Iraqi conscripts who came out on the other end of our high-tech meat grinder. Among American veterans, Gulf War Syndrome is now in the old pathology bucket with Agent Orange. And of course, whether it's Iraq I or Iraq II, few pay any mind to the literally uncounted civilians, living and dead, chalked up as "collateral damage." The only reason the interim horror show in Somalia sneaked into consciousness seems to have been the result of some video footage getting loose of jubilant bad guys dragging around the body of a dead American Ranger. Somebody wrote a book about it, which of course was made into a Hollywood movie, with GIs getting turned into hoo-ah kids and sammies getting shot down and blown away in droves. Every hint was washed away of the policy confusion and incredible command incompetence that rushed Americans and Somalis alike to their deaths. It was like John Wayne meets Super Mario or the Terminator, nothing that an R Rating for "graphic violence" couldn't take care of.

The latest battle screening, Shock and Awe in Baghdad, with "embedded reporters," was easily the smartest PR idea the military has conceived in the last fifty or sixty years, hearkening back to the old "good war," with-the-troops, foxhole, and beachhead journalism of a Richard Tregaskis or an Ernie Pyle. For thus neatly could be avoided an atmosphere of critique arising either from the adversarial reporting of Vietnam or from the top-down blackout during Desert Storm devised to make the television and newspaper war look so faultlessly cool, laser guided, and antiseptic. On CNN and CNBC—and on the big four commercial networks, spliced in with the Academy Awards and the NCAA basketball tournament—with now infinitesimal electronic delays, we received talking heads in Kuwait City, Qatar, or Abu Dhabi, in turn summoning up grainy satellite images of dusty men and women with camera crews and microphones traveling in clouds of tanks, trucks, Humvees, Amtracs, ACAVs, and Bradley fighting vehicles. (On the Fox News Channel, an extra layer of desk commentary was worked in to inveigh against any voice with the temerity to object to anything about the war.) As opposed to the headquarters four-star supremo, a media magnet like a Westy or a Stormin' Norman, the commander this time was Tommy Franks, the nearly invisible "GI general," summoning up humbler memories of an Omar Bradley or a Creighton Abrams. The briefing officer was a really smart, articulate, correspondent-friendly West Point brigadier who just happened to be African American. The GIs looked good, although we seldom saw a badly wounded or dead one.

However, in the spirit of September 11, 2001, formal portraiture abounded concerning those lost, with elaborate display made of name, face, rank, branch of service, and various pieces of hometown information. As for the Iraqis, military or civilian, aside from the occasional newspaper image of heaped bodies or of someone bowed, crouched, or sprawled amid the wreckage of warfare, it was as if people by that name did not exist. Again, as to combatants, the military has not permitted a single image of what must have been the astonishing destruction wrought by U.S. airpower on the alleged five mechanized divisions arrayed in the desert in defense of Baghdad—all reduced (or "degraded," according to the current euphemism, which seems to have replaced "attrited") to a half or possibly a third of their strength from above before they ever saw an American ground unit.

As I think about all this, it has now become, I realize, in a way most of us never dreamed of after World War II, the cold war, Vietnam, *or* the First Persian Gulf War, a new time of foreseeably endless global combat. American civilians, in the thousands, have joined the legions of the blown up and the incinerated—in Mogadishu, in Gaza City, in Kirkuk and Nasiriyah. Our enemies, or those who will continue to see themselves as such for the interminable future, are hard people, maybe as hard and fanatical and faceless a lot as has ever arrayed itself on the planet. Our government has committed us to taking action abroad against terrorists and regimes deemed to be harboring them or in sympathy with them and at home has begun the long-term process of radically restructuring the whole apparatus of national security.

As to cultural memory, however, what might be called the prime-timing of American consciousness seems now triumphantly complete. For a few weeks nonstop video and print media squeezed out the maximum amount of flapdoodle and public weeping over the victims of September 11, 2001, including all kinds of talk about "a nation challenged" and a new "twilight struggle." Along with the Delta Force, the Green Berets, the Rangers, and the Airborne, a posse of network anchors hied themselves off briefly to the field for a flurry of coverage on the hunt for Bin Laden. For a few months we read profiles and biographies in the *New York Times* and articles and books about the hijacked planes and the skyscraper heroes and heroines. In fall 2002 came the predictable media orgy of commemoration. But then, slightly more than a year later, after some military housecleaning in Afghanistan, instant amnesia took hold and we moved on to Baghdad, with the same media drill over a new set of heroes and heroines, victims and villains. OK, OK, so what if we wind up looking to the rest of the world like a bunch of fossil-fuel crack heads knocking over a 7–11 so that we can support our habit for a few more weeks, when we're really just the kind of country that wants to eat at Burger King and watch reality TV while eighteen-year-old grunts and twenty-one-year-old lieutenants go out and dig ragheads out of bunker complexes? Barely one year. Barely a year since the single most deadly and catastrophic assault by an enemy power on American citizens in the history of the Republic, and nobody could remember enough to care about what happened in Washington and New York and in the sky over western Pennsylvania, let alone give much of a damn about the war in Iraq that would turn out to be next. Start a new war? Bulldoze Congress? Ignore the United Nations? Oh, OK, go ahead, just as long as it's not my kid, or my husband, or my brother shooting his way into the center square of Baghdad. Just remember how dead American bodies freak us out and make us want to change the channel. And while you're at it, we'd just as soon not see any cooked or blown-apart enemies either. How about making it look like that big video game the way you did the last time around? We can relate to that.

At the same time, God help me, I admit it, I'm an old soldier. Like most Americans, I honestly do want to see us put a boot up the asses of the people who availed themselves of the freedoms and opportunities of the most open society in the history of the planet to kill thousands of our people. We ought to understand, however, what other people around the world think when they see those eight- to twelve-miles-per-gallon Sierras and Tahoes, the Palm Pilots and the designer handbags, the two-million-dollar McMansions on half-acre lots and the obscene pay packages for college football coaches and corporate executives. It's almost as if the whole country got together and tried to come up with the most swinish and ignorant possible way of saying to the rest of the world, "Fuck you, buddy, and fuck the history you rode in on. We've got ours."

A lot of the time, actually, I feel like the Frederic March character in *The Best Years of Our Lives*. "Last year it was kill Japs," he says, half plastered at a welcome-home civic banquet. "This year it is make money." Now that I'm in my late fifties, looking back at my parents' generation with my memories of watching them grow older, I honestly wonder how the World War II people got over their war. On the one hand, we thought we had it bad because we came home to a place where people could not have cared less about what we had just spent a year doing. On the other, maybe invisibility was what got us through, giving us the chance to come home and devise the separate peace most of us found ourselves forced to invent, knowing that we were taking up our lives again in a time and place where no one cared enough about the war to hear about it or what we saw and did there. Here the World War II veterans were, after all those years of being away, of being scared, lonely, and miserable, knowing that they were racing death for the duration, come home to a nation safe and well fed, utterly oblivious to the mass destruction wrought across most of Europe and Asia, the Atlantic and the Pacific, everybody expecting them to sit right down around the victory-culture celebration table with all the happy civilians. Like the March character, with his Twenty-fifth Division "Tropic Lightning" patch telling anyone who knows about the army just which floors of lower hell in the Pacific he got to explore, I still almost get lonesome for a time out on the ass end of III Corps where everybody knew who everybody was.

Actually now, I believe many times it's the hoo-ah kids I'm thinking about on most days in America. Part of this, I am sure, is an old soldier's reflex, what William Manchester, quoting Siegfried Sassoon, calls his urge to give the modern world the slip. But the other part of my queer nostalgia for the battlefield, I remain convinced, is the result of a particular history and the overwhelming sadness I feel for what passes as life in America amid riches and power beyond any human dreams: when I stand waiting in line for my morning decaf behind eighteen-year-olds with eating disorders ordering low-fat, sugar-free, five-dollar dessert drinks; when I read about the people who packed the Galleria parking lot in Birmingham so that they could get into the stores at one o'clock in the morning the day after Thanksgiving and catch the early Christmas bargains; when I'm out for a long, slow, old man's afternoon run, giving thanks that I'm still alive and whole after all these years, with all systems more or less pumping, navigating an intersection at SUV gridlock, with everybody on a cell phone telling somebody else on a cell phone how pissed they are about being stuck at the intersection of Fifteenth and University. Oh, you can tell we're on a war footing. The Jesus fish on the backs of the expensive cars now have to share the display scheme with the American flags on the front and sides. The yellow ribbons are all over the place again. (Does no one remember at all that the original song was about a guy coming home from the slammer?) I'm honestly surprised they haven't recycled the hairy little Nashville cockroach with the "Proud to be an American" bullshit.

Meanwhile, I find myself doing a lot of generational noticing these days, although I suspect there are not many of us to whom the concept of generation means much any more. Lynda Van Devanter, a Vietnam veteran of the army nurse corps who opened the door to women's narratives of the war, died this year. She caught all kinds of negative publicity for her memoir of her time in the evacuation hospitals, all the drinking and partying between the ripped bowels and stumps in the triage rooms and the dying kids on the operating tables; she died at fifty-five, of a chronic vascular disease possibly caused by exposure to Agent Orange. Philip Berrigan, a World War II combat marine who became a priest and then a late-life husband and father, made it to seventy-seven, after a lifetime in and out of jail for a career of offenses connected with a procession of American wars. They made a play of the Catonsville Nine, burning stolen draft records in a parking lot with homemade napalm. Berrigan didn't get to see it, one obituary noted, because he was in jail for hammering in the nose cones of missiles. Max Cleland, a Vietnam triple amputee, got voted out of the Senate. The cause of his alleged unfitness, according to his patriotic opponent, was that he was soft on national security. His offense seems to have been that he voted against a congressional measure, rather like the Gulf of Tonkin resolution, that totally surrendered war-making power over Iraq to the executive branch. My guess is that Colin Powell will soon get the door as well, the last guy in government with any institutional memory of Vietnam still holed up against all the REMF bastard fire-eaters in the White House and the Defense Department, a retired general, a former chairman of the Joint Chiefs of Staff, and one of the primary engineers of victory in the 1990 Gulf War, who actually believes that the exercise of unprecedented national power still has something to do with global community.

In late 2002 and early 2003, there were limited showings, in selected major cities, of a new film version of Graham Greene's *The Quiet American,* with Michael Caine as Fowler, the cynical English journalist, and Brendan Fraser as the titular apostle of freedom and democratic enlightenment. Like *We Were Soldiers,* it, too, had been scheduled for a much earlier release but was delayed, in its particular case because the depiction of Americans as arrogant and blindly self-righteous would look unpatriotic. Apparently, the only reason it even went to a handful of theaters before 2002 ended was to move Caine under the wire for the Academy Awards, although early reviews noted that Fraser may indeed have done the definitive performance of Pyle. The mass release to theaters was deferred indefinitely until the new Gulf War was more or less in the win column, and we were waiting to invade Damascus or Tehran or Pyongyang. It's a great way to do history: make the movie, miss the

Acknowledgments

Excerpts from John Balaban's poetry in "Wanting to Be John Balaban" appear courtesy of John Balaban and are from his book *Locusts at the Edge of Summer: New and Selected Poems* (Copper Canyon Press, 1997). "Solatium" originally appeared in the *Michigan Quarterly Review* and was reprinted in *The Pushcart Prize XXVII* (2003). "Calley's Ghost" was first published in *Virginia Quarterly Review* and "Viet Pulp" in *War, Literature and the Arts* 14, no. 1–2 (2002). "Just Like in the Movies: Richard Nixon and *Patton*" originally appeared in the *Georgia Review* 49, no. 3 (1995), © 1995 by The University of Georgia / © 1995 by Philip D. Beidler, and is reprinted by permission of Philip D. Beidler and the *Georgia Review*.